STORMY PETREL:

The Life and Times of

General Benjamin F. Butler, 1818-1893

STORMY PETREL:

The Life and Times of

General Benjamin F. Butler
1818-1893

★★★★★★★★★★★★★★★★★★★

by

HOWARD P. NASH, JR

Rutherford • *Madison* • *Teaneck*
Fairleigh Dickinson University Press

Associated University Presses, Inc.
Cranbury, New Jersey 08512

SBN: 8386–7383–X
Printed in the United States of America

To
Joan

Preface

A biographer inevitably comes to have personal feelings about his subject and the nature of those feelings should be stated so that readers may take them into account. I must, therefore, confess that my study of General Butler's life has led me to like him. However, I have tried to write about him objectively. Even with the best will in the world this has not been an easy task because few of his contemporaries ever attempted such a thing. Most of what they said or wrote about him is either as laudatory as James Parton's and T. A. Bland's biographies or as violently denunciatory as *The Record of Benjamin F. Butler* (published anonymously) and the newspapers of his day praised or condemned him according to their political attitudes.

Although I have consulted the Butler manuscripts in the Library of Congress, I have, for the convenience of the reader who may wish to check my sources, cited the more readily available Jesse Ames Marshall's *Private and Official Correspondence of Benjamin F. Butler During the Period of the Civil War,* privately issued, 1917, except that where the text of an original document differs from the text in Mrs. Marshall's compilation the original is cited.

Contents

Contents

STORMY PETREL:

The Life and Times of

General Benjamin F. Butler, 1818-1893

1

****

Meet General Butler

Ben Butler was one of the best loved and worst hated men of the nineteenth century. His friends, while he lived and those who remembered him fondly, were mostly "common people," for he was truly a democrat and always a fighter on the side of the poor and lowly. Most of his enemies during his lifetime, like those who reviled him after his death, were wealthy businessmen and their political retainers.

Before the Civil War began Butler's name was almost a household word in New England. After 1861 everybody who had ever heard of Abraham Lincoln had also heard of Benjamin F. Butler, for the activities of both of them were discussed all over the civilized world. When Butler died in January, 1893 lengthy obituaries were published in every newspaper in the United States and in metropolitan journals in Canada, England, Scotland, Wales, France, Holland, Italy, South Africa, and Turkey.

As the years passed Butler grew from a slender boy into a corpulent, but not clumsy, man. His features were somewhat heavy; his complexion fair; his skin smooth and slightly flushed; his eyes were clear and bright, with a noticeable cast in the left one. Almost bald-headed, he wore what hair he still possessed long, in the manner General George A. Custer and William Jennings Bryan did. Although Butler cannot be described as anything other than homely, his looks were apt to be forgotten when his face became animated, particularly if he smiled.

Butler's personality, like everybody's, included both pleasant and unpleasant characteristics.

His most striking trait was a delight in conflict. Like the stormy petrel he was a figure of turbulence. A contemporary who likened

13

him to a full rigged man-of-war, with decks always cleared for action and guns double-shotted, said "The hottest battles, the roughest weather, the most perilous adventures were pleasant for him, . . . in them he found his native element."[1]

Hot battles, rough weather, and perilous adventures literally proved Butler was a man of great physical courage, yet, as a military officer, he could never bring himself to order a movement of troops without feeling concerned about the casualties they would suffer.

Although Butler was quick to take offense and somewhat vindictive, he also remembered friendly acts, was generous to a fault, and was ready to apologize if he found an apology justly due.

Titles and important persons never awed Butler. He spoke his mind to Presidents, governors, high ranking military or naval officers, etc., as readily and pungently as to anyone.

Besides being insatiably curious about all sorts of things Butler had an enormous intellectual capacity and a retentive memory. He could discuss such topics as a steam locomotive with a railroad engineer, Hebrew history with a theological student, and medical theory with a doctor.

Few men have been more persevering than Butler. He first sought to become governor of Massachusetts in 1858; 24 years later his seventh try for that office resulted in his election to it.

The least likeable of Butler's qualities was his intense egotism. This led him sometimes to claim credit where he deserved none and caused him extensively to rationalize his occasional failures. Offsetting this trait, he had a sense of humor strong enough to enable him to laugh even when the joke was on him. During one of his political campaigns a little girl recognized him because, as she said, he was cockeyed. Laughing harder at this statement than anybody else present, he commented, as he gave the child a kiss and a dollar, "Such is fame." In the same vein is the story of a protest made by an opposing lawyer that Butler was looking at the jury while reading a citation of law to the court. With a

---

[1] Russell H. Conwell, *Address before the Aurora Club,* July 31, 1874 (Published by the Aurora Club [Boston, 1874]), pp. 5–6.

grimace unmistakably directed toward the jurors, he remarked, "You can't tell which way I am looking."[2]

Quick-witted himself, Butler enjoyed quick-wit in others. While he was in command of the Army of the Gulf in New Orleans during the Civil War a Union soldier of Irish extraction died. The man's comrades prepared to bury him in St. Patrick's (Roman Catholic) Cemetery, but neglected to consult the parish priest, Father Mullen, in the matter. Not having been given any evidence that the man was entitled to a Catholic funeral, Father Mullen refused permission for the digging of a grave in the cemetery. A complaint lodged against Father Mullen led to his being ordered to appear before General Butler. The priest reported and asked why he had been summoned. The General said he had been credibly informed that Father Mullen had refused to bury a Union soldier. Butler was highly amused at the priest's reply: "Your information is all wrong; I assure that nothing would give me more pleasure than to bury you all."[3]

From the time Butler first began to practice law he was always ready to do legal work for those who needed a lawyer's services but could not afford to pay a lawyer's fees and he served these clients as zealously as he did his wealthiest ones. In politics he was always on the side of labor. His professional and political activities early won him the reputation of being "a levelling democrat of the worst sort," and a host of followers who were so blindly devoted to him that they were aptly described as "Butlerolatrous."

If there was Butlerolatry there was also "Butlerphobia," for a certain class of persons (the kind who unsmilingly referred to themselves as the better element) gathered at frequent intervals "to the hunting of Butler, as men in primitive communities gather in the hunting of a dangerous beast."[4] Those who hunted Butler

2 Joseph Willard, *Half a Century with Judges and Lawyers* (Houghton Mifflin and Company [Boston], 1895), pp. 249–50.

3 Thomas McManus, *The Battle Fields of Louisiana Revisited a Second Time* (The Fowler & Miller Co. [Hartford, Conn., 1898]), p. 8.

4 John T. Morse, Jr., *Memoir of Colonel Henry Lee* (Little, Brown and Company [Boston, 1905]), p. 95.

included financiers such as Colonel Henry Lee and John Murray
Forbes and conservative politicians like Judge Ebenezer Rockwood
Hoar, his brother Senator George Frisbee Hoar, and Senator
William B. Washburn. Such men hated Butler as intensely as
others of the same sort hated Theodore Roosevelt and his cousin
Franklin D. Roosevelt and for the same reasons—each of them
seemed to threaten the privileges enjoyed by the business class
of his day.

Butlerphobia naturally originated in Massachusetts where Butler's political career began, and it always raged most violently
there. As Gail Hamilton (Mary Abigail Dodge) once commented: "Massachusetts was more afraid of [Butler] than of
any other man, and no sooner did he appear on the horizon than
all Boston stood aghast."[5] After the Civil War hostility toward
Butler spread, along with his fame beyond Massachusetts. In
1882 the editors of the *Nation* remarked that between 1867 and
1874 "hardly a week passed in which [they] did not call attention
to [what they regarded as Butler's] vices and defects, both personal and political."[6]

Another who frequently spoke ill of Butler was the historian
James Ford Rhodes. For the most part Rhodes wrote about Butler not in the manner of an objective historian, but in that of a
partisan editor blackguarding a member of the opposition. Indeed
Rhodes often deliberately twisted evidence or disregarded facts
known to him in order to belittle or besmirch Butler.

Rhodes's behavior in this matter is puzzling. Apparently he
had no grounds for any personal animus against Butler, such as
he may have had against Stephen A. Douglas,[7] whom he also
treated unfairly. Rhodes's business class background may account
for his attitude toward Butler. Another possibility is that when
Rhodes moved from the Midwest to Massachusetts he found abuse

---

[5] H. Augusta Dodge, *Gail Hamilton's Life in Letters* (Lee and Shepard
[Boston, 1901]), II, 817.

[6] *Nation,* November 9, 1882, p. 391.

[7] George Fort Milton, *The Age of Hate* (Coward-McCann, Inc. [New
York, 1930]), pp. 145–46.

of Butler highly fashionable among the Brahmins and, craving the Brahmins' approval, he outdid some of them in abusing the General.

There were, it is worth noting, some conservative businessmen who were not Butlerphobes. One of them was Samuel Bowles, Jr., proprietor of the Springfield, Massachusetts *Republican*. In 1878, when Bowles lay mortally ill (as it turned out) he received a letter from Butler expressing his "cordial regard and good wishes." Bowles instructed his secretary to "write to Mr. Butler and say that while Mr. Bowles . . . has always differed with him in politics, he has never failed to recognize his high qualities, and to appreciate his many personal attractions."[8]

The editors of the Boston *Globe* (a newspaper that maintained a dispassionate attitude toward Butler) once wondered why his errors and pecadilloes were so remarkably well remembered while those of other public men were so easily and quickly forgotten. A partial answer, if not a complete one, to that question may be gathered from a comment made by Senator Hoar to the effect that the elder statesmen of Massachusetts did not take kindly to Nathaniel P. Banks (governor of Massachusetts, 1851–61; member of Congress at intervals between 1853 and 1891; Speaker of the House of Representatives, 1856–57) because he was a man of the people.[9] Banks, who became a dutiful conservative, was eventually forgiven his origin. Butler, who remained a man of the people, was always hated by the "upper classes," although he was beloved by thousands of inarticulate ordinary men, by labor leaders and labor reformers, and, after the Civil War, by all the Negroes of his day.

In a period when scratching a ticket was a rare thing Butler changed political parties, as one man put it, "somewhere nearly as frequently as a snake does its skin."[10] He began his political

---

[8] George S. Merriam, *The Life and Times of Samuel Bowles* (The Century Co. [New York, 1885]), II, 435–36.

[9] George F. Hoar, *Autobiography of Seventy Years* (Charles Scribner's Sons [New York, 1903]), I, 123.

[10] Harry Pratt Judson, "American Politics: A study of Four Careers," *Review of Reviews,* March, 1893, p. 72.

career as a Democrat; after the Civil War he became a Republican (with strong Greenback-Labor leanings); then he returned to the Democracy; and made his last political appearance (in 1884) as presidential candidate of the Anti-Monopoly and Greenback-Labor parties. This sort of conduct did not endear him to his politically more stable contemporaries.

Butler answered those who criticized him as politically inconsistent by arguing that despite his moves from party to party his political principles did not change over the years. Toward the end of what he called "a lifetime of the closest study of, and connection with, national and state affairs and practical politics," he described his political principles in these words:

> As to the powers and duties of the government of the United States, I am a Hamiltonian Federalist. As to the rights and privileges of the citizen, I am a Jeffersonian Democrat. I hold that the full and only end of government is to care for the people in their rights and liberties, and that they have the right and privilege to call on either the State or the United States, or both, to protect them in equality of powers, equality of rights, equality of privileges, and equality of burdens under the law, by carefully and energetically enforced provisions of equal laws justly applicable to every citizen.[11]

This point of view is not unlike that held by Herbert Croly, founder of the *New Republic,* and adopted by Theodore Roosevelt and his Progressive party followers.

Butler had a habit, for which other politicians disliked him, of honestly admitting that he ran for office because he wanted to be elected. In his day it was customary for a politician covertly to seek preferment within his own party and having been nominated (perhaps after a hard fight) to pretend to be in the field only because he could not resist the importunities of his friends. If Butler wanted a nomination and it was not tendered to him he sought it openly. As he once said he was not like a coy maiden

---

[11] Benjamin F. Butler, *Butler's Book* (A. M. Thayer & Co. [Boston, 1892]), pp. 85–86.

who timidly conceals her desires, but more like a widow who
knows what she wants and does not fear to ask for it. This remark
earned him the nickname "Widow Butler" and the hostility of
many politicians who preferred to act like coy maidens.

Another thing that helped Butler to gain enemies was his almost unmatched ability as a rough-and-tumble political fighter.
Besides having a caustic wit, to which he gave free rein, he was
master of all the expedients of debate at any level of logic and
nothing ever disturbed his aplomb. One of many defamatory
stories told about him by Butlerphobes was that he had stolen a
set of silver spoons from the house he occupied in New Orleans
during the Civil War. Occasionally his political opponents sought
to interrupt his campaign speeches by producing silver colored
wooden spoons, usually about four feet long. If he was speaking
out of doors they might be lowered from a tree; if in a building,
from a trap door in the ceiling or over a balcony rail. In whatever way they appeared his reaction was always to grab them
with some variation of the remark: "I guess that's one I didn't
get before."

2

****

As the Twig is Bent . . .

As an American of colonial ancestry General Butler was what New Englanders sometimes call a "swamp Yankee." The first Butler to reach America, Nicholas, emigrated from Eastwell, Kent, England, in 1637. One of his descendants, Zephaniah Butler, born at Windham, Connecticut, was General Butler's grandfather. His paternal grandmother, Abigail Cilley, was a daughter of General Joseph Cilley (sometimes spelled Seelye), a lawyer, farmer, and businessman, whose military title was gained during the Revolutionary War.

John Butler, Ben's father, who was born at Nottingham, New Hampshire, was the youngest boy in his family. In manhood he moved to Deerfield, New Hampshire, and became a Democratic-Republican. He and seven more of Thomas Jefferson's followers "formed a little brotherhood, apart from their fellow townsmen, shunned by the federalists [sic] as men who would have been dangerous for their principles if they had not been despicable for their fewness."[1]

Ben Butler's mother, Charlotte Ellison (John Butler's second wife, whom he married in 1811) was a daughter of Richard Ellison whose ancestors had emigrated from Northern Ireland after the Battle of the Boyne, fought in 1690.

For some years John Butler engaged, with moderate success, in trading to the West Indies. In the course of time he rose from

---

[1] James Parton, *General Butler in New Orleans* (Mason Brothers [New York, 1864]), p. 14.

supercargo to ship's captain, and later to merchant trading on his own account. Early in the War of 1812 he was commissioned captain of a company of dragoons he had raised. While serving with his company on the northern frontier he suffered a broken leg. His injury was so badly treated that he was never again able to wear a boot on that foot. A cavalryman who could not wear a pair of boots was not of much use so he resigned his commission. A short time later he outfitted a privateer in which he sailed from Portsmouth, New Hampshire. It fell to his lot to carry dispatches to General Andrew Jackson at New Orleans. Learning to like the General, he named his first son Andrew Jackson Butler. His other son, born at Nottingham late in the afternoon of November 5, 1818, was named after another famous American, Benjamin Franklin. Unlike a number of his contemporaries who were also destined to attain political prominence Ben Butler was not born in a log cabin, but in a good sized, comfortable looking farm-house flanked by substantial outbuildings.

After the War of 1812 John Butler returned to the West Indian trade and took out letters of marque under Simon Bolivar, liberator of several Spanish colonies in South America and first President of the Republic of Bolivia. In later years John Butler was occasionally described as having been a pirate. His son Benjamin wrote: "My father's services on the South American coast, under a commission from the hand of a republic not having fully achieved its independence, were of much the same kind that [John] Paul Jones rendered for our Revolutionary fathers on the coast of Scotland under like circumstances."[2] In sober truth, as General Butler would have realized if he had not been carried away by filial piety, the North American privateers on the South American coast were legally pirates under the provisions of a treaty between the United States and Spain. However, they were applauded everywhere in this country during the time John Butler was of their number.

---

[2] Benjamin F. Butler, *Butler's Book* (A. M. Thayer & Co. [Boston, 1892]), p. 43.

Before Ben Butler was six months old his father died of yellow fever at St. Kitts, the British West Indies, leaving his widow in a state of comparative poverty. Andrew Butler was sent to live with an uncle; young Ben was kept at home where he was brought up by his mother and his grandmother Butler. The latter was a robust woman, who stood nearly six feet tall, and was able when nearly 80 years old to carry herself erectly, although she had to walk with a cane. An imperious person, with "a most inflexible will," who rarely yielded to others but made them do things her way, she strongly influenced her grandson during his earliest, most plastic years. The old lady taught the boy her political beliefs, which were, so far as he could understand them, "that there ought not to be any kings, princes, barons, nobles, or knights." However, she did admit the existence of an aristocracy and often boasted that her family was one of the best in New Hampshire.[3]

These ideas deeply impressed Butler. Toward the end of his life he said he had always believed in democratic government and personal aristocracy and during his long political career he invariably appeared at nighttime meetings aristocratically arrayed in evening clothes to appeal frankly for the support of labor class voters whose interests he upheld religiously.

At the age of four Ben began attending school at Nottingham Square, a two mile walk from his home. Having already been taught the alphabet by his mother he learned during the summer term of six weeks to read moderately well. He quickly became and always remained an avid reader. In fact he was so fond of books that while he was a child, errands—such as bringing home the cows from the pasture a mile distant—had to be invented in order to force him to spend any time at all out of doors and some little pressure had to be used to get him to do his chores.

In the fall of 1822 the village shoemaker gave young Ben a copy of *Robinson Crusoe*—the first book he ever owned. His mother, a strict Calvinist, did not want her son to read only secular literature so she struck a bargain with him whereby she

---

[3] Ibid., pp. 48–49.

helped him to read and understand a page of his new book every time he memorized a verse from the Bible. Apparently he had a photographic memory and by the time he finished *Robinson Crusoe* he had learned by heart the first four gospels, including, as he said, "the first eighteen verses of the first chapter of Matthew, where everybody begat everybody else."[4]

Because books were scarce in northern New England in the early nineteenth century young Ben read the few he possessed or could borrow so often that he came to know large parts of them word for word. He developed a particular interest in the history of the Revolutionary War because two of his family's neighbors happened to be veterans of that conflict. Listening to them, as he often did, he came to believe "that the highest achievement in life was to get behind a stone wall and shoot a Britisher, and . . . longed for the time when [he] should grow up to do it." Many years later he wrote: "So thoroughly was this drilled into me that in after life it was a matter of reasoning on my part whether I should treat an Englishman decently."[5]

Charlotte Butler wanted her younger son to become a Methodist preacher, but the family's financial resources were so limited it seemed unlikely he could be given a college education—a necessary preparation for the ministry. However, not long before the end of his last year in grade school a family consultation was held and it was decided that he should be sent to Phillips Exeter Academy to be prepared for college with a hope that a scholarship might be found for him. He was recommended to the president and trustees of the Academy in 1827, but he did not enter it until 1829.

In his own opinion he did not learn much at Exeter. "To be sure," he said, "I acquired the Latin grammar with a certainty of memory that was excelled only by my uncertainty as to the meanings of the rules it contained. My learning was nothing but memorizing. It was the same thing with the study of Greek."[6]

4 Ibid., pp. 44–45, 57.
5 Ibid., pp. 47–48.
6 Ibid., p. 51.

About the time young Ben matriculated at Exeter his mother moved to Lowell, Massachusetts, to become matron in one of the city's famous boardinghouses. Lowell was then the biggest manufacturing center in the United States, producing chiefly cotton textiles. Most of the mill workers were girls in their teens or early twenties. They came from a radius of 100 miles around Lowell to work for a while in order to save some money before they married, to help to put a brother through college, or for a variety of such reasons. To provide for strict supervision of the morals of these girls and for their physical care the mills maintained boardinghouses, managed by carefully selected women—often widows. There were separate establishments for men and women. Their use was optional for men, but compulsory for unmarried women. Girls coming to work in the mills of Lowell had to agree, in writing, to live in a company boardinghouse, to behave in a strictly moral manner, and to attend church regularly. To make it easier for the young ladies to conduct themselves properly the boardinghouses locked their doors promptly at 10 P.M. If a girl wanted to stay out later than that she had to obtain special permission from the matron. Lamps were never lighted in the boardinghouses on Saturday nights lest the young ladies might sit up late enough to be too tired to attend church the next morning. (The Secretary of the National Association of Cotton Manufacturers commented in 1923: "The influence which this system of boardinghouses exerted upon the good order and morals of the inhabitants, was, by all accounts, very great. It enabled the superintendent to exert his care and influence over the operatives not only while they were in the mill but while they were away from it.")[7]

(Incidentally, with wages ranging from $3.00 to $4.00 a week men paid $1.75 a week for room and board; women, $1.25 a week.)[8]

---

[7] H. C. Meserve, *Lowell—an industrial dream come true* (The National Association of Cotton Manufacturers [New Bedford, Massachusetts, 1923]), p. 62.

[8] Ibid., p. 61.

Young Butler, apparently unable to afford to stay at Exeter, joined his mother in Lowell, probably in the spring of 1830. He said in his autobiography that he left the Academy at the end of the winter term of 1828.[9] Since he is officially recorded as having entered Exeter in 1829 he either suffered a lapse of memory, pardonable enough in connection with an event more than 60 years in the past, or he did some careless proofreading.

After leaving Exeter, Ben studied Latin at home with the kindly help of Seth Ames, a lawyer who later became a justice of the Supreme Court of Massachusetts. About this time it became necessary for the boy to earn some money so he worked for several months as clerk in the only bookstore then existing in Lowell. Late in 1830 he entered the new Lowell High School. When he graduated in 1834 his heart was set upon going to West Point—perhaps he thought he might get a chance to shoot a few Britishers. He probably could have secured an appointment to the Military Academy from Caleb Cushing of Massachusetts or Isaac Hill of New Hampshire, two of his father's old friends. Unfortunately for the boy's aspirations his mother consulted her clergyman, the Reverend Enoch W. Freeman, a narrow-minded man all too typical of the cloth of his day. Freeman, mistaking Ben's ability to quote long passages from the Bible for true scholarship, assumed that the boy had a religious bent. At West Point, as Freeman understood, there was a great deal of freethinking among the cadets. He feared that if Ben went there he might become a freethinker—a horrible thing for a preacher to contemplate. The best place for a boy of Ben's (supposed) inclinations and talents to go, the minister argued, would be the then 21-year-old Baptist college at Waterville, Maine. In Freeman's view, one of the advantages of this institution was that it had a labor department, hence the boy could earn part of the money he would need. So Ben went to Waterville (now Colby) College in the fall of 1834. An uncle gave him some financial help, he spent three hours a day making chairs in the college's labor department,

---

[9] Butler, op. cit., p. 52.

and he taught school during winter vacations. Despite all he could
do to earn money he was $1,200 in debt when he graduated.

Waterville was in fact a Protestant parochial school. Its president and many of its professors were clergymen, more interested
in making good Baptists than in making scholars out of their
pupils. Attendance at church on Sundays and at daily prayers,
held about daybreak in the chapel, was compulsory. Absences
from any of these services were penalized by fines of ten cents
and demerit marks which detracted from a student's standing as
determined by his proficiency in his lessons. Butler was finally
provoked into open rebellion against this system by a series of
doctrinal sermons preached by the Reverend Samuel Smith, best
remembered as author of the hymn *America*. The gravamen of
Smith's discourses was that only the elect, hardly more than one
in 100 of so-called Christians would escape eternal damnation
and the heathen would be given more consideration by the Almighty on Judgment Day than would those nominal Christians
who had heard, but not heeded, the word of God. Unwilling to
accept such teachings because he considered them both stupid and
bigoted, Buter asked to be excused from compulsory attendance
at church and chapel. His petition, couched in respectful language,
stated that according to the Reverend Professor Smith's figure not
more than six persons at the college could possibly be saved. Inasmuch as the faculty contained nine doctors of divinity it seemed
to him to be most unlikely that any of the students would escape
eternal damnation and he was willing to admit that his chances
of doing so were among the poorest of them all. Therefore, he
argued, he would only make his own doom more terrible by continuing to attend religious services. As might be predicted, the
faculty was not amused; indeed he came uncomfortably close to
being expelled for irreverence. In the circumstances he probably
did well to graduate from Waterville at all, let alone to do so
with a mark of 7.5 out of a possible 10, "prayers deducted."

In the 1830's, as ever since, college boys indulged in "bull
sessions." Those at Waterville were commonly religious discus-

sions and because of his detailed knowledge of the Bible, Butler found it easy to pose questions his fellow students could not answer. Apparently he began doing this sort of thing purely as a form of intellectual exercise, but the act of raising such questions tended to weaken his own, not too strong, faith. Before the end of his freshman year he decided that whatever else might happen he would not become a minister.

While he was in college young Butler did not spend all of his spare time in theological disputes either with the faculty or his fellow students. He found and utilized opportunities to engage in a normal amount of boyish mischief. A story he liked to tell in later years concerns the way he and some other boys broke up an abolitionist meeting. They trapped a number of sparrows, took them to the church where the meeting was to be held, and stationed themselves in various parts of the auditorium. The church was lighted with whale oil lamps (which never had chimneys). At a signal given by one of the students all the birds were let loose. They flew at the lights and put them out. In the dark the boys each kissed a girl or two, "and they of course shrieked," as Butler gleefully remembered. When the sexton came through the door carrying a torch he was struck by an unidentified flying object. Shouting something about spirits he took to his heels. With the students leading the way, the place was abandoned in great haste.[10]

Another tale of Butler's college days deals with a wooden sign he transferred from its place outside of a store to the wall of his room. Somehow the town constable came to suspect who the pilferer was and acted accordingly. By luck Butler caught sight of the minion of the law coming up the stairs to his room. Hastily breaking up the sign he stuffed the pieces into the fireplace and lighted them. Well aware that the constable would be upon him before the evidence was destroyed Butler took emergency action. He began praying in a tone of voice he was sure could be heard

---

[10] I am indebted for knowledge of this story to Miss Frances Perkins of Colby College. It appeared in an unidentified newspaper in March, 1883.

beyond the closed door. Although the constable was suspicious, he waited for the lengthy prayer to end. When he finally entered the room he found an innocent looking boy and a pile of hot ashes, but nothing to justify an arrest.[11] (This story may be apocryphal since it is also told about a Harvard student, or it may be true in both cases.)

For some time after Butler decided against becoming a minister he was uncertain how he did want to earn his living. A great interest in the natural sciences, particularly chemistry, led him to think seriously of studying medicine. However, he happened one day during the latter part of his junior year at Waterville to visit a court where Jeremiah Mason was appearing as counsel. Mason, a commanding figure at the New England bar for half a century, was regarded by some of his contemporaries as quite as able a lawyer as the more famous Daniel Webster. In fact Webster himself rated Mason as the greatest lawyer in the United States. On the day he first saw Mason, Butler decided that the law was a higher calling than medicine.

A few weeks before commencement day Butler went swimming in the Kennebec River. It can be cold in Maine in May and he used a cake of ice, two feet thick, he said, for a seat while undressing and dressing. Not surprisingly he caught a severe cold. His weight quickly dropped to 97 pounds. To recover his health he sailed on a codfishing voyage in a vessel (probably a schooner out of Gloucester, Massachusetts) owned by one of his father's friends. As fish were caught their livers were thrown into a barrel where the heat of the sun separated the oil they contained. Butler drank large quantities of clear, raw cod-liver oil and by the time he reached home he had gained 25 pounds. Throughout the rest of his long life he enjoyed remarkably fine health.

During the early part of the nineteenth century there were few professional schools except those for training clergymen. Usually

---

[11] From an article in the *Colby Alumnus,* third quarter, 1930–31, a copy of which was sent to me by Miss Perkins.

a young man who wanted to become a doctor or lawyer served an apprenticeship under some practitioner willing to instruct him. After returning from the Grand Banks early in the fall of 1838 Butler began reading law in the office of William Smith of Lowell. Smith made little effort to direct Butler's reading, although the older man did answer the younger one's questions kindly and carefully. Butler spent about 13½ hours a day in Smith's office—from 7:30 A.M., to 10 P.M., with a break at noon and another at suppertime. For recreation and exercise he rode horseback "four or five nights a week for an hour or two, . . . about the suburbs of the city and lonely ways of the neighborhood, meanwhile . . . reciting snatches of poetry, especially from Byron and Moore . . . and sometimes from Pope and Scott."[12]

About a year after Butler began reading law he joined the Lowell City Guard, a company of the Fifth Regiment, Massachusetts Volunteer Militia. In 1843 he was commissioned third lieutenant of Company D, Fifth Regiment. He was promoted to second lieutenant in April, 1847 and advanced to captain the following October. He became a major in September, 1848, was made lieutenant colonel in July, 1850, and colonel, commanding the Fifth Regiment, in October, 1852. Because of the peculiar shape of his left eye his subordinates inevitably nicknamed him "Old Cockeye."

One of the Fifth Regiment's companies—the Jackson Musketeers—was composed of men who had either been born in Ireland or were of Irish descent and were all Roman Catholics. When the (nativist, anti-Catholic) Know-Nothing party swept Massachusetts in 1854 Governor-elect Henry J. Gardner promised to rid the state militia of all companies of men of foreign birth or extraction. A few days after his inauguration Gardner ordered seven such outfits, including the Jackson Musketeers, to be disbanded. Colonel Butler flatly refused to obey the order applicable to the Jackson Musketeers. He informed the Governor, politely but firmly, that he had issued an unlawful order—some-

[12] Butler, op. cit., pp. 71–72.

thing to be obeyed by an officer of the militia at his own peril. The Governor promptly threatened to discharge Butler. The latter wrote to the Governor saying that an officer could not be discharged until a court-martial had found him guilty of a military offense and that disobedience of an illegal order in peace time was not such an offense. This letter must have been intended to befuddle Gardner, for, as Butler certainly must have known, the law provided several ways for removing an officer other than by court-martial. One was by address of the General Court, or state legislature. (There was some thought of using this method to dispose of Colonel Butler.) The Governor, with the advice and consent of his Council, could also dismiss an officer upon the petition of one or more of his superiors. (Since Colonel Butler had recently invoked this provision against a subordinate he would have been in no position to have fought its application to himself.) In the end the Governor accomplished his purpose by reorganizing the militia in such a way that it contained no place for Colonel Butler. However, Butler took the last trick. At that time officers of the Massachusetts Volunteer Militia were elected by the men serving under them. Thus privates elected company officers who in turn elected regimental officers and so on until brigade officers elected their generals. In May, 1855, Butler succeeded, apparently without any difficulty, in being elected a brigadier general. He had the mischievous pleasure of receiving his commission from Governor Gardner who had no choice except to sign and deliver it.

Butler was extremely proud of the Massachusetts Volunteer Militia. In his opinion its members could drill and parade better than any similar body of men except the cadets at West Point. He also believed the militia officers received excellent training during their drill periods and annual encampments. Describing his military experience prior to the Civil War, he said he had camped from five to nine days with his company or regiment every year from 1840 to 1855 and with his brigade from 1856 to 1860. Therefore, he claimed he had actually "commanded a larger body of troops, duly uniformed and equipped, than any general of the United States Army then living except General

[Winfield] Scott." In 1860 all of the troops of the state—nearly 6,000 men—were mustered at Concord. Having spent five days with them, Butler had, he remarked, "seen together for discipline, instruction, and military movement, a larger body of troops than even General Scott had seen together, for he never had so many men in one body in Mexico."[13]

It never seems to have occurred to Butler that seeing, even commanding, a large number of troops assembled for training in peaceful times did not necessarily endow an officer with ability to command on a battlefield.

Interestingly, in view of things that were to happen a few years later, Butler expressed a strong opposition to the enrollment of Negroes in the militia as late as 1859. At that time he argued Negroes were not, and could not become, citizens of the United States, hence they were ineligible for service in the militia. Furthermore, he said, if Negroes could join the militia he and other white men who wanted to bear arms in defense of their country would have to degrade themselves by training side by side with black men.

During the fall of 1839 Butler earned some much needed money by teaching school in an academy in Dracut, Massachusetts, a small town near Lowell. When he took this job the school had an enrollment of 21 boys and girls. Because the teacher's pay was based upon the number of pupils it was to Butler's interest to keep the number high. However, many of the boys had been expelled from various schools in Lowell and Butler, naturally a strict disciplinarian, soon lost 11 students. But, as he said, "No one of them had gone away without a thrashing, the remembrance of which would last him a lifetime." In the end he gained by his strictness. It brought in some more girls and boys of a different sort. Within three moths he had 26 students under his charge.[14]

While he was teaching at this school Butler managed to read law for six hours a day, but he felt this was not time enough so he refused to renew his contract at the end of the term.

---

[13] Ibid., pp. 123, 127.
[14] Ibid., p. 73.

Even before Butler was admitted to the bar he began practicing law in a small way. Most of his early clients were mill workers whose cases often stemmed from differences with their corporate employers. They came to him partly because they could not afford to pay the fees a full fledged attorney would have charged them, and partly because he was willing to represent them, something not many lawyers in Lowell would do. Those who could paid him money for his services; others gave him only their thanks.

The Honorable Joseph Locke, the police court judge before whom Butler often appeared in his early days, insisted that all proceedings be conducted with absolute regularity and due observance of all the forms and rules of law. As Butler put it: "He made the young gentlemen who generally practiced before him know what the law applicable in their cases was."[15] This was invaluable training. Throughout his professional life Butler always knew what the law was in cases he tried.

After Butler had been reading law for about two years he was advised by Smith to seek admission to the bar and offered a partnership. In those days any young man who could procure a certificate to the effect that he had been reading law for three years was automatically admitted to the bar, but anyone who had spent less time in a lawyer's office had to be examined by a judge of one of the higher courts before admission. On Smith's recommendation Judge Charles Warren examined Butler one evening in September, 1840. In his autobiography Butler characteristically told how, at his examination, he enlightened Judge Warren on a point of law.[16]

In his early days at the bar Butler was socially ignored by other young lawyers, scions of wealthy families and graduates of Harvard College, who felt themselves far superior to the son of a boardinghouse keeper. In these circumstances he found time carefully to study the federal bankruptcy act of 1841, the first such law passed by Congress in more than 40 years. He familiarized

15 Ibid., p. 72.
16 Ibid., pp. 75–76.

himself with the new measure, decisions under the old one, and relevant English decisions. His reward for his studies came quickly in the form of calls from his seniors at the bar for help in handling their bankruptcy cases. He took another step up the professional ladder in 1845 when he was admitted, on the motion of Levi Woodbury of New Hampshire, to practice before the Supreme Court of the United States. (Abraham Lincoln of Illinois and William H. Seward of New York were admitted during the same term.)

Most of Butler's countemporaries, including many who disliked him because they were his political or professional rivals, conceded that he had great intellectual and legal ability. However, George Frisbee Hoar, a political foe of Butler (and brother of one of his professional competitors) said:

> Compared with other men of equal ability and distinction, he was never a very successful advocate. Quiet and modest men who had the confidence of the courts and juries used to win verdicts from him in fairly even cases. He was fertile in resources. He liked audacious surprises. He was seldom content to try a simple case in a simple way. So that while he succeeded in some desperate cases, he threw away a good many which with wise management he might have gained.[17]

He cannot have thrown away too many cases for he was certainly successful according to the standards by which success is usually measured. His practice was worth about $18,000 a year by 1860—a considerable sum in those days. After the Civil War he made as much as $150,000 annually. In 1893 he left an estate having an estimated value of $7,000,000.

Like most lawyers, Butler rationalized his professional conduct by arguing that it was no concern of his, as attorney, whether a law was good or bad; that if laws needed to be changed legislators should change them. He always held it to be a lawyer's duty to save his clients from penalty, be they guilty or innocent, and he actually enjoyed taking advantage of legal technicalities to win

[17] George F. Hoar, *Autobiography of Seventy Years* (Charles Scribner's Sons [New York, 1903]), I, 330.

acquittals for persons he knew to be guilty. An illustrative story told by James A. Parton (who may well have heard it from Butler himself) deals with the defense of a kleptomaniac, a Bostonian of respectable connections and some wealth. This man was indicted on four counts. If found guilty on all of them he would have been liable to a sentence of 60 years in prison. The case came to trial on a hot day when everybody present, including the elderly judge, wanted to get away from court as quickly as possible. Butler agreed to have his client plead guilty to one particular count if the other three were dropped. The prosecuting attorney gladly accepted this proposition. The defendant pleaded guilty to the specified count and the prosecutor moved for sentence. Butler then called attention to a technical error in the indictment on which the trial was proceeding and his client was set free.[18]

Another of many stories about Butler's legal craftiness still to be heard in and around Lowell is that early in his career he took up a small wage claim against a textile mill and enforced it by placing an attachment on the plant's water wheel. Since the plant could not operate if the water wheel could not be used, the client is said quickly to have been paid. Butler denied this tale through Parton in 1864, and again, with an explanation of how it originated, in his autobiography.[19]

One remarkable case in which Butler did play a part was the defense of a railroad against a claim for damages allegedly resulting from negligence. Several persons, including the son of President Franklin Pierce, were killed in a train wreck near Andover, Massachusetts. Suit was brought against the railroad on account of the death of another passenger. Pierce retained Butler to assist in defending the railroad because Mrs. Pierce, a fanatically religious woman, believed the boy's death had resulted from an act of God designed to take away the President's son so that he might be better prepared to devote himself wholly to the duties of his great office.

---

[18] James Parton, *General Butler in New Orleans* (Mason Brothers, [New York, 1864]), pp. 32–33.

[19] Parton, op. cit., 25–26; Butler, op. cit., 1031–33.

After practicing law in Lowell for ten years, with frequent appearances in the courts of Boston, Butler opened a Boston office. Thereafter he maintained two offices, with different partners in each one. Usually he spent his days in Boston, working in Lowell at night. He left Lowell at 7 A.M., and started home at 5 P.M. The trip took an hour each way.

In 1839, presumably while teaching school, Butler became acquainted with Fisher Ames Hildreth, only son of Dr. Israel Hildreth, of Dracut. Through Fisher, Butler met the Doctor's six daughters. He found himself strongly attracted to the second oldest of the girls, Sarah, who was a couple of years his senior.

Sarah Hildreth had learned from her father to know and admire Shakespeare's works. With her father's consent she became an actress. She made her debut in August, 1837 at the Park Theater in New York as Marianna in *The Wife*. Later she played a season each at Charleston and Columbia, South Carolina, and brief engagements at Savannah, Georgia, Wilmington and Fayetteville, South Carolina, Norfolk and Portsmouth, Virginia. She was then engaged by J. N. Weston and Company as leading lady of the Cincinnati National Theater, where she first appeared as Rosalind in *As You Like It*.

Although an affectionate feeling developed between the two young people, Miss Hildreth refused to abandon her career until Butler had "won his spurs" professionally and could provide a home for them. In the spring of 1843 he visited her in Cincinnati. Their engagement was announced soon afterward and they were married on May 16, 1844 in St. Anne's (Episcopal) Church in Lowell. They had ample means for comfortable, even luxurious living. The house they owned in Lowell was a large and (for its day) a beautiful one. They lived enjoyably together until Mrs. Butler's death in 1876.

The Butlers had four children. Paul, their first born, died in April, 1850, a little less than five years old. Blanche, who was born in 1847, married Major General Adelbert Ames and had six children of her own. Another boy named Paul was born in 1852. The last child, Ben Israel, was born in 1854.

Paul went into business after he graduated from Harvard, where his father said:

> I sent him . . . not because I deemed it the best school in the country, but because I could not foretell what might be his future, and I chose that he should not be hindered, as his father had been by the fact that he was not a graduate of Harvard. A class of Massachusetts people believe that a course at that college is indispensable to advancement in almost any pursuit in life, especially political; and as soon as a graduate obtains political preferment he is hailed as the "scholar in politics."[20]

(The "scholar in politics" to whom Butler referred was Senator Henry Cabot Lodge of Massachusetts who graduated from and taught at Harvard before entering politics. His grandson and namesake was also a senator from Massachusetts, United States Ambassador to the United Nations, and Republican vice-presidential candidate in 1960.)

Ben Israel attended West Point, "graduated with honor, and was directed by his father to accept a lieutenantcy in a regiment of colored troops which was stationed on the Plains [to fight Indians], that he might have in addition to his instruction at the academy, the knowledge of the movement and care of troops in actual service."[21]

After spending a few years in the Army, Ben Israel resigned his commission and studied law at Columbia University. He died on September 1, 1881, the day before he was to have become his father's junior partner.

[20] Butler, op. cit., pp. 81–82.
[21] Ibid., p. 80.

3

★★★★★★★★★★★★

A Practical Politician

Butler's political career began on his 21st birthday, it ended 45 years later. To his eternal credit he never pretended to that much abused title "statesman." By his own admission he never concerned himself deeply with such broad problems as "how far the Virginia resolution of [17]98 should guide the future of this country, . . . or whether the doctrines of [Alexander] Hamilton should obtain," but he was always interested in what he called the "practical politics which dealt with the condition and welfare of the citizen,"[1] or, as it has been more crudely phrased, the question of who gets what.

Because he took a particular interest in the condition and welfare of citizens of the working class he gained great popularity with laborers. The mill hands in Lowell and its vicinity, who became personally acquainted with him, liked him because he so obviously liked them as individuals. They, and many other workingmen who never knew him personally, also liked him both for the clear pro-labor record he established and because he had a singular capacity for expressing their convictions in words they could easily understand. In an age of bombast and loquacity his speeches were comparatively brief and were delivered in a crisp, even racy, style and in plain language.

At first Butler kept his political activities within bounds calculated not to interfere with the enlargement of his law practice, but it took him less than ten years to become the acknowledged

---

[1] Benjamin F. Butler, *Butler's Book* (A. M. Thayer & Co. [Boston, 1892]), p. 85.

leader of the Democratic party in Lowell. In 1848 he was a delegate to the party's presidential nominating convention, held in Baltimore, Maryland. On this occasion he voted hopefully and often for the nomination of Levi Woodbury of New Hampshire who had sponsored his admission to practice before the Supreme Court of the United States.

A year later Butler helped to create a state-wide coalition of Democrats and Free-Soilers. This coalition (which almost amounted to a distinct party) was formed as a result of the discovery that the Democrats and Free-Soilers together could outvote the Whigs.

In addition to their common hostility to the Whigs the Democrats and Free-Soilers were interested in securing a secret ballot law. At the time every political party printed its own ballots, or "tickets," at its own expense. Since these ballots were printed on distinctively colored paper it was easy for political bosses, employers of labor, or anyone who might be interested in the matter, to determine who voted for whom. In these circumstances "every man who was in fear of his employer's displeasure . . . [as most workingmen inevitably were] voted in accordance with that employer's orders."[2]

Most of the large employers in Massachusetts were Whigs and it was often alleged by Democrats and Free-Soilers that economic pressure had been used to influence their votes. It was also said in Lowell that men who did not vote "right" were likely to be discharged whenever their services could be spared and that known Democrats or Free-Soilers could not secure wage increases even during the busiest seasons.

In 1850 the Coalitionists pushed a secret ballot law through the state legislature in spite of vigorous opposition by the Whigs. This law provided that the state should furnish voters with envelopes of uniform size and style in which ballots had to be enclosed before they could be cast. Two or three elections were held under the provisions of this law; then a Whig-controlled legisla-

---

2 Joseph B. Bishop, "The Secret Ballot in Thirty-three States," *The Forum*, January, 1892, XII, 590.

ture amended it in such a manner as to make the use of envelopes optional. While the envelope system of voting was in force employers often tried to control their employees' votes by handing them sealed envelopes containing Whig ballots and marching them to the polls in groups. Where this was done men could, and often did, substitute for the envelopes given them by their employers other envelopes, prepared beforehand, containing ballots of the sort they really wanted to cast. When the optional system came into effect employers suspected that men who enclosed their ballots in envelopes might not be voting "right." This being the case the use of envelopes was discouraged and secret voting was abandoned in Massachusetts to all intents and purposes until that state adopted the Australian ballot in 1888.

Butler was a strong advocate of the secret ballot, but even after he had retired from politics he considered the envelope system of voting to be far superior to the Australian ballot—the latter could be used only by literate persons, which not all of his supporters were.

In 1851 the election returns seemed to indicate that most of Lowell's Coalitionist candidates for seats in the Massachusetts House of Representatives had won by small majorities. While the Coalitionists were still celebrating their supposed victory it was discovered that the election clerks in one ward had made a small and easily explicable error in compiling their returns. Although an amended return was promptly offered, the city officials, all of whom were Whigs, many of them supervisors in the mills, declared the election void and ordered a new one to be held two weeks later. Both parties immediately began looking for ways to strengthen their positions. Butler persuaded the Coalitionists to present themselves as "ten-hour men," or advocates of legislation limiting a day's work for factory laborers to ten hours.

At this time the mill operatives in Lowell were working 13½ hours a day, six days a week. They started at 5 A.M., were allowed half an hour for breakfast, another half an hour for lunch, and finished for the day at 7:30 P.M. By means of carefully regulated clocks all of the mills' bells, used to summon the employees in the morning and to dismiss them at night, were struck as nearly in unison as possible.

Butler claimed to have become an advocate of the ten-hour day purely from humanitarian reasons. As a young man, he explained, he "became socially intimate with a very able and very accomplished physician of the most conservative views, . . . who had no concern with the mills in Lowell or with their operatives, save when called as a doctor." The doctor told Butler "that the hours of labor . . . were too great a strain on the life-powers of the operatives," that their hurriedly eaten meals could not be properly digested, and that although the work they did was not generally heavy, it required their constant attention. "While this long day was not immediately destructive," the doctor added, "it certainly permitted 'the survival of the fittest' only, and in the end deteriorated the physical strength of the whole population."[3]

Another story, told by Parton in 1864, probably at Butler's suggestion, almost certainly with his approval, concerns a strike for a shorter workday begun by some 3,000 mill girls. They asked Butler, whom they regarded as their good friend, for advice. Their grievances were great and their demands reasonable, he said, but he thought they were not at all likely to bring their employers to terms by the means they were using. "A strike," he told them, "is a doubtful and generally a desperate measure, . . . only to be resolved upon as a last resort, when oppression is no longer endurable, or otherwise curable." He suggested that the girls return to work, discuss things with their employers, and appeal to the General Court for legislation limiting their hours of labor if their employers would not listen to reason. His own words, spoken on this occasion, are supposed to have converted him into a ten-hour law enthusiast.[4]

Whatever motive or mixture of motives really led Butler to enlist in the ten-hour movement he served it loyally and tem-

---

[3] Butler, op. cit., p. 91.
[4] James Parton, *General Butler in New Orleans* (Mason Brothers [New York, 1864]), p. 26.

pestuously. However, he always recognized that the opposition of the mill owners and mill managers to the ten-hour movement was logical from their point of view. Their premise was that if the mills in Massachusetts ran only ten hours a day they could not compete with mills in other states running more time. Butler argued that the same employees could do more work per hour in a shorter, less tiring day, hence there would be no loss of production and that other states would follow Massachusetts in enacting ten-hour laws. Significantly, he believed his own propaganda. When he became a mill owner he established a ten-hour day in his plant and was well satisfied with the results obtained. (Interestingly, the conclusion which Butler reached intuitively was proved sound by experience gained by manufacturers during World War II showing that a 50 hour, six day week results in maximum production.)

The ten-hour movement was a quarter of a century old when Butler interested the Lowell Coalitionists in it. The Democratic party in Massachusetts, as well as in most other industrialized states, had more or less enthusiastically advocated the ten-hour day ever since Butler was a small boy. This being so he had no great trouble in bringing the Democratic members of the Coalition around to his way of thinking. The Free-Soilers, who were strongly opposed to the spread of slavery beyond the Mason-Dixon line, but were inclined to be somewhat conservative on other issues, probably accepted his advice only after being made to realize that supporting the ten-hour movement would be an excellent way to attract votes—particularly toward the end of a year in which there had been much local unemployment, a condition that would lend force to the make-work argument in favor of a shorter workday.

Of course, the mill owners, mostly residents of Boston, and their surrogates in Lowell, bitterly opposed the ten-hour day and fought its advocates tooth and nail. Notices were posted in the mills advising their male employees that anyone voting the "Ben Butler ten-hour ticket" would be discharged. Since no mill in Lowell would hire anybody who could not show a "clear discharge," signed by his or her last employer, the men did not need specifically to be told that they would also be blacklisted.

A committee of three Coalitionist candidates interviewed Linus Child, agent of the Boott Corporation. Child, who seems to have been the noisiest, most belligerent opponent of the ten-hour system, in Lowell at least, told his callers that to the best of his knowledge (which was amazingly scant in the particular connection) there was absolutely no one in his employ who favored a ten-hour law. And, he said, more emphatically than grammatically,

> If there was anyone who would enter into any combination, political or otherwise, with a view to produce results so disastrous to the Mills, as the proposed scheme would be or who considered themselves oppressed by [the existing] scale of wages, or hours of labor, such persons would be of no value to the Company and [he] certainly would not retain them.[5]

After their interview with Child the members of the committee met with the rest of the local Coalition leaders. Most of those present were of the opinion that they might as well abandon the ten-hour movement at once. Some of them worked in the mills. Many of the others, for business reasons, did not care to incur the wrath of the powerful mill agents. Only Butler and a few others felt they could afford to continue the fight. They issued an unsigned handbill calling upon the workingmen of Lowell to attend a meeting at the city hall the following Saturday night when Butler would be the principal speaker.

Apparently no contemporaneous accounts of Butler's speech were published. However, when Butler wrote his autobiography some 40 years later he recalled that he had said,

> Our fathers fought the battles of the Revolution . . . to establish . . . the right to govern themselves. . . . If the workingmen can be deprived of their freedom and rights by threats of starvation of themselves and their wives and children, when

---

[5] Susan M. Kingsbury (editor), *Labor Laws and their Enforcement* (Longmans, Green, and Co. [New York, 1911]), p. 71.

they act according to the laws and their own judgment, then they had better be slaves indeed, having kind masters, instead of being . . . only at liberty to do what their taskmasters impose upon them, or starve. And this question must be settled here and now. . . . I know the power of these corporations. I know many of the men who have been in charge. They have made a mistake in the appeal to force. When that weapon is tried, they are weak and you are strong. They have their mills and machinery, their bricks and mortar. . . . You have your right arms and your torches, and by them we will blot out this accursed outrage. As God lives and I live, by the living Jehovah! if one man is driven from his employment . . . because of his vote, I will lead you to make Lowell what it was twenty-five years ago,—a sheep pasture and a fishing place; and I will commence by applying the torch to my own house. Let them come on. As we are not the aggressors, we seek not this awful contest.[6]

Butler's story cannot be fully corroborated and he certainly would not have remembered the part he played as any less heroic than it really was. However, there are bits of evidence indicating that his memory of his speech was essentially accurate. An overseer at the Boott mill testified before a committee of the Massachusetts House of Representatives that he had heard talk of tearing the mills down and rumors "that Butler had got eight hundred men he could call at any time." It is also to be noted that William S. Robinson of the Lowell *American,* who had the reputation of being a calm, well balanced man, said, after reviewing events prior to the second election, "If open war is to be declared between the people and the Factory Agents, the responsibility will rest upon those who began the warfare by oppressing their workmen, and woe be unto those men against whom the people rise."[7]

In the end all the excitement turned out to have been unnecessary. The General Court decided that the men who had received majorities at the first election should be seated, despite "informalities and errors in making up the record and return in one of the wards." By this time, however, Butler had become

---

[6] Butler, op. cit., pp. 101–4.

[7] Kingsbury, 72.

identified as "the leader of the Anti-Corporation Ten-Hour Law Democracy of Lowell; the confidant and legal adviser of all abused overseers, second-hands [assistant overseers], understrappers, and factory girls; the stump orator who swayed the tumultuous mob . . . against the agents of the mills;" etc.[8]

During the canvass a Lowell newspaper published an editorial, headed simply "Ben Butler," which referred to Butler's inflammatory speech and read in part:

> This notorious demagogue and political scoundrel, having swilled three or four extra glasses of liquor, spread himself at whole length in City Hall last night. . . . The only wonder is that a character so foolish, so grovelling and obscene, can for a moment be admitted into decent society anywhere out of the pale of prostitutes and débauchés.[9]

In later years Butler disregarded remarks almost as ugly as that one; this time he sued the editor for libel. Judge Ebenezer Rockwood Hoar, before whom the matter was tried, effectively secured the editor's acquittal by charging the jury that in order to make his case good the plaintiff would have to prove beyond any doubt, not merely a reasonable doubt, that the editorial referred specifically to the Ben Butler whose full name was Benjamin F. Butler. Hoar made sure that the jury did not miss his meaning by adding that there was nothing but the editorial itself to prove to whom it applied and this did not seem to him to be conclusive evidence on the point.[10]

Butler never forgave Hoar for that day's work. Seventeen years later the Judge was nominated to fill a vacancy in the Supreme Court of the United States. Butler, then a congressman, successfully used his influence to prevent Hoar's confirmation by the Senate. Still angry in 1876 Butler said in an open letter to Hoar,

---

[8] *Robinson Scrap Books,* Book No. 7, p. 230.

[9] Quoted in Butler, op. cit., p. 108.

[10] Frank W. Grinnell, "The Judicial System and the Bar (1820–1861)," in *Commonwealth History of Massachusetts* (The States History Company [New York, 1930]), IV, 68.

I am bound by candor to say that I never heard any criticism upon your conduct as a judge, save that the infirmity of your temper, the peculiarity of your mind, and the state of your stomach were so unfortunate, that it was said of you by a very distinguished member of the bar, that you were in a continual condition of ill-manners on the bench, both toward your associates, the members of the bar, and the suitors before your court; because you could not gratify the bitterness in your heart by giving judgment against both parties in every case.[11]

Late in 1851 it began to seem fairly certain that the next year's presidential election would end the Whigs' second brief period of power. In these circumstances a number of Democratic politicians started scrambling and intriguing to control their party's choice of a presidential candidate. A group of New Englanders, including Senator Hannibal Hamlin of Maine; Charles G. Atherton, Charles H. Peaslee, and ex-Senator Franklin Pierce of New Hampshire; Isaac O. Barnes, Charles L. Woodbury, Caleb Cushing, and Butler, of Massachusetts planned, not too secretly, to spring Levi Woodbury's name upon the convention if it became deadlocked, as they anticipated it would. Woodbury's chief asset was that his six years (1845–51) as associate justice of the Supreme Court had enabled him to keep out of any recent political squabbles. Within a short time politicians from as far away as Virginia and Missouri were collaborating with the New Englanders, either because they, too, were fond of Woodbury, or, more probably, because he seemed likely to be nominated and they wanted seats on the band wagon.

Woodbury's sudden death made it necessary for the group to find another protégé. After shopping around for a while they decided to support one of their own number—Franklin Pierce. They must have chosen him because he was so little known that no one could possibly have any feelings against him; certainly nothing else could have recommended him.

By the time the Democratic convention met, on June 1, 1852, the leading contenders for the nomination—Senator Lewis Cass

---

[11] Benjamin F. Butler, *Letter of Gen. Benjamin F. Butler to Hon. E. R. Hoar.*

of Michigan, former Secretary of State James Buchanan of Pennsylvania, Senator Stephen A. Douglas of Illinois, former Secretary of War William L. Marcy of New York, Senator Sam Houston of Texas, and William O. Butler of Kentucky—had succeeded remarkably well in their efforts to kill each others' chances. Pierce was nominated on the 49th ballot.

Although Butler's part in effecting Pierce's nomination was not too great, he had travelled quite a distance, politically speaking, for a man still in his early thirties.

In 1852 Butler was nominated as Democratic candidate for two different offices—representative in the United States Congress and representative in the General Court of Massachusetts. He ran a poor third in the congressional race, but was elected to the state legislature.

Soon after he took his seat in the General Court he remarked that the pay of a Massachusetts legislator—$2.00 a day—was not enough to carry him home. A Whig newspaper immediately proposed that a fund be raised to pay him to stay home.

Early in 1853 Butler presented to the House of Representatives a petition for a ten-hour law signed by 800 Lowell mill workers. A motion he made to have this petition referred to a special committee was tabled on the grounds that the matter of ten-hour legislation was already under consideration by another committee. The latter committee reported that it was inexpedient to enact a ten-hour law. A minority took a different view and presented a bill providing that ten hours should constitute a day's work for employees of corporations. Butler was absent on the day this bill was first read and he did not speak in favor of it at any time. Perhaps he felt that his attitude in the matter was too well-known to need amplification. For some reason he also failed to vote for the bill. The anonymous author of a political tract entitled *Gen. Benjamin F. Butler's True Record* wrote in 1879 that he was "necessarily absent on military duty on the day of the passage of the bill." This may be so; however it is equally likely that he was busy in court somewhere on that day, for, except during the Civil War, he never let his public duties interfere seriously with his law practice. Even while he was governor of Massachusetts he frequently absented himself from the state to prosecute cases in various federal courts. Because he failed to vote for this bill his enemies often took occasion to say that he gave the cause of labor more vocal than practical support. Nevertheless, most laborers were satisfied with his record.

The Senate, with malice aforethought, amended the bill to provide that ten hours should constitute a day's work for all classes of employees unless otherwise provided by contract. Making the law applicable to all classes was designed to render it potentially unconstitutional. Little doubt was entertained at the time that the legislature could regulate the employment practices of corporations—the legislature's own creatures; no such opinion was held about unincorporated businesses, which were, in the aggregate, the largest employers of labor. Everybody knew the special contract provision would make the law utterly ineffectual; New Hampshire's experience with a law containing such a provision had proved that fact. Butler logically moved nonconcurrence on the part of the House with this amendment. The sponsor of the bill supported Butler's motion which was carried.

Butler also attempted early in his legislative career to rectify what seemed to him to be an injustice of longstanding. In 1844 an anti-Catholic mob had burned an Ursuline convent in Charlestown, near Boston. On several occasions the Ursuline Order had appealed to the General Court for funds to rebuild the convent, claiming that its destruction had resulted from the supineness of the town's authorities. No attention was ever paid to these petitions until Butler entered the legislature. Perhaps as an act of simple justice, perhaps with an eye to the large and rapidly growing number of Roman Catholics in his district, he introduced a bill to reimburse the Ursulines. He thought this bill ought to be referred to a special committee. One member of the House facetiously suggested its reference to the liquor committee. Others, whose animus it is not hard to deduce, offered bills to reimburse any and all sufferers at the hands of mobs, including the women who had been present when an abolitionist meeting was riotously broken up in 1853. These witticisms led Butler pointedly to comment that the people of Massachusetts could not consistently complain of religious intolerance in other countries nor could the General Court logically ask, as it had recently done, that privileges be extended to Protestants abroad until atonement was made to the Ursuline Order.

Butler's bill was finally passed by the House on a Friday. Since the legislature did not meet on Saturdays the measure had to wait until Monday for consideration by the Senate. He never doubted that if the bill had gone to the Senate earlier in the week it would have been passed by that chamber. However, a large number of Protestant clergymen criticized it adversely in sermons they preached on the Sunday before the Senate considered it and it was allowed to die, never to be revived.

In 1853 Butler was chosen to represent Lowell at a convention called for the purpose of revising the state constitution. The "great power of will, strength of mind and industry" he demonstrated at the convention favorably impressed one of his most unfriendly contemporaries,[12] but another said "he brought to [the convention's] partisan disputes the pugnacity which was hereafter to be displayed in national scenes."[13]

For some years before the convention was held there had been a widespread feeling that the constitution, adopted in 1820, needed to be changed in several particulars. The two most important things in the eyes of the populace were apportionment of the House of Representatives and the judiciary. The state's cities, particularly Boston, were thought to have too large a number of representatives and there was considerable sentiment in favor of having judges elected for comparatively short terms instead of their being appointed for life.

---

[12] Charles Francis Adams, *Richard Henry Dana* (Houghton, Mifflin and Company [Boston, 1890]), I, 249.

[13] Edward L. Pierce, *Memoir and Letters of Charles Sumner* (Roberts Brothers [Boston, 1877, 1883]), III, 328.

The Whigs, opposed on principle to changes of any sort, and a few Free-Soilers who disliked the idea of an elected judiciary, collaborated in the General Court to prevent any action looking toward constitutional reform as long as they could. Finally, in 1852, a Coalitionist-controlled legislature submitted to the voters a proposition for a constitutional convention with its delegates to be chosen by secret ballot. In the election held that fall the people voted in favor of a convention and returned a small majority of Whigs to the General Court. The Whigs' victory went to their heads. When the legislature met in January 1853 they undertook to rescind the call for the convention. This scheme roused so much resentment that it was rather quickly abandoned, but the provision for the secret election of delegates was repealed. Butler led the fight against this reactionary step.

Butler remarked in his autobiography, and many of his contemporaries agreed with him, that as a rule the debates in the convention were distinguished by fairness and courtesy, with "scarcely a distasteful personal allusion . . . made."[14] The official records of the proceedings of the convention bear out this statement, but he forgot, or chose not to remember, an exchange that was not recorded. Butler spoke critically of the harsh, rough manner in which Chief Justice Lemuel Shaw often treated attorneys appearing in the state's Supreme Court. George S. Hillard, a Whig leader, pointed to Butler and said, "While we have jackals and hyenas at the bar, we want the old lion on the bench, with one blow of his huge paw to bring their scalps over their eyes."[15]

A witticism of Butler's may also have been regarded with some distaste by at least 15 delegates. Somebody moved that the 16 different plans for reorganizing the House of Representatives presented to the convention be referred to a committee made up of their various sponsors. Butler, who had offered one of the plans, commented that 16 babies might as well be sent to their

[14] Butler, op. cit., p. 118.
[15] George F. Hoar, *Autobiography of Seventy Years* (Charles Scribner's Sons [New York, 1903]), I, 178–79.

mothers for a unanimous report as to which was the prettiest.

One of the problems discussed by the convention was the fact that in Massachusetts, as elsewhere in New England, a candidate for a state office had to secure an absolute majority of the votes cast in order to be elected. When there were three or more parties in the field, as was often the case after the Anti-Masonic party appeared in 1832, a number of elections sometimes had to be held before a choice was made. On one occasion the citizens of Rhode Island voted five times for a governor before one was finally elected. Massachusetts could solve this annoying and expensive problem, Butler suggested, by means of a tripartite amendment to the state constitution. Its first provision was that if no candidate for any of the so-called constitutional offices (i.e., governor, lieutenant governor, secretary of state, treasurer, auditor, and attorney general) received a majority the House of Representatives should choose the names of two of the three men having the most votes and send them to the Senate to select one of them for the office in question. The second provision was that senators and members of the Governor's Council should be chosen by a plurality. The last provision was that when no candidate for a seat in the House of Representatives had a majority in an election anyone getting a plurality in a run-off should be the winner. These proposals would have worked to the advantage of the Coalition—and that may be why the convention rejected them.

In 1903 George Frisbee Hoar, who had been a Free-Soil member of the General Court in 1852, wrote that a bare majority of the House of Representatives had voted for the constitutional convention only after a specific pledge had been given "that there should be no meddling with the judiciary."[16] If such a promise really was made it was not kept. In Hoar's opinion it was broken at the instigation of Butler and Josiah G. Abbott, another politically active Democratic lawyer. As Hoar told the story in his autobiography Butler and Abbott tried a case before Judge Pliny Merrick while the convention was in session, became angry at

---

[16] Ibid., I, 172.

some action taken or some remark made, by the Judge, and returned to the convention "determined to do something to curb the independent power of the Judges."[17]

Although this tale is characteristic of the way the conservatives of Butler's day blamed him for nearly everything they disliked, its only factual basis is that Butler did have a tiff with a judge in 1853. The facts, as contemporaneously reported, are that Butler and Abbott appeared before a judge named Bigelow, with E. R. Hoar, the Senator's brother, as opposing counsel. Judge Bigelow, "who seems to have been in an ill-humor," interrupted Butler to say he had been questioning a witness for half an hour. Butler said this could not be so because the court had been in session for only 25 minutes. The Judge's answer evoked a sharp retort from Butler. The Judge ordered Butler to apologize for his remark or leave the courtroom. He did not apologize,[18] but he did not go back to the convention any more interested in the judiciary than he had previously been. In his view reapportionment of the House of Representatives was the most important matter to be considered by the convention. Actually it was a Free-Soiler, Henry Wilson, the Natick cobbler, who became the 19th Vice-President of the United States, not Butler, who was chiefly responsible for the judicial reform proposed by the convention. Wilson moved that justices of the Supreme Court be appointed for ten year terms and judges of the inferior courts for seven years, with reappointment possible, but with retirement compulsory for all judges at the age of 70. All of the Whig delegates and some of the Free-Soilers opposed this motion. Butler took no part in the first day's debate about it. When he did come to its support he said he did so at the calculated risk of being called a sickly hyena by some sickly conservative. The convention finally voted in favor of ten year terms for justices of the Supreme Court and of the Court of Common Pleas, with three year terms for other judges.

---

[17] Ibid., I, 174–75.
[18] *Robinson Scrapbooks,* Bk. No. 4, p. 329.

From the time it was first mentioned Butler opposed a provision that no money raised by taxation should ever be granted to any private school maintained by a religious sect. He claimed to see no need for such a thing and to have heard no call for it. If he had not heard a public cry for a provision of this sort he was wilfully deaf. Nobody interested in current affairs could have avoided knowing that for some time past Bishop John J. Hughes of New York had been more or less openly seeking to have the Roman Catholic parochial schools of that state given control of what he called "their share" of tax funds. The Protestants of Massachusetts were up in arms to prevent the diversion of any tax money to the parochial schools in their state. Many of the delegates to the convention hinted broadly at their desire to make sure that no Roman Catholic school should ever get any public funds. One man from Boston frankly stated that such was the purpose of the sectarian school amendment. An overwhelming majority (159 out of 183) of the delegates agreed that the provision should be included in the constitution to be submitted to the electorate.

The constitution, as revised by the convention, was rejected by a vote of about 67,000 to 65,000. Butler believed the Roman Catholic bishop of Boston was responsible for this result because he advised the Catholics of the state to vote against the proposed constitution on account of its sectarian school provision.[19] However, a number of Whigs and Free-Soilers (with not a Roman Catholic among them) also wrote and spoke against the proposed constitution because they disliked limited terms for judges. In the circumstances nobody can say with any assurance whose propaganda was more influential.

In September, 1855 Butler was chosen as one of four delegates at large to the Democratic party's presidential nominating convention to be held the next year at Cincinnati, Ohio. At the convention he attracted the notice of a reporter for the Cincinnati *Commercial* by his habit of springing to his feet "with wonderful

[19] Butler, op. cit., pp. 119–20.

quickness," and ripping out the words, " 'Mr. Chairman,' in a tone like the sound of a file on a cross-cut saw," while gesturing "as if he proposed to stab the presiding officer if he did not devote his attention instantly to 'the gentleman from Massachusetts.' "[20]

During the campaign of 1856 Butler attended a rally in Huntington Hall, a large room on the second floor of the Lowell railroad station. In the midst of a speech by Rufus Choate a loud cracking noise threw the audience into a near panic. Butler stepped to the front of the platform, calmed the crowd, and said that he and the building's architect, who happened to be present, would examine the structure and report their findings. They discovered that the building was almost ready to collapse. The architect prudently left the place. Butler returned to the platform, quietly said the hall was somewhat overcrowded and ought to be cleared. With Butler bringing up the rear the crowd filed out in an orderly manner. (In fairness to Butler it must be noted that he never told this story publicly. It was first published by the Boston *Post,* probably at Choate's suggestion, a few days after the event.) From that day on nobody ever questioned Butler's physical courage or his readiness to face emergencies.

Striving onward and upward, Butler was a candidate for a seat in the state Senate in 1857. Although he ran ahead of the rest of the Democratic ticket, he was beaten by a few hundred votes. A year later he lost the Democratic gubernatorial nomination to Erasmus D. Beach, but was chosen to run for two other offices—representative in Congress and state senator. He was thoroughly trounced in the congressional race, but won the other by a moderate plurality.

As state senator, Butler turned his attention to the judicial system of Massachusetts. He was primarily responsible for the passage of an act by which the Court of Common Pleas was abol-

---

[20] Murat Halstead, *National Political Conventions of the Current Presidential Campaign* (Follett, Foster and Company [Columbus, Ohio, 1860]), p. 22.

ished and the Superior Court was established in its stead. Some Massachusetts lawyers believed, though none of them cared to say it out loud, that many of the legislators who voted for Butler's bill did so because they considered the judges of the Court of Common Pleas incompetent. Theoretically the judges could have been removed individually by impeachment, but this method was practically useless so they were removed collectively by the elimination of their court. There was also a feeling among the state's lawyers that Butler had done a good thing in this matter. Frank W. Grinnell, secretary of the Massachusetts Bar Association, wrote in 1930 that Butler deserved great credit for his constructive service in drafting the Judiciary Act of 1859.[21]

At Butler's instigation, chiefly, the Judiciary Act of 1859 provided that judges might charge juries only as to matters of law. Hitherto judges had been free to express their opinions about facts, the credibility of witnesses, weight of evidence, etc., when charging juries. Jurors were supposed clearly to be informed that they were not bound to accept a judge's views, but a judge could usually evoke the sort of verdict he desired, as Judge Hoar did in the previously mentioned libel suit brought by Butler. There can be little doubt that Butler had this case in mind when he drafted the Judiciary Act.

It also seems likely that in 1903 Senator Hoar mentally jumbled Butler's connection with the Judiciary Act of 1859 and the judicial reforms proposed by the constitutional convention of 1853. Such an unconscious synthesis could have led Hoar to assert that Butler was responsible for what the convention did at Wilson's suggestion.

While Butler was in the state Senate he received two votes when the General Court met to choose a United States senator. One of these votes was cast by Jonas French, the other by Caleb Cushing. French may have been paying Butler a compliment or even have had some hope of seeing him elected. Cushing, who got 25 votes, probably voted for Butler in order to vote for somebody other than himself without voting for anyone who might win.

---

[21] Grinnell, loc. cit., p. 67.

When the Democratic state convention met in September, 1859 Butler was chosen, practically without opposition, as the party's candidate for governor. His only potentially serious rival, Benjamin F. Hallett, somewhat ungraciously withdrew in Butler's favor. After saying that he had "rather committed himself to support Mr. Butler, who was true on popular sovereignty," Hallett moved Butler's nomination by acclamation. According to the (Republican) Boston *Journal* a few votes were cast in the negative; the (Democratic) Boston *Post* reported that Hallett's motion was received with wild applause and adopted amid deafening cheers. The press of both sides agreed that Butler had been nominated.

In describing Butler as true on popular sovereignty Hallett meant that Butler agreed with Senator Stephen A. Douglas of Illinois that the settlers in any particular territory in the West could and should decide by popular vote whether or not to permit slavery within the territory. Douglas and his followers continued to argue that slavery could be excluded from any territory by unfriendly police regulations even after the Dred Scott decision, rendered by the Supreme Court in 1857, had undermined this theory.

Although Butler refrained from making the fact clear to his fellow Democrats, he was of the opinion that Douglas's doctrine was incompatible with the federal Constitution. Since the Constitution permitted slavery to exist Butler thought it necessarily guaranteed slave property, like any other property, against interference from, or expropriation by, any individual or agency, including federal, state, and territorial governments.

While concealing his real attitude about popular sovereignty, Butler did make it clear that his attachment to the Union far exceeded his concern with slavery. In connection with the discussion evoked by John Brown's crackbrained adventure at Harper's Ferry in October, 1859, Butler said publicly,

> Let us proclaim to all men that the Union, first and fairest of all the good gifts of God, must and shall be preserved. . . . [that] this Union, this Republic, this great experiment of equal

rights, this power of self-government by the people, this great instrument of civilization, the banding together of the intellectual and political power of those races which are to civilize the world by their energy of action, is not to fail, and human progress to be set back a thousand years, because of a difference of opinion as to the supposed rights and interests of a few Negroes.[22]

Probably no Democrat could have made any better race for the governorship in 1859 than Butler did, but when the returns came in it was found that Nathaniel P. Banks, the Republican incumbent, had received some 58,000 votes; Butler, 35,000; and the Know-Nothing candidate 14,000.

A remarkably prescient editorial published in the Taunton, Massachusetts, *Gazette* soon after the election said Butler was not the sort of politician to be killed off by one defeat. A missionary who left the United States during the campaign of 1859 returned 23 years and a few weeks later to learn that Butler had just been elected governor of Massachusetts.

---

[22] Quoted in T. A. Bland, *Life of Benjamin F. Butler* (Lee and Shepard [Boston, 1879]), p. 25.

4

★★★★★★★★★★★★

The Democratic Conventions of 1860

In 1859 Butler was chosen to represent his district at the Democratic national convention scheduled to open in Charleston, South Carolina, on April 23, 1860. Because the Democrats in Lowell were so heartily in favor of the nomination of Senator Stephen A. Douglas for the presidency that no one known to feel differently could even have hoped to be a delegate to the convention Butler concealed the fact that he really wanted to see James M. Guthrie of Kentucky nominated. Guthrie, who had been Secretary of the Treasury in Pierce's Cabinet, was a hard worker, a capable executive, and a successful businessman, but he was not well-known outside of his own state. However, Butler, who had recently played a small part in making an equally obscure and even less able man a presidential candidate, assumed that if he only got to the convention he could do singlehandedly for Guthrie what a numerous and fairly powerful group had done for Pierce.

Never having taken much interest in the slavery question Butler completely failed to appreciate that the platform, rather than the candidate, would be the big issue at the convention. At this time the Democracy was divided, like all Gaul, into three parts. A southern faction wanted a platform calling for enactment by the next (Thirty-seventh) Congress of legislation not only permitting but practically endorsing slavery in the still unorganized territories in the West and Southwest. Douglas's followers, almost exclusively northerners, desired a platform endorsing popular sovereignty. The third faction, comprising both northerners and southerners, thought that if the slavery issue were straddled the Democratic party could retain control of the federal government, as that party had done since 1801 except for the duration of two presidential terms.

Although few, if any, of the other delegates from Massachusetts were aware of the fact, Butler was among those who favored an evasive treatment of the slavery question. In the belief that he agreed with their views the pro-Douglas members of the delegation helped unanimously to choose Butler to represent Massachusetts on the platform committee, consisting of one man from each of the 33 states then in the Union.

The platform committee sat almost continuously for three days and nights, arguing all the while about the proposals advanced by the proslavery faction and those advocated by the Douglasites. During one stormy session Butler suggested that, for the sake of harmony, the Democracy should pledge itself to stand by the Constitution and the Union. A Texas fire-eater moved that this proposition be referred to the convention of the Constitutional Union party which was soon to meet in Baltimore. Butler hotly informed the Texan that he could not insult a man from Massachusetts with impunity. Such a retort might well have led to a challenge to a duel; in this case it evoked an apology. However, Butler would not have refused a challenge and in view of his military training he probably could have given a good account of himself fighting with a cavalry saber. (As the challenged party he would have been entitled to make the choice of weapons.)

The platform committee finally offered the convention a majority report and two minority reports. All three reports were based upon the platform adopted by the Democratic party in 1856 (known as the Cincinnati platform). That platform had asserted that Congress had no constitutional power to interfere with slavery in any state. It had characterized the efforts of Abolitionists and others (meaning the then recently formed Republican party) to persuade Congress to take "incipient steps in relation" to slavery as inimical to the happiness of the people and dangerous to the stability of the Union. It had promised that the Democratic party would abide by the Compromise of 1850, including the Fugitive Slave Law, and would resist all attempts anywhere and in any guise toward agitation against slavery.

William W. Avery of North Carolina, speaking for 17 southern members of the committee, proposed the addition of several planks to the Cincinnati platform. One would state that neither Congress nor any territorial legislature could prohibit slavery in any territory. Another would say that enactments of any state legislature (such as the Personal Liberty Laws of Massachusetts) designed to nullify the Fugitive Slave Law were subversive of the federal Constitution and revolutionary in their effects. A third would proclaim it to be the duty of the federal government to protect property (including slaves) and the rights of persons in the territories and wherever else its jurisdiction extended. Two others held that the federal government should protect naturalized citizens and that the United States ought to acquire Cuba at the earliest possible moment.

Henry B. Payne of Ohio, as spokesman for 15 (Douglasite) committeemen, proposed adding to the Cincinnati platform statements that all questions about property rights (including the right to hold slaves anywhere in the United States) ought to be left for settlement by the Supreme Court; that equal protection should be extended to native and naturalized citizens; that the federal government ought to assist in the construction of a transcontinental railroad (a matter of great personal and political interest to Douglas); that Cuba ought to be acquired by the United States; and that resistance to the Fugitive Slave Law was subversive and revolutionary.

Butler, speaking for himself as a minority of one, proposed reaffirmation of the Cincinnati platform "without addition or alteration" except for a plank stating that the United States owed equal protection to naturalized and native-born citizens.

(All of the reports mentioned equal protection for naturalized citizens because when the Know-Nothing party disintegrated in 1856 most of its former adherents became Republicans. Thus the Democracy could reasonably hope to gain something by stressing its long-standing friendliness toward newcomers.)

Butler's proposal practically coincided with the Administration's desire for readoption of the Cincinnati platform "pure and simple." Apparently he agreed with President James Buchanan that if the most important issue of the day was ignored the country could ride out the storm of sectionalism sweeping up from the South. The men who formed the Constitutional Union party, based as its delightfully brief platform stated upon "no political principle other than the Union and the law," had the same idea. So did the 589,000 men who voted for the Constitutional Union party's presidential candidate.

The platform committee's various reports were exhaustively debated. The dreary discussion about them was enlivened only by Butler's ferocious dissection of Avery's and Payne's proposals.

Avery argued that the Cincinnati platform could be interpreted in different ways. Butler replied:

If the Cincinnati platform is so defective, why did you give it such enthusiastic support in 1856? [You say] that it is capable of two interpretations. . . . For almost two thousand years men have been engaged in giving different interpretations of [divine] law, and they have sealed their faith in their own interpretations with their blood. They have burned each other at the stake as evidence of the sincerity of their faith.[1]

Turning to the Payne report, Butler said,

Suppose, gentlemen of the North, the Supreme Court should decide that slavery exists in Massachusetts, that it was forced upon us by the Constitution of the United States: what would you do about it?

And you, gentlemen of the South, suppose in the course of a few years the Supreme Court should become anti-slavery, and make a decision that slavery nowhere exists by natural law and that men can hold no property in man: what then? Are you prepared to abide by the decision?[2]

---

[1] T. A. Bland, *Life of Benjamin F. Butler* (Lee and Shepard [Boston, 1879]), p. 27.
[2] Ibid., pp. 27–28.

A would-be peacemaker suggested asking the platform committee to reconsider its several reports in the hope that a compromise could be reached. A motion this gentleman made to
recommit the reports was carried by a majority of one vote. Some
hours later three reports essentially similar to the original ones
were presented. Butler again offered the Cincinnati platform
"pure and undefiled." There followed what Murat Halstead
called "the most tedious and tasteless, flat, stale and unprofitable
debate" it had ever been his misfortune to hear. "It was," he
wrote, "worse than when the House of Representatives resolves
itself into a debating society and fifth-rate members draw on each
other, . . . to the dismay of the galleries, reams of foolscap filled
with essays on the slavery question."[3]

When the flood of twaddle finally ended the convention voted
on the reports, beginning with Butler's. Just as the clerk was
about to announce the count a man in a seat on the main floor
complained to the chairman that the people in the galleries were
spitting on the heads of those below. "The gentlemen in the galleries were respectfully requested not to use the heads of the
gentlemen below for spittoons, and not to wear their hats in the
presence of the uncovered Convention."[4] After this "privileged
question" had been settled it was announced that Butler's proposed platform had been rejected by a vote of 198 to 105. The
distribution of votes did not follow sectional lines. Some southern and some northern delegations divided their votes upon it;
other delegations from both sections voted solidly against it. Massachusetts cast eight votes for and five against it. Many of the
delegates were ready for some sort of compromise, but more of
them had been firmly instructed as to what kind of platform to
support—and it was not one such as Butler had proposed. Some
of them may also have thought that evasion of the slavery issue
was no longer possible, or, perhaps, even desirable.

[3] Murat Halstead, *National Political Conventions of the Current Presidential Campaign* (Follett, Foster and Company [Columbus, Ohio, 1860]),
p. 69.
[4] Ibid., p. 62.

The Payne, or Douglasite, report was next put to a vote. Although it had commanded the support of only a minority of the platform committee, it was approved by a majority (165 to 138) of the convention. As soon as the result of the vote was announced Butler moved adoption of a resolution "that we, the Democracy of the Union in convention assembled, hereby declare our affirmance of the resolutions unanimously adopted and declared as a platform of principles by the Democratic convention at Cincinnati in the year 1856; believing that Democratic principles are unchangeable in their nature when applied to the same subject matters." Because this literally meaningless plank was adopted by a vote of 273½ to 65 Butler always claimed to have persuaded the convention of 1860 to readopt the Cincinnati platform.

The approval of the Douglasite platform, as amended by Butler, led the pro-slavery extremists to bolt the convention. All of the delegates from Alabama, Mississippi, Florida, and Texas withdrew immediately, as did all except three from South Carolina, three from Arkansas, two from Louisiana, two from Delaware, and one from North Carolina. Twenty-six of Georgia's 33 delegates left the next day.

The delegates who remained in their seats undertook to choose presidential and vice-presidential candidates, but they saddled themselves with an impossible task by deciding that a vote equivalent to a two-thirds majority of a full convention should be necessary to effect a nomination. (Hitherto the two-thirds rule had regularly been taken to mean two-thirds of those voting, not of those present, much less of all of the delegates to a convention.)

Before the voting began W. B. Gaulden of Georgia, a tall, hatchet-faced, dark-complexioned, high-nosed, big-eyed, scraggly-bearded, black-haired man, who was both a slave dealer and a large slaveholder delivered a remarkable harangue. Speaking forcefully and in deadly earnest, he proclaimed himself to be "a slavery-extension, a slave-trade man." In his opinion "the institution" was "right socially, politically, morally and religiously." The abolition of slavery, he said, would cause civilization to "go back two hundred years." The law (passed by Congress in March,

1807) prohibiting the importation of slaves "had put an end to all hope of extending slavery at the present time." Therefore the only remedy immediately available for the evils of which the South complained was a reopening of the African slave trade. In this matter he looked to the northern Democracy for help. He told the delegates "that the African slave-trade man is the Union man—the true Christian man." He described "the slave-trade of Virginia" as "more inhuman, more unchristian, in every point of view, than the African slave-trade; for, the African slave-trader goes to a heathen land and brings the savage here and Christianizes him, and sends him down to posterity a happy man." By contrast, he declared "that the Virginia slave-trader, who tears a slave family asunder from those ties which cluster around civilization, . . . was far more open to rebuke than the man who brought the African from a land where he has no ties of country or family around him."[5]

During the various roll calls Butler voted first for Douglas, switched to Senator Jefferson Davis of Mississippi, tried the magic of Guthrie's name a few times, then went back to Davis. After the 57th ballot had failed to result in a nomination the convention adjourned, to meet again at Baltimore six weeks later.

Since Douglas had well over a majority on every roll call, but never came close to having a two-thirds majority of the full number of delegates entitled to seats, Butler's defection did no real harm to Douglas. Nevertheless, Butler's conduct brought the wrath of his constituents down upon his head. He was hooted through the streets of Lowell and a mob prevented him from addressing a meeting at which he sought to give an accounting of his stewardship. Later, when he managed to obtain a hearing, he said in extenuation of his behavior at the convention,

With the facts before me, and impressing me with the conviction that the nomination of Judge Douglas could not be made with any hope of safety to the Democratic party, what was I to do? Yielding to your preferences, I voted seven times for

[5] Ibid., pp. 77–78.

Judge Douglas, although my judgment told me that my votes
were worse than useless, as they gave him an appearance of
strength in the convention which I felt he had not in the party.
   I then looked about me . . . [and] saw a statesman of national fame, who had led his regiment to victory at Buena Vista
[during the Mexican War], a Democrat with whom I disagreed in some things, but with whom I could act in most—
loving his country first, his section next, but just to all. . . . I
thought such a man worthy of the compliment of a vote from
Massachusetts; therefore I threw my vote for Jefferson Davis
of Mississippi. I make no apology for that vote. I believe I
was guided by an intelligent view of the situation.[6]

Butler never thought Davis should or would be nominated. He
simply used Davis as a stalking horse for Guthrie. However, the
fact that he had voted many times for Davis, who subsequently
became President of the Confederate States of America, was often
brought up against Butler after the Civil War. But, as he asserted,
there was nothing offensive to a northern Democrat in Davis's
record up to 1860. Indeed, *Harper's Weekly,* an ardently Republican journal, published a calm discussion of Davis as a possible Democratic nominee only two days before the Charleston
convention was called to order.[7]

By the time the Democrats reassembled at the Front Street
Theater in Baltimore on June 18, 1860 the Republicans had
named their presidential and vice-presidential candidates. Every
reason, therefore, existed for the Democrats to iron out their fac-
tional differences. Instead of doing so they took the Kilkenny cats
for their model. Before the Charleston convention adjourned a
motion was adopted that new delegates be chosen in place of those
who had bolted in order to have a full convention at Baltimore.
A number of states sent two sets of delegates—one pro-Douglas,
the other anti-Douglas—to Baltimore. The credentials committee
wrangled for several days about the conflicting claims of the

6 Bland, op. cit., p. 29.
7 Benjamin F. Butler, *Butler's Book* (A. M. Thayer & Co. [Boston,
1892]), p. 140: *Harper's Weekly,* April 21, 1860, p. 250.

various delegates, then decided for the most part in favor of the Douglas men.

Just as the chairman of the credentials committee was about to read his report the stage collapsed, tossing a lot of bigwigs into a heap and almost causing a panic. Butler certainly had a rare faculty for being in collapsible buildings.

As soon as the credentials committee's report was read Virginia's delegates bolted. They were quickly followed by all or most of the delegates from North Carolina, Tennessee, California, Delaware, Maryland, Kentucky, Missouri, and Massachusetts.

Before the Massachusetts men left the hall Butler addressed what was left of the convention. At first the delegates refused to let him speak. However, he insisted upon being heard despite hoots, catcalls, and hisses. He and some of the others from Massachusetts were leaving, he said, in protest against a ruling made by the credentials committee in the case of Benjamin F. Hallett versus R. L. Chafee. Hallett had been named a delegate to the Charleston convention. Finding it impossible to attend that gathering he had notified his alternate, Chafee, who had gone to Charleston. When Hallett appeared at Baltimore, Chafee challenged his right to a seat. The credentials committee ruled in favor of Chafee. Hallett's friends, who were opposed to Douglas, refused to accept this decision and, led by Butler, they marched out of the hall.

Because Gaulden had repeated his slave trade harangue Butler also said, speaking for himself personally, "I will not sit in a convention where the African slave-trade—which is piracy by the laws of my country—is approvingly advocated."[8] He does not seem to have told anyone then or later why Gaulden's speech had not bothered him at Charleston but did so at Baltimore.

The bolting delegates gathered at the Maryland Institute in Baltimore, adopted the pro slavery platform rejected by the Charleston convention, and nominated John C. Breckenridge of Kentucky for President and Joseph Lane of Oregon for Vice-President. After deciding to call themselves the National Demo-

---

[8] Halstead, op. cit., pp. 205–6.

cratic party the delegates recommended that local tickets be entered in as many states as possible.

In September a convention attended by more than 1,000 Breckenridge Democrats met in Boston to make up a state ticket. Butler was nominated by acclamation as the party's candidate for governor.

Butler's opponents in the 1860 gubernatorial race were John A. Andrew (Republican), Amos A. Lawrence (Constitutional Unionist), and Erasmus D. Beach (Douglas Democrat). Butler was too much of a political realist to have expected to win, yet it is to be doubted that he foresaw how badly he would be beaten. He got less than 6,000 votes to 23,000 for Lawrence, 24,-000 for Beach, and nearly 102,000 for Andrew.

Late in December, 1860 Butler attended a conference of Breckenridge leaders in Washington. He asked some of the southerners present what action their section intended to take in view of Abraham Lincoln's election. Most of them answered that their states would soon follow the example of South Carolina and secede from the Union. Butler then inquired if the South was ready for war. On being told there would be no war he replied that the North would fight to its last man and its last dollar against secession. "And," he said, "you may be assured if war comes slavery ends."[9]

While Butler was in Washington three commissioners appointed by the self-styled "sovereign and independent State of South Carolina" reached the capital. These gentlemen were empowered to treat with the government of the United States for the delivery of the forts, magazines, lighthouses, and other real estate, with their appurtenances, in the limits of South Carolina; for an apportionment of the public debt; and for a division of other property held by the government of the United States, of which South Carolina had been a member until recently.

It seemed to Butler that the arrival of the South Carolinians

---

[9] Isaac N. Arnold, *Abraham Lincoln and the Overthrow of Slavery* (Clarke & Co. [Chicago, 1866]), p. 183.

offered President Buchanan a golden opportunity to resolve a question that was gravely troubling him. Buchanan deplored secession, but he was unable to conceive of anything he could do about it because he did not believe the federal government could constitutionally coerce a state. Butler thought the President could clear the air by causing the arrest of the commissioners on a charge of treason at the moment they officially presented their demands on behalf of South Carolina. Secession, Butler said to Buchanan, "is either a riot or treason." If it were only a riot the sooner that fact was established, "in the highest form of knowledge, a decision by the Supreme Court," the better. Personally Butler considered secession definitely to be treason and thought that the presentation by the commissioners of "an official call by . . . representatives of an armed combination of citizens . . . [for] the surrender of a portion of the territory of the United States to a foreign nation" would be an overt act of treason. Therefore, he suggested that the commissioners be arrested and indicted by a grand jury or that they be examined by the Supreme Court with all the form and ceremony that had attended the trial of Aaron Burr in 1807. If they were sentenced for treason and the sentence executed it would, Butler believed, "stop secession for the present generation at least." If they were acquitted something would "have been done toward leaving a clear path for the incoming Administration," time would have been gained, and Buchanan would have "put the question in the best form to learn the power and duty of the United States as to the rights of secession." The greatest advantage of his plan seemed to Butler to be that while both sides paused to "watch this high and dignified proceeding" prejudice would be stayed and the passions of men would cool.[10]

As Butler commented later: "Of course it was impossible for a man of Mr. Buchanan's temperament and training, however honest and conscientious [he might be] to adopt so decisive a course. He thought it would lead to great agitation."[11]

Even if Buchanan had caused the arrest of the commissioners

---

[10] Butler, op. cit., pp. 152–55, 156 ftn.

[11] Ibid., p. 155.

one doubts that the test case Butler proposed would have slowed the secession movement in the least degree. With Lincoln's election political power passed from the hands of the conservative southern planter class, whose members were opposed to the free distribution of the public domain and favorable to free trade, into the hands of a mildly radical farmer-labor party which was determined to secure (as it soon did) both a homestead law and a protective tariff. Secession was the southern leaders' counterrevolutionary response to a revolution at the ballot box. Revolutionists and counterrevolutionists have never been willing to settle their differences legalistically.

Butler left Washington on December 28, 1860. Because of a heavy snow storm he did not reach Boston until January 3, 1861. Early the following morning he called upon Governor-elect Andrew to warn him of the imminent danger of a sectional war. Undoubtedly Butler realized the seriousness of the situation caused by the Republicans' electoral victory considerably sooner than many other northerners did, but he was by no means alone in fearing war. The Adjutant General of Massachusetts, William Schouler, for one, had already suggested to Andrew that the state's militia be brought up to full strength.[12]

Several times during the first few months of 1861 Butler conferred with and wrote to Governor Andrew, urging that the militia be made ready for war. In mid-January the field and company officers of the Sixth Massachusetts Regiment (formerly the Fifth Regiment, Butler's old command) met at the American House in Lowell and unanimously adopted a resolution suggested to them by Butler: "That Colonel [Edward F.] Jones be authorized and requested forthwith to tender the services of the Sixth Regiment to the Commander in Chief and the legislature, when such services may become desirable. . . ."[13]

---

[12] P. C. Headley, *Massachusetts in the Rebellion* (Walker, Fuller and Company [Boston, 1866]), pp. 91–92.
[13] Quoted in Butler, op. cit., p. 163.

Possibly, though hardly probably, neither Butler nor any of the Sixth Regiment's officers knew that five days earlier the officers of the Seventh New York Regiment had adopted a resolution instructing their commanding officer to offer the services of the regiment to the governor of New York for such duty as he might prescribe in case of need.[14]

It is impossible to estimate how much Butler's advice really influenced Andrew. However, it is certain that Butler was satisfied to the end of his days that he played a highly important part, if not the principal one, in causing Massachusetts to be prepared immediately to answer President Lincoln's call for troops when the Civil War began. "With foresight and persistent effort," he said in his autobiography, " I caused the Massachusetts Volunteer Militia to be made so ready that they were the first organized armed force to march to Washington for its defense."[15] He also felt that the things he had done in this connection were not sufficiently appreciated. Indeed, he asserted that there was something close to a conspiracy to deny him credit for what he considered the great value of his actions. He claimed that William Schouler's *History of Massachusetts in the Civil War* deliberately belittled his efforts "to put the troops in perfect order, or to have done anything which would enable Massachusetts troops to be the first of all to get into the field."[16] On becoming governor (in 1883) he discovered, as he proclaimed, that the several volumes of Governor Andrew's military correspondence contained no items dated earlier than April 15, 1861, hence they omitted all that had passed between him and Andrew prior to that time. This fact indicated to Butler's satisfaction that the Governor's correspondence had purposely been manipulated to prevent anybody from learning from it what Butler had done "or tried to do before that date to prepare Massachusetts and her troops for war."[17]

---

[14] William Swinton, *History of the Seventh Regiment* (Fields, Osgood, & Co., [New York and Boston, 1870]), p. 23.

[15] Butler, op. cit., p. 1034.

[16] Ibid., pp. 168–69.

[17] Boston *Globe,* August 21, 1883: Butler, op. cit., p. 169.

The truth, as Butler ought to have known, and perhaps did, is that few, if any governors of Massachusetts had kept copies of outgoing correspondence until Andrew began doing so on April 16, 1861, probably at the suggestion of his military secretary, Lieutenant Colonel Albert G. Browne.[18] (Before carbon paper was invented it was not easy to make copies of letters. Doing so involved either making a handwritten transcript of each letter or the use of special ink and a copying press—a cumbersome machine resembling a Gutenberg printing press.)

---

[18] Boston *Traveller,* August 21, 1883: Boston *Transcript,* August 21, 1883.

★★★★★★★★★★★★

5

Off to the Wars

While on his way to Boston, Monday, April 15, 1861, Butler learned from the morning papers that Fort Sumter had been surrendered, President Lincoln had issued a proclamation calling 75,000 militiamen into the service of the United States, and Senator Henry Wilson had telegraphed to Governor Andrew that Massachusetts would be asked to send four companies to Washington.

As soon as Butler reached Boston he offered his services to the Governor and telegraphed Wilson: "See [Secretary of War Simon] Cameron and have a brigadier asked for, and I will see to it that I am detailed."[1]

Some of Butler's contemporaries thought his eagerness to serve the federal government went far to prevent the "war between the states" from also becoming a war between political parties. His conduct was described by George Frisbee Hoar as having been "in honorable contrast to that of some of his influential political associates and that of some of the old Whigs who never got over their chagrin at the success of the Republican party."[2]

There was really no reason for Hoar or anyone else to have been surprised about Butler's conduct. He had always stood on the side of law and order. Even his Lowell City Hall speech of

---

[1] Butler to William Schouler, July 10, 1871, as quoted in Jessie Ames Marshall (compiler) *Private and Official Correspondence of Gen. Benjamin F. Butler* (Privately issued [Boston, 1917]), I, 12 (Hereafter cited as POC).

[2] George Frisbee Hoar, *Autobiography of Seventy Years* (Charles Scribner's Sons, [New York, 1903]), I, 332.

1851—violent though it was—had been evoked by the efforts of
the mill managers to deprive men of their constitutional rights.
He was no more willing in 1861 to countenance resistance to duly
constituted federal authority on the part of his erstwhile political,
and in some cases personal, friends than he would have been to
countenance such behavior in anybody else.

During the afternoon of April 15 Governor Andrew received
an official request from the Secretary of War for four regiments
of Massachusetts troops, to be commanded by a brigadier general.
The Governor immediately ordered the Third, Fourth, Sixth,
and Eighth Regiments to muster on Boston Common the following day. Colonel Edward F. Jones, commanding the Sixth Regiment, took his orders to Butler, who was in court, for transmission through channels. Endorsing Jones's orders and hastily
securing an adjournment of the case he was trying, Butler caught
the 5:30 P.M. train for Lowell.

Governor Andrew's choice of a commanding officer for the
Massachusetts brigade lay between Brigadier Generals Ebenezer
W. Pierce and Butler. From a purely military point of view
Butler was more deserving of the assignment. Pierce owed his
high rank chiefly to his long connection with the militia. Butler's
ability as an officer has been described by one of his severest critics
as "beyond dispute." According to the same man his brigade "was
one of the best in the State." If Butler had not been a Breckenridge Democrat the Governor probably would not have hesitated
a moment before appointing him. After considering the matter
for two days Andrew chose Butler, perhaps in the belief that
having a man of his political complexion in command of the
Massachusetts troops would demonstrate the state's unity.[3]

The Boston *Advertiser* (April 18) said, possibly at Andrew's
inspiration, that Butler's appointment was due to the early tender
of his services and did not reflect in the slightest degree upon
the ability of any other officer.

---

[3] Henry Greenleaf Pearson, *The Life of John A. Andrew* (Houghton,
Mifflin and Company [Boston, 1904]), I, 183–84.

Whatever may have been the reason for Andrew's decision his choice of Butler pleased the Constitutional Unionists and Democrats of the state. William Gray, an ultraconservative Boston merchant, wrote to the Governor:

I feel very great gratification at the designation of Brigadier General Butler. . . . It offers the people of the whole country the highest evidence that Massachusetts knows no party but stands as one man, when the liberties of the Union, and the perpetuity of the Government are assailed.[4]

However, one Breckenridge Democrat was all the Governor could tolerate. Caleb Cushing's services were curtly refused a few days after Butler's were accepted.

On being made commanding officer of the Massachusetts brigade Butler established headquarters at the State House where he worked day and night helping to get the troops started for the various places the War Department wanted them to be sent.

The Sixth and Eighth Regiments were ordered to Washington; the Third and Fourth Regiments to Fortress Monroe (now called Fort Monroe), on Old Point Comfort, Virginia, at the entrance to Chesapeake Bay.

Since there were only about 50 regular soldiers and a few hundred marines in or near Washington the War Department's decision to send two regiments elsewhere than to the capital was a daring thing. It was a calculated risk, taken because Fortress Monroe commanded the approaches to Baltimore (via Chesapeake Bay), to Washington (via Chesapeake Bay and the Potomac River), and to much of the interior of Virginia (via the Rappahannock and James Rivers).

The Fourth Regiment traveled by the Old Colony Railroad to Fall River, Massachusetts, where it boarded the steamer *State of Maine*. The Third Regiment sailed from Boston's Central Wharf in the S.S. *Spaulding*.

A visit Butler paid to the *Spaulding* to assure himself that his

---

[4] Ibid., I, 196.

men were being made as comfortable as possible is characteristic
of the sort of conduct that endeared him to most of those who
served under him at various times and places.

Governor Andrew and his military aides had considered whether
an overland or a sea route would be better for sending troops to
Washington in the event of a sectional war. The quicker way,
overland by rail, involved "changing cars" twice. The first train
ran from Boston to New York. At New York it was necessary
to cross the Hudson River by ferryboat and take another train
from Jersey City, New Jersey, to Philadelphia. The third train
ran all the way from Philadelphia to Washington, but the cars
were uncoupled and reassembled twice en route between the two
cities. This happened first at the Susquehanna River where the
cars were ferried from Perryville, Pennsylvania, to Havre de
Grace, Maryland. At Baltimore the cars were again separated
and drawn, by four horses each, over tracks running along Pratt
Street from the President Street Station to the Camden Street
Station, a distance of about 1½ miles. Militarily the bad features
of this route were the ease with which the crossing of the Susquehanna River could be impeded and the necessity of passing through
Baltimore—a city many northerners feared would sympathize with
the South if it ever came to actual fighting. The sea route did not
look much better because the Potomac River could be commanded
by batteries erected along the Virginia shore which might be (as
it did become) hostile territory. Governor Andrew finally sent
a staff officer to Washington to stay there until he had come to
an understanding as to the route to be used in case of a call for
Massachusetts troops. The War Department decided that it would
be best for them to go by sea to Annapolis, Maryland, and by
train from there to the capital. Butler was, of course, informed
of this plan as soon as he was put in command of the Massachusetts brigade.

When the time actually came for the troops to start for Washington the Secretary of War telegraphed to Governor Andrew:

"Send [them] by railroad; they will arrive quicker, the route through Baltimore is now open."[5]

The Sixth Regiment was ready to leave Boston on Wednesday, April 17. The men exchanged their smoothbore guns for "modern rifled muskets," then had lunch and marched through the sleet and rain to "take the cars" for New York. Their train started at 7:15 P.M. ("Hurry up and wait" is not a recent addition to standard operating procedure.) They reached New York early the following morning. Divided into three parties they breakfasted sumptuously at the Fifth Avenue Hotel, the Hotel St. Nicholas, and the Astor House. The ovation given them as they marched to the Hudson River ferry surpassed anything remembered by the city's oldest inhabitants.

At Jersey City there was a long, tiring delay. Finally, worn and weary, the regiment reached Philadelphia at 7 P.M., Thursday, April 18, and "camped" in the new and hitherto unoccupied Girard House.

While the men slept Colonel Jones conferred with Brigadier General P. L. Davis, of the Massachusetts Volunteer Militia, who had been sent ahead by Governor Andrew to arrange for the subsistence and transportation of the troops, and with S. M. Felton, president of the Philadelphia, Wilmington, and Baltimore Railroad. Davis and Felton were less confident of the availability of the Baltimore route than the War Department was. Davis warned Jones of the possibility of trouble at Baltimore, but declined to take the responsibility of ordering the regiment to proceed or to wait at Philadelphia for more information. Felton mentioned that damage might have been done to the railroad's tracks or bridges in Maryland. Jones decided for himself that his orders to proceed to Washington were peremptory and must be obeyed at all cost. He asked only to have a pilot engine precede his troop train.

[5] William Schouler, *A History of Massachusetts in the Civil War* (E. P. Dutton & Co. [Boston, 1868]), I, 58.

In the hope of reaching Baltimore early enough in the day to avoid trouble Jones started from Philadelphia at 1 A.M., April 19. Just before that time Felton received a telegram saying that part of an unarmed Pennsylvania regiment had passed through Baltimore with no opposition except for a few hisses. (Actually the Pennsylvanians had been stoned by a mob. One of them, a Negro named Nick Biddle, was literally, and most appropriately, the first man to shed his blood during the Civil War.)

Felton gave such scanty information as he had to Jones and the principal officers of the Massachusetts regiment. He also told them "of the dangers they would probably encounter, and advised that each soldier should load his musket before leaving [Philadelphia], and be ready for any emergency."[6]

A railroad official suggested to Jones that, to save time, the regiment should be detrained and marched from one station to the other at Baltimore instead of having the cars hauled across town in the usual way. Agreeing to this proposition, Jones went through the cars, had the men load their pieces, and issued the following orders:

> The regiment will march through Baltimore [with] arms at will. You will undoubtedly be insulted, abused, and perhaps assaulted, to which you must pay no attention whatever, but march with your faces square to the front, and pay no attention to the mob, even if they throw stones, bricks, or other missiles; but if you are fired upon, and any one of you are [sic] hit, your officers will order you to fire. Do not fire into any promiscuous crowd, but select any man you see aiming at you, and be sure to drop him.[7]

When the train reached Baltimore the railroad people decided to haul the cars across the city with the men in them, but Jones was not informed of this change of plan. The horses were hitched up so quickly that the Colonel, who had stepped from the train to form the regiment, had to board a moving car. He learned even-

---

[6] Ibid., I, 92.
[7] Ibid., I, 94.

tually that because the train had arrived so much earlier than
expected the railroad officials thought the transit could be made
before the populace learned of the troops' presence. After a number of cars had made their way to the Camden Street Station
without any trouble one was stopped by a barricade made of
paving stones, a cart load of sand, and several anchors brought
from a nearby wharf. The driver discreetly took the car back to
the President Street Station and the rest of the cars were forced
to turn back, or, if they had not started, to remain at the station.
The cars thus stopped contained four companies—a total of about
200 men. Because the cars had not been taken from the ferryboat
at Havre de Grace in the same order they had been put on board
at Perryville the stranded companies had no regimental officers
with them. Captain Albert S. Follansbee, commanding Company
C, took charge of the separated companies, formed them on President Street and started marching toward the Camden Street Station. The troops were quickly surrounded by a large, menacing
crowd. As the soldiers moved forward the mob, shouting insults
and cheering for the Confederacy, pressed close upon them. By
the time they had marched a couple of blocks, to the corner of
Fawn and President streets, two soldiers had been hit with stones
and seriously hurt. Then, as the New York *Tribune* reported, the
mob passed rapidly from hooting and yelling to throwing showers
of paving stones and "at last wore out the patience of the troops
by shooting three of them dead and wounding several others,"
one of them mortally.[8]

The men killed at Baltimore—Charles Taylor, a painter from
Boston, Luther C. Ladd and Addison C. Whitney, both workingmen from Lowell, and Sumner H. Needham of Lawrence, a
plasterer by trade—were the first who died in the Civil War, but
the shots fired at Baltimore on April 19 were not the first shots
of the war. The first shooting was done by a sentry at Fort San
Carlos in Florida several days before Fort Sumter fell.

A Maryland historian wrote that the municipal authorities of

8 New York *Tribune,* April 20, 1861.

Baltimore ought to have been notifed when, where, and in what numbers the Massachusetts troops were to arrive so that they could have been given police protection.[9] However, the Massachusetts Volunteer Militia had been especially trained for street fighting and the men of the Sixth Regiment demonstrated their ability to protect themselves by inflicting far heavier casualties on the mob than the regiment suffered. No exact figures are available, but the regimental chaplain estimated that the troops fired about 1,000 rounds and killed 100 persons.[10] Assuming these figures to be reasonably accurate, the men gave a good account of themselves, particularly as they had never been under fire before.

There would inevitably have been some trouble at Baltimore. However, it might have been less severe than it was if some officer, whose identity remains unknown, had not blundered egregiously by ordering his men to march at double time to close a gap in the ranks. Considering the militia's special training for riot duty he ought to have foreseen that this apparent flight would embolden the mob and worsen the situation.

The four separated companies fought their way to the Camden Street Station and the regiment finally reached Washington late in the afternoon of April 19. It was joyfully welcomed by the authorities who had spent the preceding four and a half days in constant expectation of an attack. Some of the men were assigned to guard the White House, the others were billetted, under arms, in the Senate chamber.

At 11 P.M., April 19, the mayor of Baltimore sent a committee of three prominent citizens to Washington by special train with a signed message saying that it would be impossible for any more northern troops to pass through the city without having to fight every step of the way. Maryland's governor, Thomas H. Hicks, concurred in writing with this statement.

---

[9] Matthew Page Andrews, *History of Maryland* (Doubleday, Doran & Company [New York, 1929]), p. 13.

[10] John W. Hanson, *The Sixth Massachusetts Regiment* (Lee and Shepard [Boston, 1866]), pp. 36, 39.

President Lincoln and General Winfield Scott had already conferred about the problem of getting more troops to Washington in view of what had happened in Baltimore. Scott had suggested bringing them around Baltimore so Lincoln diplomatically assured the mayor's representatives that no more soldiers would come through their city if they could by-pass it without being molested. The three Baltimoreans were not at all satisfied with this answer. They did not want any more Yankees to set foot in any part of Maryland whatsoever. Nevertheless, Lincoln handed them a note addressed to the mayor and the governor saying that troops must and would be brought to Washington, but he would not make a point of their coming through Baltimore. Governor Hicks responded to this tactful message by iterating the committee's demand that no more troops cross Maryland anywhere. He also suggested to the President that the British minister to the United States be asked to mediate between the federal government and the government of the newly formed Confederate States of America.

Meanwhile, the mayor of Baltimore had taken steps to prevent any more troops from even reaching the city. With the governor's consent, if not at his special instructions, the mayor caused a number of wooden railroad bridges north and west of Baltimore to be burned during the night of April 18–19. One of the demolition parties was led by the city's chief of police. By the morning of April 20 every rail connection between Baltimore and the North had been broken. All telegraph lines north and west of the city were cut the next day. Thus Washington was almost completely isolated. For nearly a week the only communication between the capital and the rest of the country was by means of couriers and they had great trouble traveling through Maryland. One day President Lincoln said to some members of the Sixth Massachusetts Regiment, "I begin to believe there is no North. . . . The Seventh [New York] Regiment is a myth. Rhode Island is another. You are the only real thing."[11]

11 John G. Nicolay and John Hay, *Abraham Lincoln* (The Century Co. [New York, 1890]), IV, 153.

This remark must have gratified Governor Andrew. He had made a particular effort to hasten troops from Massachusetts, partly because he realized how truly desperate the situation was at Washington, partly, perhaps mostly, to demonstrate that his state could mobilize its militia faster than Rhode Island or New York could. When the Colonel of the Fourth Regiment (bound for Fortress Monroe) protested that the *State of Maine* was overloaded Andrew answered: "Push steamer on without stopping. Massachusetts must be first on the ground."[12]

As soon as the Sixth Regiment left Boston, Butler, who had not been home since the previous Monday morning, dashed to Lowell by special train for an overnight stay. On April 18 he departed from Boston with his staff and the Eighth Regiment, intending to follow the route taken by the Sixth Regiment.

Governor Andrew, of course, delivered a farewell address, full of patriotic sentiments, to the Eighth Regiment similar to one he had made to the Sixth Regiment the day before. Butler's reply, on behalf of the troops, was studded with such sentences as: "We will bring back our shields or be brought back on them;" and "We will not turn back till we show those who have laid their hands upon the fabric of the Union that there is but one thought in the North—the Union of these states, now and forever, one and inseparable." Like an Indian war dance, this ceremony roused great enthusiasm among those present.

At the conclusion of Mr. [sic] Butler's remarks [reported the Boston *Advertiser*], without regard to the sentry or the police, gentlemen crowded upon him to exchange greetings with him. One member of the [Governor's] Council exclaimed "God bless you." Cheers without number were given for the Eighth, the Union, Old Essex [County], . . . and for a time the most thrilling excitement pervaded the large concourse. The troops

---

[12] Pearson, op. cit., I, 188; Sarah Forbes Hughes, *Letters and Recollections of John Murray Forbes* (Houghton, Mifflin and Company [Boston, 1899]), I, 211.

then took up their line of march, . . . cheered on every hand as they passed through the streets.[13]

The Eighth Regiment reached New York on the morning of April 19, a few hours before the Sixth Regiment arrived at Baltimore. As the troops marched down Broadway to the Jersey City ferry, "General Butler, who walked with steady step and erect head, was the observed of all, and recognized by hundreds, was the subject of a personal ovation of the most complimentary character."[14]

There was a delay at Jersey City because the railroad people did not know where they could get enough cars to carry the regiment without interfering with their regular passenger trains. Butler angrily insisted that the troops must be sent forward no matter what happened to the passenger service.

Leaving Jersey City about 11 A.M., the Eighth Regiment reached Philadelphia late the same afternoon. Here Butler heard for the first time of the trouble the Sixth Regiment had encountered in Baltimore. As quickly as he could gather reliable information about the affair he relayed it, by telegraph, to Governor Andrew. Since it was known in Boston only that something appalling had happened in Baltimore, Butler's dispatches were eagerly read by the Governor and his aides and such parts of them as it seemed safe to publish were given out as official bulletins.

Back in Philadelphia, Butler faced the problem of how to proceed to Washington. Felton and Captain Samuel F. Du Pont, commanding officer of the local navy yard, both urged the General to disregard his orders to go via Baltimore and to travel by rail to Perryville and to sail from there to Annapolis in the Philadelphia, Wilmington and Baltimore Railroad's car ferry *Maryland*. At first Butler refused to hear of this plan, although it was

---

[13] Boston *Advertiser,* April 19, 1861.
[14] Mary A. Hedrick, *Incidents of the Civil War* (S. W. Huse & Co., [Lowell, Mass., 1888]), p. 32.

not unlike the one previously considered by the Massachusetts authorities and described to him before he left Boston. Insisting that he would push on through Baltimore, he told Felton "he would go that way and if they fired upon him from any house he would raze that house to the ground, by the help of God, or leave his bones and ashes in the streets of the City."[15]

After considerable discussion Butler decided to follow the advice given him by Felton and Du Pont. If his movement had not turned out well he probably would have told the world who suggested it; everything worked remarkably well and he always credited himself with having originated the plan.

About 2 A.M., April 20, the handsomely appointed Seventh New York Regiment arrived at Philadelphia bound for Washington via Baltimore. Felton quickly got in touch with the commanding officer, Colonel Marshall Lefferts, and informed him that he could not possibly use his intended route. Felton advised Lefferts to accompany Butler to Perryville and Annapolis. For a little while Lefferts seemed inclined to accept this advice. Then he heard (as Butler also had) that the *Maryland* had been sunk by southern sympathizers. Butler did not believe this rumor: Lefferts did. Lefferts, therefore, decided to sail from Philadelphia directly to Washington in the steamer *Boston,* put at his disposal by Felton.

Probably General Butler tried to "pull rank" on Colonel Lefferts,[16] and the latter, to show his independence, set out to reach Washington by another route than Butler was going to take. Lefferts was in a position to do this because he and Butler were acting under different commanders in chief.

On being notified of Lefferts' intention Butler wrote to Governor Andrew:

Colonel Lefferts has refused to march with me. I go alone at

---

15 Schouler, op. cit., I, 102.

16 William Swinton, *History of the Seventh Regiment . . . of New York* (Fields, Osgood, & Co. [New York and Boston, 1870]), pp. 85 ff.; see also Benjamin F. Butler, *Butler's Book* (A. M. Thayer & Co. [Boston, 1892]), 199, and Nicolay and Hay, op. cit., IV, 134–35.

3 o'clock P.M., to execute this imperfectly written plan [of sailing from Perryville to Annapolis and going by train, as he then expected, from Annapolis to Washington]. If I succeed, success will justify me. If I fail purity of intention will excuse want of judgment or rashness.[17]

After leaving Philadelphia, Butler heard that nearly 2,000 men were waiting at Perryville to prevent his force of less than 1,000 from taking possession of the *Maryland*. Thus forewarned, he detrained the regiment about a mile north of Perryville and arranged his men with a view to surmounting a street barricade. The van consisted of a company of Zouaves deployed as skirmishers. They were followed by a demolition party of 100 men equipped with axes, picks, etc. Next came a support company, ready to lay down a covering fire for the demolition party. The rest of the regiment marched in a solid column under orders to push forward by sheer weight of numbers. As it turned out these precautions were unnecessary; the Zouaves rattled onto the ferry without any opposition.

However, the *Maryland* was found to be out of fuel and drinking water and without an engine room crew. Some 20 members of the regiment responded to a call for engineers and firemen, the vessel was hastily coaled, the troops were packed on board as tightly as subway passengers in the rush hour, and Butler ordered the captain to steer for Annapolis at the lower end of Chesapeake Bay. Most of the men dropped wearily onto the decks where they slept, some of them so soundly they did not wake up when inadvertently stepped on. Butler stayed awake to keep watch over the captain and crew whose loyalty to the Union he gravely doubted. Whether his suspicions were justified or not they were natural in view of recent events in Baltimore and the known temper of much of the populace of Maryland.

Leaving Perryville about 6 P.M., the *Maryland* reached Annapolis toward midnight. Butler had planned to land his men quietly and he hoped to have control of the town by the time its

[17] Butler to Andrew, April 20, 1861; POC, I, 20.

residents awoke. However, as his vessel entered the harbor rockets were fired from various places, lights sprang up along the shore, and the cadets at the Naval Academy were called to quarters. Uncertain who held the town and particularly concerned about who occupied the Naval Academy, Butler had the *Maryland* anchored in midstream. A boat soon came alongside carrying a naval officer with a message from Governor Hicks addressed "To the Commander of the Volunteer troops aboard the steamer," reading: "The excitement here is very great and I think it prudent you should take your men elsewhere." The Governor also said he had telegraphed to the Secretary of War protesting against the landing of any troops at Annapolis. Butler courteously replied that "finding the ordinary means of communication cut off by the burning of railroad bridges by a mob," he had been obliged to make a detour, and there was "no cause for excitement in the mind of any good citizen."[18]

(Hicks's telegram to the Secretary of War probably brought Washington its first intimation that reinforcements were within 40 miles, but Scott did not dare to send any troops away from the capital to establish contact with Annapolis. Of eight couriers who were dispatched only two finally got through to Butler.)

The superintendent of the Naval Academy was afraid the frigate *Constitution's* 30-man crew might be overcome and the vessel seized for use as a Confederate privateer or warship. He asked Butler if his instructions would permit him to take out the *Constitution's* guns, tow her to the outer harbor, and place a guard on board. "To this," Butler wrote to Governor Andrew, "I replied that your Excy's instructions left me a latitude for the exercise of my discretion & I thought it indispensible to save the 'Constitution,' whether the ship or form of government, from the enemies of the country."[19] He detailed the Salem Zouaves, the best drilled company in the regiment, as he thought, to guard the *Constitution* and a company of Marblehead men, fishermen by trade, to work the ship under the orders of a naval officer.

---

18 *Official Records of the Union and Confederate Armies* ([Government Printing Office, Washington, 1880–1901]), Ser. 1, I, 586–87.
19 Butler to Andrew, April 23, 1861; POC, I, 46.

After leaving the frigate at a safe anchorage the *Maryland*
went hard aground while trying to rescue a man who fell over-
board. The regiment spent the rest of the day (Sunday) and all
of that night on shipboard with little to eat except some hardtack
baked in 1848 and no drinking water at all. "But," wrote Theodore Winthrop, a private in the New York Seventh Regiment
who was soon to become a major on Butler's staff, "hungry,
thirsty, grimy, those fellows were grit."[20]

Monday morning Butler's troubles were alleviated by the arrival of the New York regiment's transport which had turned
back from the mouth of the Potomac River because Lefferts had
been informed by the captain of a lightship that the Confederates
had set up batteries on the Virginia shore of the river. Since Virginia had not yet seceded this information may not have been
correct, but it was credible in the circumstances.

The *Boston* tried to tow the *Maryland* free. Everything ingenuity or experience could suggest was done in the hope of working the stranded vessel loose. The men on board ran back and
forth on the decks (as the crew of the U.S.S. *Missouri* did when
she grounded at Hampton Roads, Virginia, in 1950), heavy equipment was jettisoned, etc., but it was all to no avail. Finally the
Boston landed the troops she had on board and came back for
Butler's men.

Before his troops began going ashore Butler received a call
from the governor of Maryland and the mayor of Annapolis.
They informed the General that the railroad tracks between
Annapolis and Washington had been torn up and the right of
way was heavily guarded by men who were fully determined to
keep him from ever reaching the capital. He believed what they
said about the damage to the tracks; he doubted absolutely the
rest of their statement. The Governor and the Mayor also said
that while no official opposition would be offered to his movements the whole state was spontaneously arming to repel his
troops and those from New York; that the populace of Annapolis
was so highly excited that it could not be restrained for long; that

[20] Theodore Winthrop, "New York Seventh Regiment," *The Atlantic
Monthly,* June, 1861, VII, 749.

a mob of Baltimoreans could be expected to descend upon him at any moment; and they ordered him to encamp at least three miles away from Annapolis.

Butler replied that the excitement of the populace was shared by the Eighth Regiment and his men would be more than delighted to meet a mob of Baltimoreans; it would afford the members of the regiment an opportunity to avenge their comrades who had been foully murdered in that city. He flatly refused to put any considerable distance between himself and the *Maryland*, his base of supplies. When he did leave Annapolis it would be, he added, at his own convenience, not at the will of anybody else.

Remarking to the mayor that the Eighth Regiment was not provisioned for a long stay in the field, Butler asked if his quartermaster might purchase supplies in Annapolis. The mayor haughtily answered that no patriotic Marylander would sell anything to the Yankee invaders. The General said, in the quiet manner of a really angry man, "I suppose there are sufficient provisions in this capital of Maryland to feed a thousand men, and if the people will not sell those provisions, a thousand hungry, armed men have other means of getting what they want to eat besides buying it." The quartermaster was allowed to purchase what he thought was needed.[21]

Although the men did not have to forage for themselves at Annapolis most of them got their first taste of living under field conditions there. Some of the things connected with their education in the realities of war greatly amused Butler. Cooking their own rations was not one of the arts in which they had been trained. At their peace time encampments they had always been allowed to hire caterers as company cooks. Their uncertainty about what to do with the salt beef, hardtack, and firewood issued by the quartermaster seemed to the General to be among the funniest incidents of the war. Another incident that ended humorously, or at least not fatally, occurred when a Massachusetts soldier, on guard duty in hostile territory for the first time in his life, challenged someone who identified himself as "Officer

----

21 Butler, op. cit., p. 195.

of the Night." As another member of the regiment told the story, the sentry, without further ado, "let squizzle and jest [sic] missed his [own captain's] ear" with a musket ball.[22]

Butler strongly suggested to Lefferts that the New York and Massachusetts regiments join forces in a march to Washington, repairing the railroad tracks as they moved forward. Lefferts, who gave more credit than Butler did to tales both of them had heard about the formidable opposition it would be necessary to overcome on their way to the capital, wrote to Butler: "Upon consultation my Officer[s] do not deem it proper under the circumstances to co-operate in the proposed march by the R. R. laying track as we go along—particularly in view of a large force hourly expected and with so little ammunition as we possess."[23]

Determined to repair the tracks with or without help from Lefferts, Butler seized the yard and station of the Annapolis and Elk Ridge Railroad, a branch line connecting at Annapolis Junction with the Baltimore and Washington Railroad. When a rusty, partly dismantled locomotive was found in a shed Butler asked if anyone could repair it. Private Charles E. Homans of the Beverly Light Guard (Company C) examined it, said it had been made in a shop where he had once worked, and he guessed he could fix "her up and run her." A gang of mechanics was quickly assembled and put to work under his supervision. Butler then called for any experienced tracklayers to step forward. About 20 men responded.

The versatility displayed by the men of the Eighth Regiment led the Washington *National Intelligencer* to comment: "We doubt whether any other single regiment in the country could furnish such a ready contingent to reconstruct a steam-engine, lay a rail track, and bend the sails of a man-of-war."[24] Winthrop enthusiastically wrote: "They were the men to make armies of. They could tailor for themselves, shoe themselves, do their black-

---

[22] Winthrop, loc. cit., p. 752.

[23] Lefferts to Butler, April 22, 1861, as copied by P. Haggerty, Butler's aide-de-camp, Butler mss, Library of Congress.

[24] *National Intelligencer,* quoted in George Lowell Austin, *The History of Massachusetts* (B. B. Russell; Estes & Lauriat [Boston, 1876]), p. 492.

smithing, gunsmithing, and all the other work that calls for
sturdy arms and nimble fingers." He thought the regiment was
so universally accomplished that if orders were given: "Poets
to the front; painters present arms; sculptors charge bayonets,"
a baker's dozen from every company would have obeyed.[25]

Governor Hicks complained to Butler that his seizure of the
railroad would make it impossible for members of the Maryland
legislature to reach the state capital if they should be called into
special session. Butler replied, with understandable acrimony;

> It might have escaped your notice, but . . . [you] expressly
> stated as a reason why I should not land, that my troops could
> not pass [over] the railroad because the company had taken
> up the rails, and they were private property. It is difficult to
> see how it can be that if my troops could not pass . . . one
> way members of the legislature could pass the other way.[26]

This answer seems to have left the Governor at a loss for words.

Before Homans and his helpers finished repairing the damaged
locomotive Lefferts, or his officers, reconsidered matters and decided to march with the Massachusetts regiment. By this time
Butler had received orders, transmitted by courier, to remain at
Annapolis with enough men to hold a beachhead there while the
rest of his force proceeded to Washington.

As Butler had expected the troops met with no opposition.
They began their march early in the morning of April 24, with
Annapolis Junction, 20 miles to the northwest, as their first objective point. A skirmish line, with scouts out on both flanks,
led the way. Next came a working party—tracklayers, etc.—
followed closely by a train, with Homans at the throttle of the
locomotive which pushed a flatcar carrying some brass cannon
belonging to the New York regiment and drew several coaches
and freight cars. Averaging about a mile an hour, listening
through the night to the tree frogs' mournful music, the troops
reached Annapolis Junction just before daybreak, April 28. In-

25 Winthrop, loc. cit., p. 747.
26 Butler, op. cit., pp. 208–9.

stead of meeting trouble there, as they had feared they might, they found that trains were running to Washington over tracks in perfect order. By noontime the New York Seventh Regiment was at the capital; the Massachusetts Eighth Regiment reached there a short time later.

When Butler first arrived at Annapolis he heard rumors of an impending Negro uprising. He immediately wrote to Governor Hicks:

> I have understood within the last hour that some apprehensions are entertained of an insurrection of the negro population of this neighborhood. I am anxious to convince all classes that the forces under my command are not here to interfere with or countenance an interference with the laws of the State. . . . I beg, therefore, that you announce publicly that any portion of the forces under my command is at your excellency's disposal to act immediately for the preservation and quietness of the peace of this community.[27]

Hicks tersely informed Butler that the citizens of the state would be fully able to cope with any possible trouble.[28]

Despite this answer Butler believed to the end of his life that his offer to Hicks allayed fears that "the troops of anti-slavery Massachusetts had . . . come to Maryland to inaugurate a servile war or promote a negro insurrection," and kept the state from seceding.[29]

Governor Andrew (whom somebody once called "a one idea'd abolitionist") sharply rebuked Butler for his part in this affair. On April 25 Andrew wrote to Butler:

> . . . I think that your action in tendering to Governor Hicks the assistance of our Massachusetts troops to suppress a threatened servile insurrection among the hostile people of Maryland, was unnecessary. . . . I think that the matter of a servile insurrection among a community in arms against the Federal

[27] Butler to Hicks, April 23, 1861; POC, I, 26–27.
[28] *Harper's Monthly,* June 1861, XIII, 123.
[29] Butler, op. cit., p. 211.

Union is no longer to be regarded . . . in a political, but solely from a military point of view, and is to be contemplated as one of the inherent weaknesses of the enemy from the disastrous operation of which we are under no obligation of a military character to guard them. . . .[30]

Answering the Governor, Butler explained that Maryland really was not enemy territory. Governor Hicks and the mayor of Annapolis had, said Butler, formally protested against his landing, but they had offered no armed opposition to it. The mayor had warned him of the danger of an attack by a mob from Baltimore, "in numbers beyond the control of the [Annapolis] police." He had replied, he told Andrew, that, "supported by the authorities of the State and City," he would "repress all hostile demonstrations against the laws of Maryland and the United States." Commenting that he could see no reason for allowing a black mob preference over a white one in a breach of law, he added: "The question seemed to me to be neither military nor political, and was not to be so treated. It was simply a question of good faith and honesty of purpose."[31]

---

[30] Andrew to Butler, April 25, 1861, Butler mss., Library of Congress.
[31] Butler to Andrew, May 9, 1861; POC, I, 38–41.

6

★★★★★★★★★★★★

Baltimore

Unlike Governor Andrew, President Lincoln found nothing objectionable in Butler's offer of assistance to Governor Hicks. A few days after it was made Butler was named commanding officer of the newly created Department of Annapolis, comprising all of the country lying 20 miles on either side of the railroad from Annapolis to Bladensburgh, Maryland (on the outskirts of Washington). In effect this was a promotion since it gave Butler control over all officers and men in or passing through this corridor which had become one of the busiest areas, militarily speaking, in the North.

There were many who thought Butler richly deserved the sort of recognition that his being made a department commander implied. "Almost any other man," said Benson J. Lossing, "would have been appalled by, and helpless before, the impediments of civil authority, hostile feeling, armed resistance and destructive malignity" thrown in his way, but he had "exhibited an illustration of the truth of the saying, 'Where there's a will there's a way.' "[1] Theodore Winthrop wrote that Washington owed its safety "1st, to General Butler, whose genius devised the circumvention of Baltimore, and . . . whose utter bravery executed the plan;—he is the Grand Yankee of this little period of the war; 2d to the other Most Worshipful Grand Yankees of the Massachusetts regiment who followed their leader as he knew they would."[2]

---

[1] Benson J. Lossing, *The Civil War in America* (George W. Childs [Philadelphia, 1866]), I, 438.

[2] Theodore Winthrop, "Washington as a Camp," *The Atlantic Monthly,* July 1861, VIII, 118.

Both of the men just quoted owed debts of gratitude to Butler
—Lossing for hospitality enjoyed, Winthrop for advancement expected—but their sentiments were echoed by others under no sort
of obligation to the General. Even Judge Hoar wrote to Governor Andrew that while Butler was not methodical or systematic
he had shown a high capacity to meet grave emergencies.[3] (Governor Andrew had sent Hoar and Dr. Samuel Gridley Howe to
Washington to investigate the health and welfare of the Massachusetts troops. Dr. Howe, who thought there was more need
of a health officer than of a chaplain, bemoaned the fact that the
Army knew of no such thing as a health officer. Hoar urged the
employment of "an agent with brains and some business skill"
to supervise the distribution of the supplies being sent to Washington by the state. He thought these qualities could be found
in the person of Charles Russell Lowell, Jr., and was sure that
Andrew would be pleased to hear that Lowell was "a Harvard
graduate and a member of a well-known Boston family.")[4]

At Annapolis, Butler displayed, as he was often to do again
during the war and afterward, an ability to carry a tremendous
work load. He was at the main building of the Naval Academy
every day, interviewing numerous callers and attending to the
manifold duties of a department commander. Usually he was
courteous, though always firm. However, there was a limit to
his politeness. One midnight a newspaper reporter asked where
he was to sleep; all of the hotels being full. "Sir," thundered
Butler, "I have done today about everything a man ever did in
this world, but I am not going to turn chambermaid."[5]

Immediately after the Baltimore riot Governor Hicks mobilized
the Maryland militia "to preserve order" until the people of the
state should have an opportunity, in a special election of members

[3] Henry Greenleaf Pearson, *The Life of John A. Andrew* (Houghton,
Mifflin and Company [Boston, 1904]), I, 217.

[4] Ibid., I, 216–18.

[5] James Parton, *General Butler in New Orleans* (Mason Brothers [New
York, 1864]), p. 194.

of Congress soon to be held, "to express their devotion to the Union, or their desire to see it broken up."[6] On April 22 the Governor issued a call for a special session of the legislature to begin at Annapolis on April 26. Before the latter date Hicks suddenly changed the meeting place to the town of Frederick, in order, as he put it, to assure the safety and comfort of the legislators in view of the extraordinary situation at the capital. These events led Butler to send "an imploring request to the President to be allowed to bag the whole nest of traitorous Maryland legislators and bring them in triumph to Washington."[7] Lincoln almost undoubtedly shared Butler's suspicions, but the President was unwilling for anything to be done that might stir up trouble with a border state. The War Department, therefore instructed Butler not to interfere with the legislature unless and until it took overt action against the federal government. However, Butler undertook to guide the legislators' deliberations by remarking within the hearing of several newspaper reporters that if the legislators passed a secession ordinance he would arrest them all. This warning can scarcely have been absent from the solons' minds when they protested against the "unconstitutional military occupation" of Maryland; expressed their sympathy with the southern states, "struggling for their rights;" and called upon the federal government to "cease this unholy war" and recognize the independence of the Confederate States of America; but agreed that existing circumstances made it inexpedient to call a convention to consider secession.

Although Maryland was not going to secede, nobody was quite sure what Baltimore would do. As the mayor wrote later: "For some days it looked very much as if Baltimore had taken her stand decisively with the South; at all events, outward expressions of Southern feeling were very emphatic." One certainly

---

[6] Frank Moore (editor), *The Rebellion Record* (G. P. Putnam [New York, 1861]), I, Doc. 65.

[7] William Roscoe Thayer, *The Life and Letters of John Hay* (Houghton, Mifflin Company [Boston, 1915]), I, 101–2.

emphatic expression of such feeling was a telegram the chief of police sent to a man in Frederick during the night following the mob's attack on the Sixth Massachusetts Regiment: "Streets red with Maryland blood; send expresses over the mountains of Maryland and Virginia for the riflemen to come without delay. Fresh hordes will be down upon us tomorrow. We will fight them and whip them or die." Another was the appropriation by the city council of $500,000, to be spent at the mayor's discretion, "for the purpose of putting the city in a complete state of defense. . . ." A third was a statement made by the Baltimore *American* that the populace was determined "to resist at all hazard the passage of [more] troops."[8]

The attack on the Sixth Massachusetts Regiment evoked a strong desire for retaliation throughout the North and the federal government could not allow Baltimore, less than 40 miles northwest of Washington, to remain in the hands of a hostile element or even to continue in what the mayor called a condition of armed neutrality. General Scott began making plans, with which the President and the Secretary of War concurred, to have four columns of 3,000 men each converge upon Baltimore as soon as enough men could be spared from the force defending Washington. Butler did not entirely approve of this scheme, though he did not openly criticize it when it was described to him as potential leader of one of the columns. He thought Baltimore could be occupied and controlled by a comparatively small force, by no more troops than would be needed to quell a severe civil disturbance such as might occur in connection with a big strike. Circumstances he helped to create soon enabled him to test his belief.

On May 4 he received orders to occupy a village, called the Relay House, strategically located at a railroad junction between Baltimore and Harper's Ferry. He set up camp there the following day. A short time later he wrote to Scott, saying he believed he could march through Baltimore with the troops he had with

---

[8] George William Brown, *Baltimore and the Nineteenth of April*, 1861 (Johns Hopkins University [Baltimore, 1887]), pp. 60–77, passim.

him at the moment. Scott ignored this broad hint. However, on May 13, Colonel Schuyler Hamilton, Scott's military secretary, who had been briefly on Butler's staff at Annapolis, wrote Butler some letters at Scott's direction, though probably not at his dictation. One of them called Butler's attention to the fact that several tons of gunpowder, believed to be intended for shipment to the Confederate States, were known to be stored in Baltimore. Another contained a statement that Baltimore was in Butler's department. Scott found nothing remarkable in these letters, if he saw them at all. As Butler interpreted them they authorized him to go to Baltimore with the force under his command.

He had promised his "old comrades of the Sixth Regiment," who were with him at the Relay House, that he would "march them through Baltimore and revenge the cowardly attack made upon them on April 19th." The regiment was eager to have this promise kept; he was eager to keep it. Being virtually certain that a direct request for permission to occupy Baltimore would be refused by Scott, Butler acted upon his interpretation of Hamilton's letters without asking if it were correct.[9]

A few hours after receiving Hamilton's letters Butler entrained 1,000 of his troops and started toward Harper's Ferry where the Confederates had been expecting him to make an attack ever since he first reached the Relay House. Just as the train got under way two men, driving fast trotting horses hitched to light buggies, were seen departing toward Baltimore. Butler had been watching these gentlemen for several days and would have had them arrested if he had not wanted them to carry word to Baltimore that he was on his way to Harper's Ferry. Because there was a steep grade between the Relay House and Harper's Ferry nobody paid any attention to the fact that one locomotive was pushing the train while another pulled it. A couple of miles from the Relay House the train was stopped and split into two sections. Two cars proceeded to Frederick with a detachment under orders to arrest Ross Winans, in whose machine shop many of the "John Brown

---

[9] Benjamin F. Butler, *Butler's Book* (A. M. Thayer & Co. [Boston, 1892]), pp. 226–27.

pikes" used in the Baltimore riot had been made. Butler was satisfied that "a military commission composed of officers of the Sixth Regiment . . . would be very likely to find such facts as would enable the commanding general [i.e. Butler], according to the laws of war to hang Mr. Winans." Much to Butler's disgust Winans was quickly released by order of Secretary of State William H. Seward who had charge of political prisoners. If Seward had not intervened Butler would have hanged Winans within 48 hours of his seizure on a scaffold in the center of Baltimore.[10] In Butler's opinion hanging Winans would quickly have checked the Rebellion because the execution of a man of such wealth and position would have struck terror throughout the South by showing that the North was in earnest.[11] (What Butler wrote and said about this matter leaves it impossible to deduce whether he thought Winans ought to have been hanged for being worth, as Butler estimated, $15,000,000, or for making the pikes and a fearful looking, but actually harmless steam gun—so-called because its projectiles were propelled by steam pressure.)

While the two cars went to Frederick the other locomotive rapidly pulled the rest of the train back past the Relay House into Baltimore. This section carried most of the Sixth Massachusetts Regiment, some horses, and several pieces of artillery.

Butler planned, on reaching Baltimore, to march his force to Federal Hill, a position overlooking the harbor and much of the city. His marching orders, issued on board the train, called for complete silence in the ranks and forbade any shooting without specific orders from an officer. If anyone fired at the troops a halt would be called and the building or buildings from which the shots came would be burned to the ground while the troops stood guard. The column was arranged with some cannon between the second and third companies, some in the center, and the rest ahead of the last two companies.

This was perfect planning for the circumstances—the placement

---

[10] Ibid., pp. 227–28.

[11] Gideon Welles, *Diary* (Houghton Mifflin and Company [Boston, 1911]), II, 269–70.

of the artillery where it could be protected by infantrymen for the short time before it could be brought into action when it could command a wide area is particularly noteworthy. Butler was certainly well schooled in the tactical use of troops for police work.

Butler intended to reach Baltimore at about sunset because, as he once explained:

When troops are taking possession of a city where there is a possibility of assault by a mob, it is always best that it should be done in the dark. The general then always knows where his troops are, and how many of them there are, while the mob can have no concerted action, and are not able to organize any in the dark. If your column is fired upon from houses, the flash will show every window from which the missiles come, and those windows can instantly be filled with returning bullets. Furthermore, the column, unless it is too long, can be protected in the street better in the dark than in daylight.[12]

As luck had it a blinding thunderstorm broke just before Butler's force arrived at the Camden Street Station between 7:30 and 8 P.M. Because the weather kept almost everybody off the streets the troops reached Federal Hill without attracting much attention and entirely without opposition.

After establishing his headquarters in a tavern on top of the hill Butler sent a message by hand to the commanding officer of Fort McHenry, guarding Baltimore Harbor:

I have taken possession of Baltimore. My troops are on Federal Hill, which I can hold with the aid of my artillery. If I am attacked tonight, please open on Monument Square with your mortars. I will keep the hill fully lighted with fires during the night so that you may know where we are and not hit us. Major [Charles] Devens [of the Massachusetts Volunteer Militia, for whom Fort Devens is named] will know my handwriting.[13]

---

[12] Butler, op. cit., pp. 373–74.
[13] Jesse Ames Marshall (compiler) *Private and Official Correspondence of General Benjamin F. Butler* (Privately issued [Boston, 1917]), I, 81 (Hereafter cited as POC.).

While the men dried their clothes and brewed coffee at the 30 fires they built to indicate their position to Fort McHenry, Butler supped on fried bacon and eggs, hardtack soaked in rain water, some powerful Limburger cheese, and strong coffee. Ordinarily he would have enjoyed a stein or two of the tavern-keeper's beer; in the existing circumstances he wanted to be able to stay awake throughout what he foresaw would be a busy night.

Early in the morning of May 14 Butler received a note from the mayor of Baltimore, saying that the sudden arrival of an armed force at the railroad station would create much surprise in the community. If the troops were going to remain at the station the mayor would, he added, instruct the police to take precautions against any disturbance of the peace. Confident that his men did not need police protection, Butler disregarded the mayor's message.

Twenty-four hours later the mayor called personally upon Butler to learn what his intentions were. Butler answered the mayor's questions by handing him a copy of an extra edition of the Baltimore *Clipper* containing the text of a proclamation the General had issued. Baltimore had been occupied, the proclamation said, for the purpose of enforcing federal laws, and upon request, state laws as well. Loyal, well-disposed persons would not be disturbed; others would be summarily arrested. Any property used, or intended to be used, to aid the Confederate States would be confiscated. (During the ensuing day 2,200 muskets sent to Baltimore from Virginia and at least 4,000 pikes made at Winans' shop were seized.) All manufacturers of arms and munitions of war were ordered to report to General Butler, "forthwith," so that the legality of their business might be understood and misconstruction of their future activities avoided. Officers of the state militia were required promptly to make themselves known to Butler to enable him to distinguish the regularly constituted troops of Maryland from other bodies of armed men. There would be no interference with the city government. Any display of Confederate flags or similar emblems was forbidden.[14]

---

[14] POC, I, 83–85.

Toward the end of his first full day in Baltimore, Butler demonstrated his contempt for the numerous assassination threats he had heard by riding, unaccompanied except by three of his staff, through the city and dining at the Gilmore House. He returned to Federal Hill to get some sleep for the first time in nearly 40 hours. Having been frequently disturbed during the night he rose on May 15 but little refreshed. At 8:30 A.M., not long after he finished breakfast, he received a telegram from General Scott, reading:

> Sir: Your hazardous occupation of Baltimore was made without my consent and, of course, without my approbation. It is a godsend that it was without conflict of arms. It is also reported that you have sent a detachment to Frederick; but this is impossible. Not a word have I received from you as to either movement. Let me hear from you.[15]

Butler did not think this sort of message ought to have been sent to an officer who had accomplished with less than 1,000 men something Scott had hoped someday to do with 12,000 men, so he ignored it despite its peremptory closing words.

Nothing else Butler did during the Civil War was more heartily applauded than his Baltimore coup. Soon after it occurred he was promoted to the rank of major general, United States Volunteers.

Butler's commission as major general, dated May 16, 1861, was in fact the first of its grade issued. Therefore, he always argued that he was the senior in his rank. However, similar commissions subsequently issued to George B. McClellan and John C. Frémont were antedated to May 14, making them technically senior to Butler. There was one distinction of which nobody robbed him. He and ex-Governor Nathaniel P. Banks of Massachusetts were the only men from their state to obtain the rank and pay of major general. (Some others from the state were brevetted to that rank.)

Scott's reprimand angered Butler to such an extent that he was

---

[15] Scott to Butler, May 14, 1861. POC, I, 85.

undecided whether to accept a commission as major general or to resign as brigadier general and let the Union Army do the best it could without him. In this frame of mind he called upon General Scott in Washington. Scott received him coldly and kept him standing while listening to a sharp rebuke. Soon finding his stock of patience exhausted, Butler turned upon Scott and concluded a series of unflattering remarks by saying he had not reported about the Baltimore expedition partly because he doubted Scott's ability to stay awake long enough to read such a report.

After his set-to with Scott, Butler went to see Secretary of War Simon Cameron and Secretary of the Treasury Salmon P. Chase to inform them that if his services were no longer needed he intended to return at once to Lowell and resume his law practice.

Cameron and Chase, both former Democrats, realized how much the loss of Butler's services would cost the Administration politically. Since they were politicians, not military experts, they probably gave no thought at all to the fact that Butler had shown more soldierly ability than anybody else had as yet. In any case, they undertook, with the liberal use of soft soap, to persuade him not to resign. Cameron told him he ought to be able to overlook the petulence of an old man like Scott. Chase insisted that Butler accept the promotion offered him because with it he was going to be given one of the Army's most important commands, the Department of Virginia and North Carolina, with headquarters at Fortress Monroe. He decided to stay in the Army.

On May 18 Butler received orders, signed by Scott, to proceed to Fortress Monroe and take charge of the volunteer troops there. No mention was made of his commanding a department nor of the real importance of the post and his orders concluded with the words:

Boldness in execution is nearly always necessary, but in planning and fitting out expeditions, great circumspection is a virtue. In important cases, where time clearly permits, be sure to submit your plans and ask for instructions from higher authority. Communicate with me often and fully on all matters important to the service.[16]

As soon as Butler finished reading his orders he sent a "friend and aide-de-campe" to the Secretary of War with a letter saying:

I have just received an order from General Scott transferring the command of the Department of Annapolis to General [George C.] Cadwallader, and ordering me to Fortress Monroe. What does this mean? Is it a censure upon my actions? Is it because I have caused Winans to be arrested? Is it because of my proving successful in bringing Baltimore to subjection and quiet? . . . If my services are no longer desired, . . . I am quite content to be relieved altogether, but I will not be disgraced. . . . To be relieved of the command of a department and sent to command a fort, without a word of comment, is something unusual at least, and I . . . [do] not understand it otherwise than . . . [as] a reproof. At least I desire a personal interview with you and the President before I accept further service.[17]

President Lincoln, who was as unready to dispense with Butler's services as Cameron and Chase were, smoothed the General's ruffled feathers and sent him off to Fortress Monroe.

[16] Scott to Butler, May 18, 1861. POC, I, 95.
[17] Butler to Cameron, May 18, 1861. POC, I, 95.

★★★★★★★★★★★★

7

General Butler's Fugitive Slave Law

Nominally the Department of Virginia and North Carolina extended from the coasts of those two states to the summit of the Blue Ridge Mountains. Actually the Union Army controlled only a small area in the immediate vicinity of Fortress Monroe. However, the fortress was the largest military structure in North America. Its granite-faced walls 25 feet high and 35 feet thick, surrounded by a moat dug 6 feet deep, enclosed 65 acres of land on which stood barracks, shops, a hospital, and other appurtenances for a war time garrison of 2,500 men. As already mentioned its strategic importance had led to its being reinforced with two Massachusetts regiments at the beginning of the Civil War and 10,000 more men had been sent there as soon as possible, making a total of 12,000 officers and men on hand when Butler took command on May 22, 1861.

Butler found much to be done at his new post. His first problem was simply to procure enough drinking water. There was neither a spring nor a well anywhere on the government reservation. Rain water, caught in cisterns, was the only sort of supply that had ever been available and it had previously failed to meet the needs of a garrison of only 400 men. Butler ordered an artesian well to be drilled and had a number of shallow wells dug near a creek. The artesian well was not finished during his time at the post and the dug wells did not furnish enough water, so for a time water had to be brought in boats from Baltimore at a cost of two cents a gallon. The erection of a distilling plant, capable of producing a pint of fresh water for each pound of coal burned, finally solved the problem.

Because there were no draught animals at Fortress Monroe when the war began all provisions and ammunition sent there had to be dragged or carried by men over a sandy road almost a mile long. Butler secured the services of one of the Pennsylvania Railroad's civil engineers who supervised the laying of tracks to various parts of the post, using rails and ties from Confederate stores captured at Alexandria, Virginia.

Much work also had to be done to put Fortress Monroe into a defensible condition on its landward side, where no need for strength had been foreseeen when it was built in 1847. In this connection a curious chain of circumstances made it necessary practically to reconstruct the moat. Delicious oysters abounded in Chesapeake Bay. With the guns withdrawn the embrasures served as windows in the officers' quarters and provided convenient places through which to dispose of oyster shells. By 1861 shells had accumulated in the moat to a depth of three feet.

Since Fortress Monroe could easily and pleasantly be reached by boat from Washington and Baltimore, Butler had to play host to many senators, congressmen, governors, editors, and other VIP's. Often he had to take time to entertain a couple of dozen such guests at once. One day, when mere chance kept Mrs. Lincoln away, the visitors included the Secretary of War and Mrs. Cameron, General Ambrose E. Burnside's wife and son, General and Mrs. Lorenzo Thomas and their daughter, two daughters of the Secretary of the Treasury, and a number of gentlemen without ladies.

As if he did not already have enough trouble, people on the home front, such as the Rev. B. F. Stead, bothered Butler by mail. Stead, the pastor of a Presbyterian church in Astoria, New York, wrote: "A lady in the village has received a letter from a soldier under your command, a reliable man, who says that one of the officers has been drunk a week. An army in which such conduct is tolerated is, of course, demoralized." Butler replied that if the reliable man would come forward, identify the officer, and testify against him everything possible would be done to punish him suitably. The General also commented pertinently that he had not appointed the officer mentioned and wondered how it happened that the state of New York had commissioned such an unfit person. Stead dropped the subject.[1]

Drinking was, however, a real problem at Fortress Monroe, as it was everywhere in both the Union and Confederate Armies during periods of inactivity. Butler issued an order prohibiting the use of intoxicating beverages at Fortress Monroe and caused the destruction of all liquor, bottled or barrelled, to be found there. He had, he candidly admitted, been using such beverages in his own quarters, but said he would abide by the rule he was applying to his subordinates.

Soon after Butler reached Fortress Monroe he began thinking of moving against Richmond by way of the peninsula between the York and James Rivers (as General George B. McClellan was later to do). In preparation for such a movement Butler had a reconnaissance of the country near Fortress Monroe made from a captive balloon on June 10, 1861.[2] (This was the first time an observation balloon was used during the Civil War. On June 18 "Professor" T. S. C. Lowe made an experimental ascent from the grounds of an armory in Washington. He made his first ascent for a military purpose near Manassas Junction on July 21, the day of the first battle of Bull Run.[3]

In the end nothing came of Butler's plan, whatever it may have been. At first his orders limited his operations to places not more than half a day's march (five miles at the most) from his headquarters. Later, as he persistently claimed, he was denied the men and equipment necessary for the sort of campaign he had in mind. Unquestionably he developed at least a mild persecution complex in regard to his treatment by his superiors at this time.

---

[1] Boston *Post,* August 2, 1861.

[2] John La Mountain to Butler, June 10, 1861; as quoted in Jesse Ames Marshall (compiler), *Private and Official Correspondence of Gen. Benjamin F. Butler* (Privately issued, [Boston, 1917]), I, 132 (Hereafter cited as POC).

[3] William W. Hassler, "Professor T. S. C. Lowe," *Civil War Times,* August 1967, VI, 14–15.

The truth is that in the early days of the war there simply was not enough matériel for everybody to have all he wanted, or perhaps even needed. Commanders had to do their best with whatever could be made available to them. There is no real evidence that Butler was treated any differently than others in the matter of supplies while he was at Fortress Monroe.

Although some northerners had long disliked slavery, the Civil War did not begin as an antislavery crusade. In fact abolitionism was detested to such an extent in 1861 that calling a man an abolitionist was about as insulting as calling him a thief. It was to save the Union, not to free slaves, that men enlisted at the outbreak of the war. Nevertheless, many slaves instinctively sought refuge with the Union armed forces whenever and wherever they found opportunities to do so.

By the time Butler reach Fortress Monroe the question of what to do with such persons was becoming serious, but the Administration had not yet decided how to deal with it. Since Army and Navy officers in the field or on blockade duty were given no instructions in the matter they behaved as they thought best. Some of them would not allow any Negroes to come within their lines or on board their vessels. Others readily permitted slave owners or their agents to search for and seize alleged fugitives. Thus many Negroes were returned to their masters, including men on active duty with the Confederate armed forces. Occasionally color alone was accepted as *prima facie* evidence of bondage. In at least two cases free Negroes were delivered to claimants under this process which was more summary than even the Fugitive Slave Law.[4]

---

[4] Lloyd Lewis, *Sherman* (Harcourt, Brace and Company [New York, 1932]), p. 245; J. G. Holland, *Life of Abraham Lincoln* (Gurdon Bill [Springfield, Mass. 1866]), p. 337.; George W. Williams, *History of the Negro Troops in the War of the Rebellion* (Harper & Brothers [New York, 1888]), p. 72; John T. Morse, Jr., *Abraham Lincoln* (Houghton, Mifflin and Company [Boston, 1899]), II, 6, 8; Edward L. Pierce, "The Contrabands at Fortress Monroe," *Atlantic Monthly,* November 1861, VIII, 628–29.

Undoubtedly it was politically wise, perhaps it was even politically necessary, for the Administration to avoid taking a definite stand about the treatment of fugitive slaves for there was no consensus on the subject. Militarily, however, evasion of the issue was a poor policy because slave labor added substantially to the South's ability to wage war.

An army officer mentioned this aspect of the "Negro problem," as it had come to be called to Butler during his first day at Fortress Monroe. Saying that a naval officer had returned several slaves to a claimant at nearby Norfolk, Virginia, the army man remarked,

> General [this] is a question you will have to decide . . . very soon; for in less than twenty-four hours deserting slaves will commence swarming into your lines. The rebels are employing their slaves in thousands in constructing batteries all around us. And, in my judgment, in view of this fact, not only slaves who take refuge within our lines are contraband, but I hold it as much our duty to seize and capture those employed, or intended to be employed, in constructing batteries, as it is to destroy the arsenals or any other war-like element of the rebels, or to capture and destroy the batteries themselves.[5]

Butler soon had occasion to recall this conversation. During his second day at Fortress Monroe he sent Colonel (later Brigadier General) John W. Phelps with part of his First Vermont Regiment on a reconnaissance toward the village of Hampton, Virginia. Somehow the local Negroes had gained an impression that the troops at Fortress Monroe were friendlier to their race than some others were. Perhaps they did so because Phelps was an old time and extremely ardent abolitionist. In any case, three Negro men decided to test their belief. Taking advantage of the confusion caused by the appearance of the Union troops they escaped and made their way to Fortress Monroe.

Interrogated separately, these men all told Butler the same story; they were slaves owned by a Colonel Mallory of the Con-

---

[5] Williams, op. cit., pp. 68–69.

federate Army and they were about to be sent farther south to work on some coastal fortifications. Butler decided to confiscate them as contraband of war, just as he would have seized any property being used by an enemy in a war against the United States. If he did not remember his recent discussion of the relative values to the Confederates of slaves, arsenals, and other warlike elements it must have influenced him subconsciously.

Soon after Butler finished questioning the slaves he was told that a Confederate officer bearing a flag of truce desired admission to the fort. (This man believed he had carried the first flag of truce used by either of the belligerents during the Civil War.)[6] When Butler and the Confederate met the latter identified himself as Major John B. Carey, in civilian life the principal of an academy at Hampton, and said he and Butler had last seen each other at the Democratic conventions in Charleston and Baltimore.

Carey sought some information as to the manner in which Butler proposed to conduct the war in the vicinity of Fortress Monroe. He asked first if citizens of Virginia who wanted to go north would be allowed to pass through the blockade. Butler answered, with irrefutable logic that one of the reasons for the blockade was "to prevent the admission of supplies and provisions into Virginia while she is hostile to the government" and passing vessels through the blockade would involve so much trouble and delay, "by way of examination to prevent fraud and abuses of the privilege," that he felt compelled to say no to Carey.[7]

Stopped in one direction, Carey tried another. "Will the [overland] passage of families desiring to go north be permitted?" he asked. That, Butler replied, was a question he would have to leave for his superiors in Washington to answer.[8]

Then, probably never dreaming of anything but ready acquiescence, Carey requested the return of Mallory's slaves. On being told they had been confiscated as contraband of war Carey spoke

[6] John B. Carey to Butler, March 9, 1891; POC, I, 103.

[7] Benjamin F. Butler, *Butler's Book* (A. M. Thayer & Co. [Boston, 1892]), p. 257.

[8] Idem.

feelingly of the Fugitive Slave Law and reminded Butler of his obligations under the federal Constitution. Butler answered that the Fugitive Slave Law, enacted by the United States Congress, could not be invoked by a foreign state, which Virginia claimed to be, and she must consider it among the infelicities of her position if she was taken at her word to some extent.

"General Butler's fugitive slave law," as Scott laughingly called the contraband of war theory, was heartily applauded by many northerners. Within a few days the phrase "contraband of war" quickly shortened to the single word "contraband," was on everybody's lips, and Republican newspapers were publishing gleeful editorials about the happy twist Butler had given to the South's often repeated claim that black men were property comparable to cattle. The New York *Herald* thought the confiscation of slaves would soon cause the South to end the war and said that Butler had "proven himself the greatest lawyer . . . between a pair of epaulets."[9] Edward L. Pierce wrote in the *Atlantic Monthly*:

> There is often great virtue in such technical phrases [as contraband of war] in shaping public opinion. They commend practical action to a class of minds . . . which would be repelled by formulas of a broader and nobler import. The venerable gentleman, who wears gold spectacles and reads a conservative daily, prefers confiscation to emancipation. He is reluctant to have slaves declared freemen, but has no objection to their being declared contraband. His whole nature rising in insurrection when [Henry Ward] Beecher preaches in a sermon that a thing ought to be done because it is a duty, . . . he yields gracefully when Butler issues an order commanding it to be done because it is a military necessity.[10]

Butler's technical phrase also suggested a course of practical action to the minds of some men who were not repelled by formulas of broad import. The Radical Republicans in the Thirty-seventh Congress urged Lincoln to cause a general application of

---

[9] New York *Herald,* May 31, 1861.
[10] Edward L. Pierce, "The Contrabands at Fortress Monroe," *Atlantic Monthly,* November 1861, VIII, 627.

the contraband doctrine as a means of effecting a partial abolition of slavery. The President disregarded this suggestion, but in August, 1861 and July, 1862 the Congress passed Confiscation Acts which provided, among other things, that owners who used their slaves or permitted them to be used for military service against the United States should forfeit all claims to their labor.

Because Lincoln's Emancipation Proclamation seized the imagination of historians it has been almost forgotten that the contraband theory promulgated by Butler "had practically emancipated thousands of slaves before Lincoln dreamed of emancipation,"[11] and that Congress, following Butler's lead, had gone further toward emancipation by the middle of 1862 than Lincoln was to do for some time to come.

Some of Butler's former political associates accused him of having sensed an antislavery wind and trimmed his sails accordingly. Actually his conduct was strictly logical. In his view property, including slaves, was constitutionally entitled to protection by federal agents in states abiding by the Constitution, but if a state seceded it abandoned the benefits of the Constitution. Thus he felt bound to offer to put down an insurrection of slaves in loyal Maryland and compelled to confiscate slaves in rebellious Virginia.

Mallory's slaves said, when they first reached Fortress Monroe, that if they were not sent back "others would understand that they were among friends and more would come the next day." They proved to be excellent prophets. Two days later there were eight male Negroes standing before Butler's quarters. All of them were confiscated. During the ensuing 24 hours 47 more persons of both sexes and all ages from three months to 85 years presented themselves. This group included half a dozen families.[12]

Within a short time Butler found that he had, at current prices, $60,000 worth of Negroes on his hands. Startled at the

---

[11] Carlos Martyn, *Wendell Phillips* (Funk & Wagnalls [New York, 1890]), p. 387.
[12] Pierce, loc. cit., p. 628.

magnitude of this figure, he wrote to his superiors in Washington seeking definite instructions by which to guide himself.

He had determined, he said, to employ the able-bodied persons, as he could usefully do. (The men were already working as laborers or officers' servants; the women as laundresses, seamstresses, etc.) He intended to issue "proper food for the support of all, . . . charging against their services the expense of care and sustenance for the non-laborers, keeping a strict account . . . of the services [as well] as the expenditures, having the worth of the services and the cost of expenditures determined by a board of survey hereafter to be detailed." He knew of no other way of disposing of this subject and the problems connected with it.[13]

Able-bodied Negroes, he continued, were of great value to the Confederacy and he thought it wise to deprive their masters of their services. But, he asked: "As a political question and a question of humanity, can I receive the services of a father and mother and not take the children?" Although he had no doubt what the humanitarian answer to this question would be, he felt he had no right to judge of its political aspects.[14]

Because his letter had as much to do with political as with military matters he sent a copy of it to the Secretary of War as well as to General Scott.[15]

Butler did not feel the need of advice from either Cameron or Scott, one a businessman, the other a professional soldier, about the legality of confiscating slaves. However, he had been rebuked by Governor Andrew for his conservative behavior in Maryland; now he wanted to be sure his radical handling of the Negro problem would not cause him more trouble.

President Lincoln and the Cabinet carefully considered Butler's letter and the Secretary of War replied to it without really answering any of the questions it contained. (It was plausibly rumored that advice given to the President by Secretary of State Seward was responsible for Cameron's evasiveness.)[16]

---

[13] Butler to Scott, May 27, 1861; POC, I, 112–13.
[14] Idem.
[15] Idem.
[16] Boston *Journal,* June 6, 1861.

Butler was told that his actions to date were approved; he was directed neither to interfere with slavery nor to return fugitive slaves to their alleged masters; he was ordered to continue to employ Negroes in the services for which they might be best adapted; and he was informed that the question of their final disposition would be reserved for future determination.[17]

[17] Cameron to Butler, May 30, 1861; POC, I, 119.

8

★★★★★★★★★★★★

Big Bethel and Hatteras Inlet

Early in June, 1861 Theodore Winthrop, who had become Butler's military secretary, learned from a contraband named George
Scott that a considerable body of Confederate troops had gathered at Little Bethel, a village consisting of a church, an old
gristmill, a blacksmith shop, and three small houses, all in a
rather dilapidated condition, near Yorktown, Virginia.

Winthrop drew up, and Butler approved, a plan for a movement based on Scott's information. Two regiments were to start
from different points, one at midnight, the other an hour later,
converge at daybreak and launch a surprise attack. The officers
detailed for this operation were given precise orders; they were
specially directed to take ample precautions to avoid a collision
between their separate forces in the darkness of the night.

A noteworthy sentence in Winthrop's plan reads: "George
Scott [is] to have a shooting iron."[1] If Scott did carry a "shooting iron" Butler was almost certainly the first Union Army commander to use the services of an armed Negro, although the Navy
had long been desegregated.

Brigadier General Pierce, Butler's former associate in the militia, now his second in command, was put in charge of the movement against Little Bethel. If Butler had had a free choice in
the matter he would have assigned the command to Phelps; Pierce
was chosen because of his rank.

The officers and men of the detachment were understandably

---

[1] As quoted in Jesse Ames Marshall (compiler), *Private and Official
Correspondence of Gen. Benjamin F. Butler* (Privately issued [Boston,
1917]), I, 133 (Hereafter cited as POC).

nervous as they set out toward Little Bethel (and for most of them) their first experience under fire. Unfortunately the colonel and staff of one of the regiments were mounted and the other colonel, knowing there was no cavalry at Fortress Monroe, mistook them for Confederates. His troops immediately opened fire; it was promptly returned. Two men were killed and eight wounded before daylight revealed the mistake. Alerted by the shooting, the Confederates abandoned Little Bethel and concentrated at Big Bethel a few miles away. Although the Confederates were substantially outnumbered, they drove off the Union troops after four hours of fighting. The Union casualties were 18 killed, 53 wounded, and 5 missing; the Confederates had one man killed (the first one on their side who died in action) and 7 wounded.

A year later such a trifling skirmish would not have been mentioned in the newspapers of either side. At the moment it was the nearest thing to a battle that had occurred so it attracted much attention. Because the Confederate commander claimed to have won a great victory it produced a degree of discouragement in the North, matched by elation in the South, out of all proportion to its real significance.

As was to happen on all too many other occasions during the Civil War the Union officers who fought at Big Bethel were more concerned with evading blame for disaster than in trying to learn what they had done wrong. Pierce wrote a letter to the Boston *Journal* attributing the outcome of the "battle" to poor planning by Butler's staff.[2] Some support for this thesis can be found in the fact that a lieutenant who was killed in action said, as he left Fortress Monroe, "This is an ill advised and badly arranged movement. I am afraid no good will come of it; and as for myself I do not think I shall come off the field alive."[3] However, the victorious Confederate general placed the responsibility for the Union defeat squarely upon Pierce's shoulders.[4] Major Winthrop

[2] Boston *Journal,* August 5, 1861.

[3] John W. Draper, *History of the American Civil War* (Harper & Brothers [New York, 1868]), II, 250.

[4] New York *Tribune,* June 17, 1861.

was killed, so he did not comment on the alleged shortcomings of his plan.

The truth really seems to be that no particular person was at fault. The troops fought well, but were badly handled by inexperienced officers.

Pierce's poor leadership moved Butler to recommend the adoption of some means other than by court-martial for weeding out inefficient militia officers who had been elected by their subordinates. "Ignorance and incompetency," he wrote to the Secretary of War, "are not crimes to be tried by court-martial, while they are great misfortunes to an officer." He suggested the creation of examining boards in each department, empowered, with the approval of department commanders, to dismiss incompetent officers without disgrace.[5]

No one can say how far Butler might have risen if at this time he had added even a minor victory to the laurels he had already gathered at Annapolis and Baltimore. When McClellan was made general in chief of the Union Armies (succeeding Scott on November 1, 1861) he had not really accomplished any more than Butler would have done if his subordinates had conducted themselves more capably at Big Bethel.

In his report on the Big Bethel affair Butler said, "I think, in the unfortunate combination of circumstances, and the result which we have experienced, we have gained more than we have lost. Our troops have learned to have confidence in themselves under fire. . . . Our officers have learned wherein their organization and drill are inefficient."[6] Butler's argument that his troops had gained more than enough in experience to offset their loss in men at Big Bethel was not widely accepted in the North. Nevertheless, he stuck to it and even repeated it after the Union disaster at Manassas Junction, near Warrenton, Virginia, in what northern historians call the battle of Bull Run. "We have heard the sad news from Manassas," he wrote to Montgomery Blair,

---

[5] Butler to Cameron, June 26, 1861; POC, I, 161.

[6] *Official Records of the Union and Confederate Armies* (Government Printing Office, [Washington, D.C., 1880–1901]), Series 1, I, 80.

"but are neither dismayed nor disheartened. It will have the same good effect upon the Army in general that Big Bethel has had upon my division, to teach us wherein we are weak and the rebels strong, and how to apply the remedy to our deficiencies."[7]

As time passed Negroes flocked to the "freedom fort," as they called Fortress Monroe, by "twenties, thirties, and forties."[8] By the middle of July 300 able-bodied men, 30 men too old to work, 175 women, and 395 children under 18 years of age had reached there. Once again Butler wrote to Cameron for advice and guidance. This time he wanted to know what was the status of these 900 individuals and what was to be done about them. Apologizing for addressing the Secretary of War directly instead of through channels and saying that he did so only because he sought answers to questions of as much political as military significance, Butler asked: "Are these men, women and children slaves? Are they free? Is their condition that of men, women and children, or of property, or is it a mixed relation?" He knew, as he thought everybody did, that they had been property according to laws prevailing before the war. Now he wanted specifically to be told what were the effects of rebellion and a state of war upon their previous condition. Personally he was satisfied that his treatment of able-bodied Negroes fit to do militarily useful work as confiscable property was constitutional and legal. (In any case it was legalized by the passage of the first Confiscation Act soon after his letter was written.) But he was disturbed by some other questions. Disregarding the Negro women, it was impossible, he wrote, to treat Negro children on the same basis as able-bodied Negro men. If the children were property they were an encumbrance upon, rather than a help to, the Confederate States, hence they could not legally be regarded as contraband of war. Therefore he asked: "Are they property?" If they were, he added, they had been deserted by their owners, "like wrecked vessels

---

[7] Quoted in T. A. Bland, *Life of Benjamin F. Butler* (Lee and Shepard [Boston, 1879]), p. 59.

[8] Edward L. Pierce, "The Contrabands at Fortress Monroe," *Atlantic Monthly,* November 1861, VIII, 628.

upon the ocean, . . . abandoned . . . to be swallowed up by the winter storm of starvation." Since they were no longer under ownership of any kind he inquired: "Have they not, by their masters' acts and the state of war, assumed the condition, which we hold to be the normal one, of those made in God's image?" His own mind compelled him, he confessed, "to look upon them as men and women, if not free born, yet free, manumitted, sent forth by the hand that held them, never to be reclaimed."[9]

If his ideas, as imperfectly as he felt he had set them forth, were correct his duty as a humane man was perfectly clear to him; he would "take the same care of these men, women and children, houseless, homeless and unprovided for, as . . . of the same number of men, women and children, who, for their attachment to the Union, had been driven or allowed to flee from the Confederate States." He was in doubt about how to conduct himself only because he had heard that General Irvin McDowell, commanding the Department of Northeastern Virginia, had recently been substantially ordered to forbid fugitive slaves to enter his lines.[10]

If he received a similar order Butler said he would be bound, as a soldier, to enforce it, "steadfastly, if not cheerfully." But, he added, he would prefer not to have to do so.[11]

Cameron replied in due time that he had given Butler's letter the "most attentive consideration." The President, Cameron said, felt that ordinary forms of judicial procedure unquestionably must be observed in loyal states. (Since Butler had not asked how to conduct himself in a loyal state this is a curious obiter dictum.) Slaves need not be returned to any claimants. If slaves belonging to loyal masters took refuge with Butler he might employ them, keeping a record of their owners' names. After the war ended Congress undoubtedly would "properly provide for all the persons thus received into the services of the Union, and for a just

---

9 Butler to Cameron, July 30, 1861; POC, I, 185–88.
10 Idem.
11 Idem.

compensation to loyal masters." He was to report at least twice a month what he was doing about Negroes.[12]

Butler's "Negro letters" delighted the abolitionists. Lewis Tappan, one of the founders of the American Anti-Slavery Society, wrote on behalf of several "friends of liberty and benevolents [sic]," seeking Butler's "advice with reference to the organization of a committee of citizens to provide for the removal of the self-emancipated negroes to the free States, where they could find employment, . . . receive wages for their labor, . . . and acquire property. . . ." Such a committee, Tappan thought, would also benefit field commanders by relieving them of the trouble of caring for Negroes. Butler answered that in his opinion "it would not be profitable to the Negroes to be sent North, . . . amid the stagnation of business [which occurred during the early months of the war], and at a season when all agricultural operations, except harvesting, are about to be suspended, to fill our towns with a new influx of people, when their labor is not wanted." Moreover, there was plenty of waste land in the South where they could be given better care at less cost than would be possible "amid the rigors of our northern winter." Anyway, he said, "The most of them would not desire to go North, if they can be assured (as I can assure them) of their safety at the South." However, the committee Tappan mentioned could help by furnishing "a number of suits of substantial, cheap clothing fit for winter service—shoes especially." Any such gifts would be distributed according to need, Butler promised.[13]

(Incidentally, Butler's arrangements for the subsistence and employment of Negroes worked so well that they were adopted almost in their entirety by the Freedmen's Bureau, established by Congress in March, 1865.)

A short time after Butler's second Negro letter was answered he was relieved as commanding officer of the Department of Vir-

[12] Cameron to Butler, August 8, 1861; POC, I, 201–3.
[13] Tappan to Butler, August 8, 1861; Butler to Tappan, August 10, 1861; POC, I, 199–200, 200–201.

ginia and North Carolina. His successor, Major General John E. Wool, was a 77-year-old veteran of the War of 1812 who had been living in virtual retirement in Troy, New York. There had been some pressure brought to bear upon Lincoln to assign Wool to an active command. *The New York Times,* for example, urged that Wool be given a place suitable to his rank, and, by inference, suitable to New York's importance. Although political considerations probably were responsible for Wool's supersedure of Butler, Butler believed he was replaced because his hammering at the Negro question had become embarrassing to Lincoln.[14]

Possibly by chance, perhaps for reasons the War Department did not care to disclose, Butler was relieved without being reassigned. Puzzled by this fact, he wrote to Montgomery Blair: "As a friend, may I ask you . . . what have I done or omitted to do? . . . . I am in the dark. Please give me 'more light.' "[15]

Soon after Wool reached Fortress Monroe he detailed Butler to take command of the 860 officers and men assigned to a joint Army-Navy expedition against Forts Clark and Hatteras, located at Hatteras Inlet some 20 miles south of Cape Hatteras. Butler asked for this duty and Wool may have granted his request as a means of showing him that his displacement as department commander had not been meant to reflect adversely on his military capacity.

Butler claimed in his autobiography that he suggested the Hatteras Inlet expedition. He had, he said, been watching the building of the forts there and had made plans to take them as soon as possible.[16] Since there is no indication in his autobiography (or anywhere else) that he controlled any seagoing vessels at this time it would be interesting to know how he watched the construction of fortifications on an island more than 100 miles

---

[14] A. Howard Meneely, *The War Department, 1861,* (Columbia University [New York, 1928]), pp. 196–97; James Parton, *General Butler in New Orleans* (Mason Brothers [New York, 1864]), p. 175.

[15] Butler to Montgomery Blair, August 11, 1861; POC, I, 206–7.

[16] Benjamin F. Butler, *Butler's Book* (A. M. Thayer & Co. [Boston, 1892]), p. 281.

(airline distance) from Fortress Monroe. He mentioned having received information from South Carolina loyalists (of whom there were remarkably few) without explaining how they communicated with him in northern Virginia. One also wonders how he proposed to transport his troops to Hatteras Inlet.

If Butler had not occasionally claimed more credit than was rightfully due him, as he did in this case, he would have had a better "image" among his contemporaries.

Actually the Hatteras Inlet expedition was conceived and put in train by the Navy Department on the basis of information furnished by Captain Daniel Campbell, master of the merchant schooner *Lydia Frances*. Early in the war the *Lydia Frances* was wrecked near Cape Hatteras and Campbell was held prisoner at Hatteras Inlet for about three months. During that time he saw many blockade runners pass through the Inlet and watched the erection of the forts designed to guard this gateway to Pimlico Sound. Escaping at last, he made his way to Norfolk and communicated with Captain Silas Stringham, commanding officer of the Atlantic Blockading Squadron. For some time past the Navy Department had been planning an attempt to capture Port Royal, South Carolina, for use as a base for the Atlantic Squadron. This was to be done as soon as the Army could and would furnish enough men to make up an expedition. Campbell's information led the Navy Department to decide to move first against Hatteras Inlet. At the request of the Secretary of the Navy, General Scott agreed to have Butler detail the necessary men from among those at Fortress Monroe. Because the Navy was not ready to undertake the expedition until after Wool had succeeded Butler it fell to Wool's lot to furnish the men. He made it an express condition that they were to be returned to Fortress Monroe as soon as possible so plans were made to take the two forts, spike their guns, and block the Inlet by sinking a schooner loaded with stone in its narrow channel.

The Navy's part of the Hatteras Inlet expedition, commanded by Stringham, comprised 11 vessels—warships, tugs, transports, and a dismasted schooner to be used as the blockship. The forts to be attacked were heavy earthworks, mounting a total of 25 guns. Although the fleet had 158 guns all told, its firepower was regarded as only slightly superior to the forts' because in those days one piece on shore was considered the equivalent of five in a ship.

The expedition departed from Hampton Roads, Virginia, about noon, Monday, August 26, 1861 and reached Hatteras Inlet late the following afternoon. As soon as their vessels anchored Stringham and Butler held a council of war at which they made plans to launch their attack at dawn Wednesday.

Before Butler turned in Tuesday night he took time to write some personal letters. In one of them he dealt with talk he had heard about the possibility of his being nominated as the Democratic candidate for governor of Massachusetts in the next election, then three months in the future. "As I have stated to you," he wrote to his brother-in-law, Fisher Ames Hildreth, "and as I have publicly repeated, when I left home I left all politics, in a party sense of the term, behind me, and I know of no politics . . . save as represented by the question—How to preserve the Union and restore the country to its integrity." This being so, Butler could not, he said, consent to the use of his name by any party. He did not agree with the principles espoused by the state and national administrations, but the Republicans had won the last election and he thought they were entitled to a fair trial. Saying; "I believe Governor Andrew has endeavored faithfully, zealously, and efficiently to put our Commonwealth on the side of the Nation and to sustain the Union," Butler concluded, "I, therefore, . . . would not desire to see a change in the executive. . . . I do not say that I would vote for Governor Andrew, but were I at home I would not vote against him."[17]

Hildreth released this letter to the press, as he was obviously meant to do, and it was widely published.

If Butler had chosen to run for governor in 1861 he probably would have been elected. On this occasion, at least, he put principle above personal advantage.

---

[17] New York *Tribune,* September 7, 1861.

At noon, Wednesday, instead of at dawn as planned, eight of Stringham's ships opened a heavy fire on the Confederate works and two other vessels cleared a beach-head several miles north of them. The troops began landing at 1 P.M., with Butler directing the operation from the deck of the revenue cutter *Harriet Lane*. Of course, he had no walkie-talkie with which to communicate instantly with the landing party, but had to rely upon signalmen who wigwagged messages back and forth between the *Harriet Lane* and the shore. The expedition's landing craft—two iron surfboats, two flat bottomed fishing boats, and some of the ships' lifeboats—were powered by oars only. A stiff southwest wind (described by Butler in his official report as a gale) sprang up in midafternoon, making it increasingly difficult to handle the boats. After about 300 men and two howitzers had been landed both of the iron surfboats had been swamped and both of the flat bottom boats had been wrecked. In these circumstances landing operations had to be suspended and, to make a bad situation worse, the ships had to stand off shore to ride out the storm.

The men fortunate or unfortunate enough to have landed were soaked to the skin, their ammunition was wet, one of their howitzers was so badly damaged as to be practically useless, they had no food with them and only what water was in their canteens. To add to their troubles the ships fired on them twice. By good luck nobody was killed as a result of this mistake, although a shell fragment struck one man's hand. Despite all of these things Fort Clark, the smaller of the two works, was taken before nightfall (chiefly because it had run out of ammunition). The food shortage was alleviated by the "acquisition" of some sheep and a few geese. These were cooked (more burned than roasted, as one man put it) on cutlasses and bayonets and eaten for supper. They were warmed over for the next morning's breakfast.

Early Thursday morning the fleet resumed its bombardment of Fort Hatteras. A few hours later Flag Officer Samuel Barron of the Confederate Navy sent word to Butler offering to surrender Fort Hatteras with all of its arms and munitions of war on condition that the officers be allowed to keep their side arms, the enlisted men to retire without arms. Barron's written message was accompanied by a verbal one to the effect that he had more than 600 men at the fort with another 1,000 within an hour's march, but he was anxious to avoid further bloodshed. Butler apparently took this statement for a poker player's bluff; he answered that he would accept nothing less than "full capitulation," with both officers and men to be treated as prisoners of war. (For some reason Butler's phrase did not attract the attention Grant's demand for the "unconditional surrender" of Fort Donelson did four months later.) While Barron was considering Butler's reply the *Harriet Lane* and the transport *Adelaide* ran aground close under the fort's guns. However, Barron did not realize to what extent conditions had changed in his favor and he accepted Butler's terms. Butler then told Barron that because the expedition was a joint affair the surrender would have to be made on board the flagship to the two commanders. A short time later Barron, Colonel Martin of the Seventh North Carolina Regiment, and a Colonel Andrews boarded the *Minnesota* where they formally surrendered Forts Clark and Hatteras. In addition to these three officers Major James A. Bradford, chief of the Confederate Army's ordnance department, 715 officers and men, 1,000 muskets, 30 cannon, a 10-inch columbiad, a brig loaded with cotton, a sloop loaded with provisions, five flags, and 150 bags of coffee were captured at Hatteras Inlet.

Butler went ashore as soon as he could to see how his troops had fared, to inspect the forts, and to embark the prisoners and the wounded. On his return to the *Minnesota* he and Stringham, who had conducted an examination of his own, decided it would be far wiser for a Union force to hold Hatteras Inlet than for it merely to be blocked. Stringham remained at the Inlet while Butler made a flying trip to Fortress Monroe where he obtained permission from Wool to go on to Washington to explain his views, and Stringham's, to the authorities there. His representations to President Lincoln and the Cabinet led the President to order the forts to be occupied permanently. In his report to Wool, Butler suggested that Fort Hatteras be renamed Fort Stringham.

Because it was the first Union victory of any sort the Hatteras Inlet affair gave a big lift to northern morale. The capture of the Inlet was also of considerable military significance. The Confederates immediately abandoned Fort Ocracoke, at Ocracoke Inlet, about 20 miles south of Hatteras Inlet, whereupon a party from the U.S.S. *Pawnee* spiked the 22 cannon there and destroyed a large amount of matériel. It also put an immediate stop to blockade running into Pamlico Sound by way of which large quantities of goods had been reaching places along the Chowan, Neuse, and Roanoke Rivers. According to Admiral David D. Porter, Hatteras Inlet was quite as important to the Confederacy as Charleston and Mobile and its capture "ultimately proved one of the most important events of the war.[18]

---

[18] David D. Porter, *Naval History of the Civil War* (The Sherman Publishing Company [New York, 1886]), pp. 44, 47.

9

★★★★★★★★★★★★

On Leave

In September 1861, with four and a half months of active duty and his part in the Hatteras Inlet expedition behind him, Butler asked for, and was granted a leave of absence.

Soon after he reached home he turned his attention to the matter of raising troops. Recruiting was being conducted in accordance with an act of the Thirty-seventh Congress which imposed the duty of organizing regiments of United States Volunteers upon the governors of the loyal states and gave them the right to choose officers.[1] Under the provisions of this law the governors appointed officers and delegated the raising of troops to them. Occasionally the President or the Secretary of War granted individual applicants permission to raise regiments and appoint officers in various states. The governors, jealous of their patronage, full of dignity and local pride, and often of states' rights sentiments (even though most of them were Republicans), protested vigorously against these special permissions. Governor Andrew, who was "a great stickler for proper form and ceremonies,"[2] was one of the loudest, most frequent complainers.

Lincoln readily admitted that the governors had much justification for their complaints, but, as he explained to two of Governor Andrews' emissaries, such special permissions as had been issued "had been extorted by the pressure of certain persons [in-

---

[1] Ch. IX, sec. 4, Acts of the Thirty-seventh Congress.

[2] Peleg W. Chandler, *Memoir of the Hon. John Albion Andrew* (John Wilson and Son [Cambridge, Mass., 1880]), p. 10.

cluding Butler?], who if they had been refused, would have accused the government of rejecting the services of many thousands of imaginary men." This pressure, he added, was of a persistency beyond the conception of anyone not subject to it. "Perhaps," he concluded, "he had been wrong in granting such independent permissions at all, even under this pressure, but . . . certainly it had not been intended to do any person or State a wrong."[3] Andrew, who had come "to think himself greater than anyone else," remained unmollified.[4]

It seemed to Butler that the governors were letting the war degenerate into a partisan affair and that they were failing to tap a big reservoir of man power by commissioning only Republicans. This feeling was by no means unreasonable. Theoretically the Army Organization Act established a purely military relationship between the federal government and the governors; in fact the law made political influence, social position, nepotism, and favoritism significant factors in the selection of officers.[5] These things did not commend Democrats to Republican governors anywhere. Democrats in Massachusetts were additionally handicapped because Governor Andrew "was disposed to think that blood and family and a college education stood for something in the way of military ability above the education of the common people."[6]

After giving the matter due consideration Butler decided that it behooved him to raise an army of New Englanders, to be officered exclusively by Democrats. Because he thought it beneath the dignity of a major general of United States Volunteers to seek permission from a governor to raise troops he penned an order, which he asked the Secretary of War to sign, author-

---

[3] *Official Records of the Union and Confederate Armies* (Government Printing Office, [Washington, D.C., 1880–1901]), Series 3, I, 813–14. (Hereafter cited as *OR*)

[4] Harriet J. H. Robinson, *"Warrington" Pen Portraits* (Published by Mrs. William S. Robinson [Boston, 1877]), p. 411.

[5] Anonymous, "Our Military Past and Future," *Atlantic Monthly,* November 1879, XLIV, 567.

[6] Robinson, op. cit., p. 409.

izing him to recruit and equip six regiments in Maine, New Hampshire, Vermont, Connecticut, and Massachusetts. He deliberately omitted Rhode Island because he understood that General Ambrose E. Burnside was enlisting men there for immediate service. Before Cameron was allowed to sign the order Butler sought President Lincoln telegraphed to the governors who would be affected: "Gen. Butler proposes raising in New England, six regiments, to be recruited & commanded by himself & to go on special service. I shall be glad if you as Gov. of [blank] will answer by telegraph that you consent."[7] All of the governors except Andrew consented cheerfully, even enthusiastically. Andrew replied: "Authorize state to raise whatever regiments you wish additional. We will first fulfill engagements with General [T. W.] Sherman ordered by Secretary of War, then add others as fast as possible. Will help General Butler to the utmost."[8]

In the belief that Andrew had given his consent, Lincoln permitted Cameron to authorize Butler to raise and prepare such New England troops as he might judge fit for the purpose of making "an expedition along the eastern shore of Virginia . . . to Cape Charles."[9]

Armed with this authorization Butler called upon Governor Andrew. The Governor behaved more cordially than Butler had expected. The General, ready to be as friendly as the Governor seemed, gladly consented to Andrew's request to postpone active recruiting in Massachusetts until Sherman's needs should have been more nearly met than was just then the case. In the meantime Butler decided to see what he could accomplish in Maine.

While Butler was in Maine, Andrew underwent a change of heart, if indeed, he had not intended all along to oppose Butler's special recruiting. Opportunely for Andrew the War Department chose this moment to issue an order for all persons having

---

[7] Roy Basler (editor), *The Collected Works of Abraham Lincoln* (Rutgers University Press [New Brunswick, New Jersey, 1955]), IV, 518.

[8] *OR,* Series 2, I, 509.

[9] Jesse Ames Marshall (compiler), *Private and Official Correspondence of Gen. Benjamin F. Butler* (Privately issued [Boston, 1917]), I, 241. (Hereafter cited as *POC*).

special permission to raise troops to put themselves at the disposal of the governors of their states. Andrew immediately forbade the formation of any new regiments or companies in Massachusetts without orders from the state's commander in chief, viz., Andrew himself.

Andrew's satisfaction at having checkmated Butler did not last long. Butler quickly secured an order from the War Department making him commanding officer, while he was engaged in recruiting, of a temporary Department of New England. Andrew fought tooth and nail to have this department abolished, but it remained in existence until February, 1862, by which time it had served Butler's purpose.

During the four and a half months this department existed Andrew, bitterly intolerant of the least diminution of his prerogatives, and Butler, who thought the Governor's states rights views were almost as bad as those of a secessionist, hurled letters containing thousands of words at each other.[10] This epistolary duel did little enough credit to either man, but some of their contemporaries believed Andrew played the worst part. Lincoln thought the Governor ought to have let the thing drop in favor of more important matters. The Philadelphia *Inquirer* called Andrew's conduct shameful, absurd, factious, and half mutinous. He seemed to be composed, the *Inquirer* commented, of equal parts of "unreasonable and unseasonable" abolitionism and ultra state's right abstractionism.[11]

A shabby thing Andrew did in his efforts to block Butler's special recruiting drive was to deny state financial aid to the families of men who enlisted under Butler's banner on the grounds that they were not members of a military force authorized by the Commonwealth. Butler believed the state legislature would overrule the Governor in this matter, but he publicly guaranteed his men's families the equivalent of state aid even if it had to be paid out of his personal funds.

At an early stage of the Andrew-Butler controversy, while it

[10] See *OR,* Series 3, I, 811–66 for transcripts of their letters.
[11] Philadelphia *Inquirer,* quoted in the Boston *Post,* May 29, 1862.

still might have been settled amicably, Butler sought a personal interview with the Governor. Andrew directed his assistant military secretary to send Butler a curt note to the effect that the Governor was extremely busy so the General would have to write. (The curtness may have been the secretary's fault, but the message was from Andrew.) Butler then asked, in a courteous, pleasant, unofficial letter to Andrew if anything personal stood in the way of a meeting. Professing to be unaware of any such difficulty, Butler hoped if one did exist it could be removed. Instead of taking time to answer by his own hand Andrew had his military secretary write: "His Excellency, Governor Andrew, has . . . [no personal reason] for not desiring an interview . . . [but] unless the subject upon which an interview is desired is of such character as to absolutely require immediate attention he would prefer at this moment that it be placed in writing."[12]

The next time Butler had occasion to write to Andrew he referred to himself as General Butler and to his correspondent as "His Excellency, Governor Andrew," with the latter title enclosed in quotation marks every time it was used. A complaint the adjutant general made about this letter gave Butler an opportunity to write to Andrew, "in the character of a citizen," most emphatically disclaiming any intentional discourtesy toward the governor of Massachusetts. "In the matter of the address in question," Butler said, "I but copied the address assumed by one of the numerous military secretaries who write me on behalf of the Governor. . . . 'His Excellency, Governor Andrew' is neither 'a baptismal, inherited, or constitutional' title, and . . . I marked it in quotation to call attention to the difference."[13]

By the time Butler finally raised the troops he wanted another general had been assigned to command the eastern Virginia expedition. However, the War Department had no trouble in finding something for Butler and his Democratic Army to do.

Although the fact was to remain unknown to Butler for some

12 Adjutant General Browne to Butler, October 8, 1861; *POC,* I, 250.
13 Butler to Andrew, December 29, 1861; *POC,* I, 307.

little time after the decision had been reached, his New England troops were chosen as the Army's contingent of a joint Army-Navy expedition against New Orleans, the Confederacy's biggest city and principal cotton shipping port.

The idea of attacking the soft underbelly of the Confederacy—to paraphrase Winston Churchill—occurred to Assistant Secretary of the Navy Gustavus V. Fox toward the middle of 1861. The Army men with whom he discussed the thing thought Mobile, Alabama, would be a better objective for a joint operation such as he envisioned. Their view was that Mobile would be easier to take; his was that New Orleans was strategically far more important. Its capture would, he argued, have three effects; it would close one of the biggest holes in the blockade, it would make it difficult for supplies from Texas to reach the eastern Confederate States, and the city could be used as a base for operations farther up the Mississippi River.

Fox, who had been an officer in the Navy and the merchant marine, insisted that a fleet of battleships could make its way past New Orleans' chief defenses, Fort St. Philip on the easterly side and Fort Jackson on the westerly side of the river, take the city, and turn it over to an army of occupation. Having sailed up the Mississippi to New Orleans in an ocean-going steamer he knew the river was navigable by large vessels at least that far from the Gulf of Mexico. His opinion, which some others shared, that a fleet could pass the forts below New Orleans was strengthened by the Union Navy's experiences at Hatteras Inlet and Port Royal. Those operations had refuted Admiral Nelson's dictum that only fools would attack stone forts with wooden ships. Fox convinced his chief, Gideon Welles, of the feasibility of his proposal. Welles discussed it with Lincoln who became mildly interested in it. However, a lack of up-to-date, detailed information about the condition of the river and the strength of New Orleans' defenses prevented the making of any firm plans at this time. Fortuitously Commander (later Admiral) David D. Porter arrived in Washington early in November, 1861. Porter, who had been on duty with the Gulf Squadron, had the needed information, gleaned from spies and escaped slaves. And, as it happens he had independently been thinking along somewhat the same lines Fox had been doing. Porter's idea was to reduce Forts St. Philip and Jackson by gunfire from floating batteries before advancing upon New Orleans. He outlined his plan to his superiors without knowing that they already had something similar to it under fairly serious consideration. His information and suggestion settled the matter. In mid-November, Fox's plan was adopted by a council of war attended by Lincoln, Welles, Fox, Porter, and McClellan, who had recently become General in Chief of the Union Armies.

Although McClellan admitted that something would eventually have to be done about New Orleans, he opposed Fox's plan as soon as it was mentioned. Ostensibly McClellan disliked the thing because he assumed that it would necessitate the use of 50,000 troops, a far larger number than he was willing to detach from the Army of the Potomac. Probably the real reason for his attitude was that the movement was planned for the near future, for he was an extreme procrastinator. (Lincoln once said McClellan seemed to be afflicted with "the slows.") He did not like the proposal any better when he was told the Navy would assume the task of taking New Orleans so he would have to furnish only 10,000 troops for an occupation force. Despite McClellan's qualms Lincoln gave definite orders to go ahead with the project. The availibility of Butler's New England Army probably had an influence, perhaps even a controlling one, on the President's decision.

Fox's plan was modified in one particular by the council before it was approved. At Porter's urging, and with McClellan's concurrence, Porter was given command of a fleet of 20 schooners, each of which was to carry a 13-inch mortar capable of firing a 285 pound shell. He promised that a 48 hour bombardment by these huge guns would render Forts St. Philip and Jackson untenable if they were not utterly destroyed.

Welles insisted that plans for the New Orleans expedition be kept secret even from the Secretary of War as long as possible to prevent them from being broadcast by the press. (Cameron was not notably discreet and there was no censorship imposed by the government nor restraint practiced by editors during the Civil War. Everything the newspapers learned was promptly published.) To mislead Cameron and the newspapers Lincoln directed the Secretary of War to have Butler prepare plans for an invasion of Texas.

Late in November, 1861 two shiploads of Butler's New England troops were sent, under the immediate command of Brigadier General Phelps, to Ship Island in the Gulf of Mexico some ten miles south of Biloxi, Mississippi. On December 5 Phelps reported his safe arrival at Ship Island to Butler and said, "Deeming it proper to make known to this people the remote object of this expedition, I have prepared a proclamation, which I shall endeavor to have distributed as early and as widely as possible, consistent with the more pressing demands of the service." This proclamation, addressed "To the Loyal Citizens of the Southwest," began: "Without any desire on my part, but contrary to my private inclinations I find myself among you as a military officer of the government. A proper respect for my fellow-countrymen renders it not out of place that I make known to you the motives and principles by which my command will be governed." This scarcely endearing introduction was followed by a statement that in Phelps' opinion slavery was incompatible with the federal Constitution. His view was that ratification of the Constitution by the 13 original states had morally obligated them to abolish slavery and that slave states admitted to the Union after ratification had been wrongfully admitted. He also voiced his conviction ("our conviction" is his actual phraseology) that slave labor was a monopoly because it excluded free labor, an essential element in free institutions, which were better adapted and more congenial to Anglo-Saxons than were the despotic tendencies of slavery.[14]

---

[14] James Parton, *General Butler in New Orleans* (Mason Brothers [New York, 1864]), pp. 198–200.

To say that Phelps was far in advance of the Administration and, generally speaking, of public opinion in the North would be a distinct understatement. Obviously Butler had these facts in mind when he wrote to the Adjutant General that he had not received an official copy of Phelps' proclamation, but information from other sources made it certain that the newspapers versions of it were nearly correct. "I need hardly say," Butler added, "that the issuing of any proclamation . . . was neither suggested nor authorized by me, and most certainly not such a one."[15]

Butler's own departure for Ship Island with the rest of his division, scheduled for the fall of 1861, was delayed because of a potentially explosive international situation. In November, 1861 Captain Charles Wilkes of the U.S.S. *San Jacinto* took two Confederate diplomatic agents out of the British mail steamer, *Trent,* bound from the West Indies to London. The British government protested this act so vigorously that for a time a war with Great Britain seemed likely to begin at any minute.

If there had been such a war Butler thought the United States would have won an easy victory. To judge from his autobiography he was more than a little disappointed by the peaceful settlement of the *Trent* affair.[16] (The poor fellow never did get a chance to shoot any Britishers.)

While the danger of an Anglo-American war lasted those of Butler's troops who had not already departed for the Gulf of Mexico were held in New England. Most of his men were on shipboard, ready to sail from various ports, when he was told to disembark them and wait for further orders. The fact that a steamship chartered at $3,000 a day was lying idle in Boston harbor led to whispers that Butler had an interest in her and was pocketing a large sum by delaying her departure. Of course, he could not defend himself by telling what the truth was.

With the *Trent* affair settled, it seemed safe by the end of the

---

15 *OR,* Series 1, VI, 465.

16 Benjamin F. Butler, *Butler's* Book (A. M. Thayer & Co. [Boston, 1892]), pp.319–23.

year to send the rest of Butler's division to the Gulf. However, McClellan was apparently determined to break up the New Orleans expedition. On January 13, 1862 he ordered a shipload of Butler's troops, bound from Boston to Ship Island, to be landed at Port Royal to reinforce General T. W. Sherman.

Fortunately for the New Orleans expedition (and for the Union cause in general) Edwin M. Stanton succeeded Cameron as Secretary of War in January 1862. Soon after Stanton took office he and Butler, who were old personal and political friends, spent several hours discussing the Gulf Coast expedition. Three days later McClellan countermanded his order for Butler's troops to land at Port Royal.

Toward the end of January, Stanton called simultaneously upon Butler to "report without delay the present state and condition of the Expedition now under his charge," the expenditures already incurred in connection with it, and "the probable expenditure required to place the Expedition at its contemplated destination," and upon McClellan to give his opinion without delay as to whether the expedition ought to go forward at all.[17]

Stanton's order to Butler may well have been intended chiefly to keep him too busy to bother the War Department about the expedition for a while. Anyway, it had such an effect during the two weeks Butler spent compiling a report that he had 2,000 men at Ship Island, 2,200 in transports bound for the Gulf, and 8,800 more ready for almost immediate embarkation at various places in New England; that expenditures had been $885,392.50; liabilities, $1,348,034.69; and that additional costs would be about $30 a man.[18]

McClellan urged that "what was known as General Butler's expedition" be suspended and the troops assigned to it be held in reserve, ready for use wherever they might be needed, with such places to be determined as active operations proceeded.[19]

[17] Stanton to Butler, January 24, 1862; POC, I, 326. George C. Gorham, *Life and Public Services of Edwin M. Stanton* (Houghton, Mifflin and Company [Boston, 1899]), I, 315.
[18] *POC,* I, 326–30.
[19] Gorham, op. cit., I, 315.

Stanton also sought advice about the proposed expedition from General J. G. Barnard, chief engineer of the Army of the Potomac. Barnard, who had helped to build Forts St. Philip and Jackson, said a force of 10,000 would be strong enough to take them if the fleet could not pass them. Stanton decided to send the expedition forward with 18,000 troops.

Early in February, Butler went to Washington to get his final orders. Their delivery was delayed longer than he thought reasonable so he wrote to the Secretary of War about them. Stanton referred the matter to McClellan with a request that it be given immediate attention. There being a still further delay, Butler decided personally to prod the General in Chief. On February 12 Butler told the Committee on the Conduct of the War that in his opinion there were no more than 65,000 Confederate troops in the vicinity of Washington—this estimate was substantially lower and, as time proved, far more nearly correct than McClellan's guess. Butler then managed to obtain an interview with McClellan during which he hinted broadly that Lincoln had offered him command of the Army of the Potomac if he would lead it in an attack upon the Confederate Army. His orders were soon issued.

They named him commanding officer of the newly created Department of the Gulf. This department was to comprise such parts of the Gulf states west of Pensacola, Florida, as he could occupy. His Army of the Gulf was to cooperate with the Navy in the advance upon New Orleans, the capture of which was the main purpose of the expedition. The route to be followed ran up the Mississippi River. The first obstacle likely to be encountered, and perhaps the only one, would be the resistance offered by Forts St. Philip and Jackson. If Porter's mortar boats reduced these works Butler was to take charge of them and garrison them securely. In the event that the Navy could not overcome them Butler's troops were to endeavor to carry them by assault. The same directions would apply in regard to the Chalmette Batteries at English Bend (where Andrew Jackson defeated the British in the War of 1812). Butler was told, parenthetically, that once the fleet had passed the Chalmette Batteries New Orleans would inevitably fall. He was to occupy the city and destroy any works guarding it. His attention should quickly be turned to Baton Rouge, Berwick Bay, and Fort Livingston, all in Louisiana. A feint at Galveston, Texas was recommended. An attempt to open communication with the Union Armies in the North, via the Mississippi River, was practically ordered, "always bearing in mind the necessity of occupying Jackson, Mississippi," as soon as it could safely be done.[20] (Jackson is somewhat more than 150 miles north of New Orleans, about 40 miles east of the Mississippi River, on a railroad from New Orleans to Richmond. This railroad was, of course, in Confederate hands.)

On paper Butler was assigned 14,400 infantrymen, 275 cavalrymen, and 500 artillerymen (including his New England division). He was supposed to be furnished enough more troops from the garrison at Key West, Florida, to bring his total force up to nearly 18,000 men and he was promised reinforcements at an early date so that he could accomplish the various things mentioned in his orders. Actually he was given about 13,500 effective officers and men and no more were sent to the Department of the Gulf while he was its commanding officer.

---

[20] *OR*, Series 1, V, 40.

10

★★★★★★★★★★★★

"Almost as Many Adventures as Jason"

Butler's final orders for the New Orleans expedition were delivered to him in Washington on Sunday, February 23, 1862. He left Hampton Roads the following Tuesday afternoon in the *Mississippi,* a chartered steamer, accompanied by Mrs. Butler, his staff, and 1,600 troops. Ordinarily the sailing time from Hampton Roads to the Gulf of Mexico was six or seven days. However the *Mississippi's* voyage took nearly three weeks, because, as Parton said with some poetic license, "In getting to Ship Island, General Butler had almost as many adventures as Jason in search of the golden fleece."[1]

Pleasant weather prevailed during the ship's first night out of port, but Wednesday morning brought a gale and seas rough enough to cause the *Mississippi* to ship a dangerous amount of water. Besides working the pumps to capacity it became necessary to bail the vessel with buckets passed from hand to hand by a line of men extending from the hold to the deck.

Butler wanted the *Mississippi* to put into Hatteras Inlet to pick up General Thomas Williams, a regular Army man Butler had asked to have assigned to the New Orleans expedition. Because of the bad weather the ship gave Cape Hatteras and the Inlet a wide berth, leaving Williams to make his way to Ship Island later.

By Thursday evening the gale blew itself out and the ship's company spent another enjoyable night. Then, about 9 A.M.,

---

[1] James A. Parton, *General Butler in New Orleans* (Mason Brothers [New York, 1864]), p. 203.

Friday, just after the Butlers had finished breakfast, the *Mississippi* struck on Frying Pan Shoals, off Cape Fear, North Carolina. When soundings showed shallow water on all sides of the vessel her anchor was dropped. Unfortunately she ran upon the anchor hard enough to punch a 5-inch hole through her bottom. Despite the best the pumps could do the water gained fast. Mrs. Butler asked the General how dangerous the situation was. "A hundredfold worse than [during] the storm, but there is no time for words, I must look after the ship," he answered. In the face of her knowledge of the ship's plight Mrs. Butler sat tranquilly on the quarter-deck busy with some needlework. Her visible serenity calmed the soldiers wonderfully. Shortly before noon a warship was sighted standing toward the stranded vessel. Luckily the stranger turned out to be the U.S.S. *Mt. Vernon* of the blockading squadron. At 3:30 P.M., after a careful approach, the *Mt. Vernon* passed a line to the *Mississippi*. For an hour and a half the *Mt. Vernon* did her best to tow the *Mississippi* free. When these efforts proved useless the captain of the *Mt. Vernon* took "Mrs. General Butler," as he called her, and about 300 soldiers on board his ship. Mrs. Butler did not want to leave her husband's side. She went only when he asked her: "Are you mad that you would risk to the children the loss of both [of us]?"[2]

After much of the *Mississippi*'s cargo and armament had been jettisoned she finally freed herself. The *Mt. Vernon* then cautiously made her way to deep water, showing lights for the guidance of the *Mississippi*. The transport, with her stern riding several feet higher than her bow, was convoyed by the *Mt. Vernon* to a comparatively safe anchorage at the mouth of the Cape Fear River. Soon after daybreak, Saturday, Mrs. Butler and the troops returned to the *Mississippi* which made her way to Port Royal without further incident except for a display of St. Elmo's fire during a thunderstorm.

---

[2] Mrs. Butler to Mrs. Heard, February 25, 1862, as quoted in Jesse Ames Marshall (compiler), *Private and Official Correspondence of Gen. Benjamin F. Butler* (Privately issued, [Boston, 1917]), I, 366. (Hereafter cited as *POC*).

(A letter, signed "Old Salt," referring to the events just described, published 21 years later in the Boston *Post* is illustrative of the lengths to which hostility to Butler drove some men. The Old Salt, who identified himself only as having been a member of the crew of the U.S.S. *Vixen* [!] when she went to the aid of the *Mississippi,* blamed Butler for that ship's trouble because, "contrary to nautical advice and experience," he ordered the captain to run too close to Cape Hatteras. Since Cape Hatteras and Hatteras Inlet, where Butler wanted to put in, are scarcely more than 20 miles apart it would have been impossible to stop at the Inlet without approaching the Cape, and even if a ship had run unnecessarily close to Cape Hatteras on one day it certainly did not cause her to go aground on Frying Pan Shoals some 150 miles farther south on another day. To make sure of thoroughly blackening Butler's reputation the Old Salt asserted that the *Mississippi*'s cargo had included several hundred barrels, or several times 3,150 gallons, of whiskey for the General's personal use.)[3]

There was no vessel at Port Royal capable of carrying the *Mississippi*'s troops to Ship Island so she had to be unloaded and repaired. As she started to leave Port Royal she went aground again. Then, after being refloated with the aid of all the tugboats in the harbor, she parted a rudder chain and grounded for the third time. At this point a board of inquiry convened by Butler deposed the captain. An officer of the *Mt. Vernon* was put in command of the *Mississippi* for the rest of her passage to Ship Island and her owners sent another captain to bring her home.

When the *Mississippi* finally cleared Port Royal she made an easy, pleasant seven days' run to the Gulf, only to encounter such violent winds there that she could not dock at Ship Island for three days.

Immediately after Butler landed at Ship Island he conferred with Captain David G. "Damn the Torpedoes" Farragut, commanding officer of the naval contingent of the New Orleans ex-

[3] Boston *Post,* November 30, 1883.

pedition. They agreed that Butler should follow in Farragut's wake, ready to hold whatever places the Navy took or to do anything else Farragut might request. The General promised to have 6,000 men on board transports, ready for action, within a week. Farragut sailed for the Southwest Pass, one of the Mississippi's several mouths, where he intended to enter the river.

Back at Ship Island, Butler divided his army into three brigades, each consisting of five or six regiments of infantry, a troop of cavalry, and at least one battery of artillery. A hundred carpenters began making scaling ladders for use if the forts had to be stormed. Another 100 men were picked to handle the 30 small boats Butler had with him in case amphibious operations became necessary.

True to his promise Butler put seven regiments and two batteries on shipboard and joined Farragut six days after reaching Ship Island. However, heavy winds and low water over the bars at Southwest Pass delayed Farragut so the transports returned to their base and the men disembarked. For the next two weeks Butler oscillated between Ship Island and the delta.

Because Ship Island could have been a staging point for an expedition bound for any place along the Gulf Coast from western Florida to western Texas the Confederates were not unduly worried about New Orleans at first. When Farragut's attempt to enter the Mississippi finally revealed the real objective of the Union force General Mansfield Lovell asked the Confederate government to add 10,000 troops to the 1,000 militiamen he had available for the defense of the city. Because the Confederacy was being severely pressed elsewhere at this time only a few men could be spared to reinforce him so he had to rely chiefly upon Forts St. Philip and Jackson with the Chalmette Batteries as a weak secondary line.

In the hope of frightening Farragut and Butler the Confederates added phantom defenses to their real ones. Southern newspapers frequently reported that the banks of the Mississippi River below New Orleans were impregnably fortified and that Lovell had 30,000 well equipped men immediately available with many more close at hand and care was taken to have these stories become known to the northern press.

Before Farragut's vessels entered the river Butler's troops were in action only once. The series of events leading to the battle (using the word loosely) they fought began when a six or seven year old girl and some sailors were picked up in a lifeboat from an abandoned blockade runner. The child's parents, who had taken to another boat, had not been found so Butler detailed his adjutant to take her to the mainland in a boat flying a flag of truce and to find somebody in Biloxi who could send her to relatives. The boat ran aground on her way back to Ship Island and some shots were fired at her. Unharmed, she floated free on the next high tide. As soon as Butler heard of what had happened he sent 600 men of the Ninth Connecticut Regiment to the mainland to avenge the insult. They returned "loaded with a whimsical variety of spoil and bubbling over with blatherskite. . . . They had landed, marched six miles into the country and broken up a camp of militia. . . . The enemy had fired two rounds without hitting anybody, and then emigrated due north at the top of their speed."[4]

Farragut's battleships and Porter's mortar schooners finally crossed the bars and entered the Mississippi on April 7. A week later Farragut notified Butler that the fleet would be ready to start upstream the following day. Butler immediately embarked eight regiments and three batteries in five transports and went with them to the head of the passes, ready to do to the best of his ability whatever Farragut might ask of him. He planned to send the transports back to Ship Island for more troops as soon as those they carried had landed.

Farragut had little faith in the utility of the mortar boats be-

---

[4] John Williams De Forest, *A Volunteer's Adventures* (Yale University Press [New Haven, 1946]), p. 9. (Quoted with the publisher's permission)

cause he knew that in 1815 a single fort standing where there were now two had held a British fleet in check for nine days while the ships fired more than 1,000 shells. Nevertheless, Porter was allowed to bombard Forts St. Philip and Jackson for six days, during which time he fired—by his own report—16,000 shells at them.

Having given Porter's pet scheme a thorough trial Farragut reverted to Fox's original plan of running past the forts without waiting for them to be reduced. He arranged with Butler that as soon as the fleet was above the forts the troops should begin moving against Fort St. Philip from its rear, or Gulf side. At 2:30 A.M., April 24, Farragut started up the river. Butler watched from the deck of his headquarters vessel, the *Saxon,* until he was sure the fleet had passed the forts, then he dashed back to where his transports were waiting, led them through Pass a l'Outre around to Sable Island in the Gulf of Mexico 12 miles east of Fort St. Philip. Here the troops were transshipped to a shallow draught gunboat which carried as many of them as it could to a landing place within six miles of the fort, and went back to the island for more soldiers. The troops made their way (in small boats as far as possible, then on foot) through the bayous and swamps to a point on the river a few miles north of the fort. (This movement was well under way by the time a messenger sent by Farragut reached Butler to suggest beginning it.) During the night of April 26–27 some of the troops were ferried across the river by a gunboat left for that purpose. Since the Union soldiers could be seen from the forts the Confederates had to face the prospect of being unable either to retreat or to obtain supplies. The officers wanted to hold out at least until they could hear from New Orleans, but they were unable to persuade the enlisted men to keep up an obviously useless struggle. With their garrisons on the verge of mutiny the forts were surrendered to Porter who happened to be the Union officer with whom it was easiest for the Confederate commanders to communicate.

The courteous thing for Porter to have done would have been to have arranged for an immediate cease fire pending a formal capitulation to him and Butler or some other Army officer (as Butler did when he and Stringham were joint commanders of the Hatteras Inlet expedition). Instead, Porter accepted the surrender of the forts and implied in his report to the Secretary of the Navy that they had been given up to him because his mortar bombardment had made them untenable. In another report, written after he had inspected the forts, he said he had found Fort Jackson "a perfect wreck, [with] everything in the shape of a building in and about it . . . burned up by the mortar shells."[5]

If Porter was not inexcusably ignorant of his profession he consciously refrained from telling the whole truth about the damage suffered by the forts as a result of his shelling. The bombardment cost the Confederates a total of 14 men killed and 39 wounded; the barracks and other wooden buildings ancillary to both forts were largely destroyed; and the levees were cut, causing some minor flooding. However, the result he had predicted and which he implied had been achieved—reduction of the forts to military impotence—was not even approached. Lieutenant Godfrey Weitzel, of the Corps of Engineers, a West Point graduate, officially reported that while Fort Jackson might seem to an inexperienced eye to be badly cut up it was in fact as strong as it had been on the day the first shell was fired at it.[6] Butler said that both works were "substantially as defensible as before the bombardment began, St. Philip precisely so."[7]

Porter never forgave Weitzel and Butler for having made those perfectly accurate statements.

Because Porter's widely published reports contained no reference whatsoever to the Army's part in capturing the forts Butler wrote to the Secretary of War, saying that while he did not want even to seem to take any credit from the officers and men of Farragut's vessels he was not willing to see someone's greed for

[5] David D. Porter, *The Naval History of the Civil War* (The Sherman Publishing Company [New York, 1886]), pp. 215, 217.

[6] Robert Underwood Johnson and Clarence Clough Buel (editors) *Battles and Leaders of the Civil War* (The Century Co. [New York, 1884–88]), II, 73.

[7] Butler to the Secretary of War, April 29, 1862; POC, I, 428.

praise detract from what was fairly due to the troops. Therefore, he asked to be permitted,

> for the sake of my brave and enduring soldiers, . . . to put
> the truth of history right before the War Department and the
> country, by the simple enumeration of the fact that it was due
> to their efforts and that [sic] of their comrades, and to those
> alone, that Forts Jackson and St. Philip surrendered when they
> did. No naval vessel or one of the mortar fleet had fired a
> shot at the forts for three days before the surrender, and not
> one of the mortar fleet was within twenty-five miles at that
> time, they having sailed out of the river . . . for fear of the
> ram *Louisiana*. . . . A majority of the garrison of Fort Jack-
> son had surrendered to my pickets the night before the officers
> made a surrender to Commodore Porter, and obtained from
> him better terms than . . . ought to have been given . . . to a
> rebel officer or soldier.[8]

Butler's assertion that the surrender of the forts was due solely
to the efforts of his troops is overstrong; his statement that the
mortar boats had left the river in fear of the *Louisiana* is incor-
rect (they had left the river bound for the Gulf to bombard Fort
Jackson from its rear, or westerly side) ; his opinion that the forts'
officers were granted unduly lenient terms is arguable; but his
belief that Porter's greed for praise had led him (as it often did)
to deprecate the accomplishments of others is well-founded.

After a ten minute delay to silence the Chalmette Batteries,
Farragut anchored his vessels off New Orleans late in the afternoon of April 25 and called upon Mayor John T. Monroe to
surrender the city. Monroe refused officially to surrender New
Orleans, but he did so in effect by saying there was no force
available to defend it. He intimated in a high-toned, belliger-
ently worded letter to Farragut that if General Lovell had not
fled with his troops the city could not have been taken easily.

Actually Lovell had removed his small force, as he reported
to his government, because he recognized "the perfect absurdity

---

[8] Butler to the Secretary of War, June 1, 1862; POC, I, 538.

of confronting more than one hundred guns, of the largest cali-
bre, well manned and served, and looking down upon the city,
with less than three thousand militia, mostly armed with indifferent shotguns." He thought it would have been senseless to
have offered enough opposition to lead "to a wanton and criminal
waste of the blood of women and children, without the possibility
of any good result, for the enemy . . . could have reduced the city
to ashes, without . . . any resistance whatever."[9]

Lovell volunteered to return to New Orleans with his whole
command, ready to fight to the last ditch when he heard of Monroe's gasconade. The mayor did not accept this heroic offer.

Although the capture of New Orleans was wholly the work
of the Navy, this fact does not detract anything from the expedition's soldiers or their commanding officer. One of Butler's
subordinates thought (as other officers and enlisted men undoubtedly did) that the Army "might storm the forts, and afterward
skirmish [its] way to New Orleans by land, scouring forests,
turning fieldworks, and ending off with a street fight."[10]

As soon as Butler learned of the forts' surrender he began to
make arrangements for occupying New Orleans. While the transports were getting back into the Mississippi he went to the city
to confer with Farragut. At this time Butler was told that an
American flag Farragut had caused to be raised over the United
States mint had been hauled down, dragged through the streets
and ripped to shreds while church services were being held in the
Union ships. The names of the men who had done this thing were
published by the New Orleans *Picayune* and Butler was heard
to say that he would make an example of those fellows if he
ever caught them.

---

[9] Lovell's report, as quoted in Frank Moore (editor), *The Rebellion
Record* (G. P. Putnam; D. Van Nostrand [New York, 1861–71]), X,
Doc. 57.

[10] De Forest, op. cit., p. 14. (Quoted with the publisher's permission.)

11

★★★★★★★★★★★★

Living Dangerously

After conferring with Farragut, Butler returned to Plaquemine Bend late in the afternoon of April 30, 1862. Leaving the Twenty-sixth Massachusetts Regiment to garrison the captured forts and Lieutenant Weitzel to supervise their repair, Butler started for New Orleans at midnight in the *Mississippi* with his wife and as many troops as the ship could carry.

While the *Mississippi* was being docked at noon the following day the crowd on the levee kept shouting for Picayune Butler. General Butler, who supposed they were calling for a popular song of that name, asked if the band could play it. There was no such song so the band could not play it. The cries referred to a Negro known as Picayune Butler who was or had been a barber in New Orleans and was reputed by some southerners and southern newspapers to be General Butler's father. As Parton heard the story told, Picayune Butler's son Benjamin,

> in early manhood emigrated to Liberia, where an indisposition for labor and some talent turned his attention to the bar, to prepare for which he repaired to Massachusetts. Having mastered his profession, he acquired a fondness for theological studies and became an active local preacher, the course of his early labors leading him to New York, where he attracted the notice of Mr. Jacob Barker, then in the zenith of his fame as financier, and who, discovering the peculiar abilities of the young mulatto, sent him to northern New York to manage a banking institution. There he divided his time between the counting-house and the court-house, the prayer-meeting and the printing office.[1]

[1] James Parton, *General Butler in New Orleans* (Mason Brothers [New York, 1864]), pp. 174–75.

Apparently the belief that Picayune Butler and General Butler were father and son was based upon the fact that there once was a religiously inclined citizen of New York named Benjamin F. Butler who "united the professions of lawyer and banker" and was connected in business with a relative named Jacob Barker who was an able financier.[2] However, the New York Butler, who died in 1858, was a white man who had been a member of the Cabinets of Presidents Andrew Jackson and Martin Van Buren. Perhaps the excited southerners of the 1860's can be forgiven for confusing the two Benjamin F. Butlers since there are modern historians and biographers who do not distinguish them in indexing their books.

A naval officer who had gone ashore a few times with messages from Farragut said to Butler, "General, I fear you are going to have a rather lawless party to govern from what I have seen in the past three or four days."[3] This remark neither surprised nor perturbed Butler. He calmly made plans to start landing his troops at sunset of the day the *Mississippi* reached New Orleans, choosing that hour to take advantage of darkness on the march to the customs house which he planned to occupy as a symbolic piece of United States property. He issued essentially the same sort of marching orders as he had at Baltimore—remarks made by the crowd were to be disregarded; if a shot came from a building a halt would be called, the inmates seized, and the place destroyed; if a shot came from the crowd the person firing it was to be captured if possible; in any case, no shooting was to be done by the troops except at an officer's orders. Looting was forbidden under the strictest penalties; and nobody, enlisted man or officer, was to absent himself from his outfit without arms or alone on any pretext whatsoever. Commanding officers of compa-

---

2 William L. Mackenzie, *The Lives and Opinions of Benj'n Franklin Butler and Jesse Hoyt* (Cook & Co. [Boston, 1845]), pp. 13–34, passim.

3 Robert Underwood Johnson and Clarence Clough Buel (editors), *Battles and Leaders of the Civil War* (The Century Co. [New York, 1884–88]), II, 94.

nies and regiments were made responsible for the strict enforcement of these orders.

The first troops who went ashore—a company from the Thirty-first Massachusetts Regiment—disembarked with loaded pieces and fixed bayonets. Although there was some swearing and jeering done by toughs of both sexes, no active resistance was offered to these soldiers as they cleared enough space on the levee for the rest of their regiment, the Fourth Wisconsin Regiment, and a battery of loaded cannon to land. Butler led the march on foot. He did not have a musical ear and some observers noted his anxiety to keep time with the band. Nobody thought he seemed concerned about anything else.

A few hours after Butler landed he sent two of his staff officers to the office of the *True Delta* to have a handbill containing a proclamation to the people of New Orleans printed. The foreman in charge of the office told Butler's representatives that he could not do any printing for them without orders from the paper's proprietors. Early the following morning the same officers called upon the proprietors. They refused to print the document. Butler then had a detail, including a sufficient number of typographers, take over the *True Delta*'s office and equipment long enough to print the document. A subsequent issue of the *True Delta* said the soldiers had effected their purpose "without offering any offense in language or behavior, or manifesting the least desire to interfere with the regular business of the office, or to injure or derange its property." Nevertheless, the editor criticized the seizure of the plant and promised that the paper would cease publication "rather than molt one feather of its independence." Butler immediately suspended the paper until further notice. He allowed it to resume publication 24 hours later, for, as he said, having demonstrated the ability of his troops to do everything necessary for the success of his plans without the aid of any citizen of New Orleans he had no desire to interfere with the press.[4]

During the night of May 1–2 the rest of the troops available for the occupation of New Orleans reached the city. They began

[4] Parton, op. cit., pp. 282–83.

landing at daybreak. While they were coming ashore Butler established his headquarters in the Hotel St. Charles, in spite of some verbal opposition on the part of a son of one of the proprietors.

Butler summoned the mayor and other members of the city government to his headquarters in the afternoon of May 2. Before their conference had proceeded far they were disturbed by an uproarious mob gathered outside of the hotel. An aide told Butler that General Williams, in command of the guard, was afraid he could not keep order. Butler sent the aide away with instructions for Williams to clear the streets with artillery. The city officials sprang to their feet, crying out against this order. Butler serenely asked: "Why this emotion, gentlemen? The cannon are not going to shoot our way and I have stood this noise and confusion as long as I choose to do." The mayor requested, and was granted, permission to try to quiet the crowd. Heedless of the mayor, the mob howled its wish to see "Old Butler." Stepping out upon a second flood balcony the General folded his arms and asked: "Do you see me?" Almost as he pronounced these words he, and those in the street, heard a loud noise coming from the direction of St. Charles Street. A moment later the Sixth Maine Battery appeared, led by a hard riding captain, with the bugler blowing the charge, and the cannoneers clinging to their seats as the guns' wheels bounced over the large, unevenly laid granite paving blocks. At this sight the crowd began to melt away. By the time the guns had swung "into battery," with three pieces at each corner of the hotel, the streets in the vicinity were almost empty. (Because of his prompt action on this occasion Butler never again had to move a man or a piece of artillery to disperse a mob in New Orleans.) After several other, less melodramatic, interruptions had occurred Butler decided to adjourn the conference with the municipal authorities until nightfall.

At the resumed conference Butler and his staff were arrayed in carefully brushed dress uniforms. The General sat near the corner of the large ladies' parlor of the hotel with his subordinates

ranged along two sides of the room behind him. The city councilmen sat along the other side, with the mayor in front of them
facing Butler. The General opened the proceedings by explaining how he hoped to conduct himself and asking to what extent
the municipal authorities would co-operate with him. If it could
be done he wanted to leave the city fathers in charge of such things
as the collection of taxes, the activities of the police, fire, and
street departments, etc., while he administered the military affairs of his department and sustained the federal government
against its enemies.

Pierre Soulé, a bombastic little man (about the size and build
of Napoleon) with long jet black hair, who had been a United
States senator and American minister to Spain, appointed himself
spokesman for the mayor and councilmen. He advised Butler
immediately to withdraw his troops from New Orleans. "The
people are not conquered and cannot be expected to act as conquered; your soldiers cannot have peace or safety in our midst,"
he truculently told Butler.[5]

Soulé and Butler, being fellow Democrats, had often met before the war, always amicably, of course. If Soulé presumed upon
their acquaintanceship he went too far. The General informed
him, with angry logic, that if New Orleans had not been conquered there would not be any Union troops there and asked:
"Did you open your arms and bid us welcome; would you not
expel us if you could?" His troops would be removed, he said,
when, but only when, the municipal authorities had demonstrated
their ability to control "the insulting, irreligious, unwashed mob"
which seemed to him to constitute the populace of New Orleans.
He also mentioned having heard of an organization whose purpose was to assassinate Yankees. If a shot were fired from any
house it would "never again shelter a mortal head," he warned.
If the perpetrator of the deed were discovered he would be appropriately punished. "I have the power," Butler said, "to suppress the unruly element in your midst. . . . I mean to use it so

---

[5] T. A. Bland, *Life of Benjamin F. Butler* (Lee and Shepard [Boston, 1879]), p. 82.

effectively that in a short period I shall be able to traverse your streets alone, free from insult or peril, or else this metropolis of the South shall be a desert from the Plains of Chalmette [on the east] to the outskirts of Carrollton [on the west]."[6]

Referring to Butler as a Yankee tyrant, the mayor urged the immediate resignation of everybody connected with the city government. A councilman argued that a mass resignation was a matter to be decided collectively. Butler told the city officials to discuss the thing among themselves. Twenty-four hours later a delegation from the council informed him that his proposals had been found acceptable. They asked only to have the troops withdrawn from the immediate vicinity of the city hall so that they might not seem to be acting under duress. This request seemed reasonable to Butler and he granted it.

By the end of his first week in New Orleans, Butler had established a routine that hardly varied while he stayed there. His day began at 6 A.M. After writing for an hour or two in his room he had breakfast. At 9 A.M. he went, with a cavalry escort, from his residence—a house owned by General David E. Twiggs of the Confederate Army—to his office at the customs house. He was saluted by a guard drawn up before his residence and by another guard on his arrival at the customs house. (This pomp and ceremony is one of so many points of resemblance between Butler's conduct at New Orleans and General Douglas MacArthur's at Tokyo 80-odd years later as to lead one to think that MacArthur must have taken Butler as an ideal model of the commanding officer of an army of occupation.) Usually Butler devoted the first hour at his office to receiving reports from his medical director, the chief of police, the labor commissioner, the relief commissioner, and various military subordinates. By the time this business was finished a large number of persons would be waiting to see him for all sorts of reasons. His callers were carefully screened. Many of them, particularly those who wanted

---

[6] Ibid., pp. 83–84.

only to apply for passes to go outside of the Union Army's lines, never saw him at all. The officer in charge of issuing passes, or as someone put it, of denying passes, said to Butler on more than one occasion, "General, you must see some of these people. . . . If you would only hear their stories, you would give them passes." "That," Butler often replied, "is precisely why I want you to see them for me."[7]

(One of the few passes Butler signed personally was sent under a flag of truce to General Pierre G. T. Beauregard of the Confederate Army, whose wife was lying fatally ill in New Orleans. The note Butler sent to Beauregard to inform him of his wife's condition was also his safe-conduct to and from the city.)

After disposing of the callers he could not avoid seeing, at an average rate of two or three a minute, Butler turned his attion to his mail. Whenever possible he took care of his letters by making notes on them to indicate how they were to be answered. Answering the letters he had to handle personally and dictating reports occupied most of the afternoon. From about 4:30 P.M. until nightfall he combined duty and recreation by riding horseback to visit outposts, review regiments, etc. At home again he wrote or dictated official letters until 10 P.M., then he turned to his private correspondence. Even though his days were long and fully occupied, he was often busy all of Sunday, struggling to keep up with his administrative duties. A special agent of the Treasury Department said, "General Butler does more work than any other man in Louisiana. Every thought seems to be given to the interest of the government, and his powers of endurance are remarkable. No other man could fill his place here."[8]

As busy as he was, Butler found time to send his 10-year-old son Paul working models of a piece of field artillery, complete with its caisson and other equipment, a mortar, and a gun mounted on a barbette carriage—of the sort used in fortifications. He

[7] Anonymous, "Our General," *Atlantic Monthly,* July 1863, XII, 108.
[8] "Diary and Correspondence of Salmon P. Chase," in the *Annual Report of the American Historical Association for the Year 1902* (Government Printing Office [Washington, D.C., 1903]), p. 316.

promised to send Benny, aged seven, something soon. A couple
of weeks after the models had been shipped he inquired in a letter to Mrs. Butler, who had gone home to escape the hot weather:
"Has Paul blown himself up with the cannon yet?"[9]

Butler found New Orleans literally on the verge of starvation. What little food there was to be had in the city was selling
at sky-high prices—flour more than $20 a barrel; common salt,
$10 for a small sack; Irish potatoes, $8 a bushel; beef, $10 a
barrel; milk, ten cents a quart; eggs, 75 cents a dozen. To alle-
viate "the suffering condition of the poor" he immediately granted
safe-conduct to vessels to go to Mobile to get flour ordered for,
but not delivered to, New Orleans before its capture. For the
same reason he authorized and ordered the management of the
Oupelousas Railroad "to run the cars over the road for the purpose of bringing provisions to supply the wants of the city."[10]
To avoid having to stop the procurement of supplies he pretended
to be unaware of the fact that his passes were being abused by a
few persons to send things to General Lovell's troops, encamped
not far from New Orleans.[11]

By forcing various business houses and wealthy individuals to
"donate" amounts ranging from $200 to $100,000 Butler secured a sum of more than $600,000 for the relief of the poor.
The names of those assessed came from a list of voluntary con-
tributors to a fund raised by a Confederate Committee of Public
Safety. Part of the money was used to provide direct relief for
the needy; part of it was spent to employ a large number of men
to clean the streets of New Orleans. The street cleaners were
paid 50 cents for a ten hour workday and were given the equiva-

---

[9] Butler to Mrs. Butler, July 15 and July 28, 1862, as quoted in Jesse
Ames Marshall (Compiler), *Private and Official Correspondence of Gen.
Benjamin F. Butler* (Privately issued [Boston, 1917]), II, 79, 115. (Here-
after cited as *POC*)

[10] General Order No. 19; *POC,* I, 442.

[11] John William De Forest, *A Volunteer's Adventures* (Yale Uni-
versity Press [New Haven, 1946]), p. 21; A. Sellow Roberts, "The Federal
Government and Confederate Cotton," *American Historical Review,*
XXXII, 256–57.

lent, every day they worked, of a Union soldier's rations. One of Butler's reasons for hiring these men was to prevent Satan from finding a cure for their idleness; another one was his belief that a cleaner city would be a healthier one.

For some time before New Orleans was taken there had been no specie in circulation. Confederate paper money, worth about 30 per cent of its face value, had been the only currency available in denominations of a dollar or more. Omnibus tickets, drinking-house shinplasters, and other forms of scrip had been used for small change. In compliance with Soulé's entreaties and the obvious exigencies of the situation Butler agreed to let such money remain in use temporarily. On May 16 he issued an order forbidding the circulation of Confederate money after May 27. Naturally this order was going to be costly to some persons and institutions. The local banks undertook to avoid being among the sufferers. They began advertising on May 17 that Confederate money not withdrawn during the ensuing ten days would be held thereafter at the risk of its depositors. Butler felt it to be his duty to interfere in this matter in order to make the banks bear their share of the cost of devaluation. On May 19 he decreed that all banks in New Orleans must immediately pay out their own bills, United States treasury notes, gold, or silver to all depositors.

Shortly before that order was issued Thomas J. "Stonewall" Jackson chased General Nathaniel P. Banks, ex-governor of Massachusetts, ignominiously out of the Shenandoah Valley. With this conjuncture of events in mind, the Charleston *Mercury* commented, under he heading "Epigram,"

> Whilst Butler plays his silly pranks,
> And closes up New Orleans Banks,
> Our Stonewall Jackson, with more cunning,
> Keeps Yankee Banks forever running.[12]

---

[12] Quoted in Frank Moore (editor) *The Rebellion Record* (G. P. Putnam; D. Van Nostrand [New York, 1861–71]), VI, 10.

Early in June, Butler reviewed the death sentences imposed by a military commission upon six Confederate prisoners of war who had violated their paroles. On learning that the men had not known the meaning of the word parole—they thought it applied only to officers, not to enlisted men like themselves—he commuted their sentences to imprisonment at hard labor during the President's pleasure. By itself this incident would not have been particularly important. However, a few days after it occurred William Mumford, ringleader of the men who had desecrated the flag raised over the New Orleans mint before Butler reached the city, was captured, tried by a military commission, and sentenced to be hanged. Mumford, who fancied himself a hero, made a grave mistake by professing to regard his trial as a farce. His friends worsened matters by loudly asserting that if Mumford should be executed Butler's life would be taken in retaliation. These threats had no influence upon Butler. Neither did he heed the pleas of his wife, of Mrs. Mumford, or of others who interceded on Mumford's behalf. He was not motivated by cruelty or sadism. Sending another man to the gallows gave him no pleasure. He simply felt he had no choice but to let Mumford hang. His lenient treatment of the parole violators had been regarded in some quarters as a sign of weakness on his part. If this attitude became widespread and the notion became prevalent that he could be cowed the populace might become uncontrollable except by a final resort to grapeshot and canister. In his mind it was a question of hanging one defiant man or of eventually having to kill many innocent persons. He chose what seemed to him to be the only possible alternative.

When Mrs. Mumford called upon Butler he said to her,

I hear Mumford believes he will not be executed, and I am told he is making no preparations for his death. Now, I think the greatest kindness you can do him is to let me ring for my carriage and send you to the jail. I will give you an order for your admission to his room, or that you and your family may meet him in any room in the jail that will be most convenient for you. I wish you to convince him that he is mistaken and

that he will be executed. Whether I live or die he will die. . . .
Let him in the few hours he has to live look to God for his
pardon.[13]

Mumford was hanged on June 7 in front of the mint in imi-
tation of the grim Spanish custom of having an execution occur
as near as possible to the place where the crime was committed.

The South proclaimed Mumford a martyr and called his execution an atrocity. The Confederate government inquired officially about the matter, but Butler refused to answer the note
sent to him because of its discourteous language. President Jefferson Davis thereupon branded Butler "an outlaw and common
enemy of mankind," to be hanged summarily if captured and ordered that no commissioned officer of the United States taken
captive should be released on parole before exchange until Butler
should have met with "due punishment for his crime." Richard
Yeardon, editor of the Charleston *Courier,* offered a reward of
$10,000 "for the capture or delivery of the said Benjamin F.
Butler, dead or alive, to any proper Confederate authority." The
Charleston *Mercury* recommended that Butler be poisoned or
stabbed if he could not be caught and hanged. This furor left
Butler unperturbed. Referring to the possibility of his own as-
sassination he said, "If they do it, it will only place General
Phelps in command; and if they are satisfied with that arrange-
ment I have nothing to say."[14]

Of course, Butler took such precautions as he could against
being assassinated. At first, when working at his desk, where he
necessarily spent much of his time, he kept a loaded revolver in
front of him. After one of his aides pointed out that somebody
could easily seize this weapon and use it against him he kept an
empty piece on the desk with a loaded one on a concealed shelf.

---

[13] Benjamin F. Butler, *Butler's Book* (A. M. Thayer & Co. [Boston,
1892]), p. 441.

[14] Moore, op. cit., VI, Doc. No. 85; E. Merton Coulter, *The Confederate
States of America* (Louisiana State University Press [Baton Rouge, La.,
1950]), p. 72; *Harper's Weekly,* July 12, 1862, January 24, 1863; New
York *Tribune,* June 14, 1862, January 24, 1863.

He always went about the streets armed and partly by luck he gained the reputation of being a crack shot. While he was riding one day he saw an orange tree with some of its branches extending over a wall surrounding a house and yard. He aimed his revolver at a twig and brought down a fine bunch of fruit. It was a shot such as he might never have equalled, but it created an impression that he was a superb marksman with a handgun. This was a useful reputation for a man who was probably threatened with assassination oftener than anybody except a Russian czar to have.

Soon after he had acted both mercifully and sternly toward Confederate offenders Butler had occasion to consider the cases of seven northerners who had been convicted of having robbed a number of houses in New Orleans while posing as Union soldiers on official duty. One of the men involved was the *Saxon*'s mate, another was a discharged Union soldier, the rest were soldiers on active duty with the Army of the Gulf. A soldier who turned state's evidence was sentenced to five years at hard labor. A young boy was given only a short sentence because of his mother's intercession with Butler. The death sentences imposed upon the other five were approved by the General and were carried out.

There was comparatively little fighting done in the Department of the Gulf while Butler was there. Almost immediately after he occupied New Orleans he detailed two infantry regiments and a battery to accompany some of Farragut's vessels in an attempt to capture Vicksburg, Mississippi. A lack of man power and a shortage of supplies brought this expedition to an unsuccessful end. Later Farragut was ordered to make another try at taking Vicksburg. This time Butler furnished six regiments and two batteries. Still lacking enough men to make a vigorous attack, Farragut called upon Major General Henry W. Halleck, commanding the Department of the Mississippi, for help. Halleck could not be prodded into moving, even by the Secretary of War, so Farragut again went back to New Orleans empty handed. There was also a battle fought at Baton Rouge, Louisiana, in which General Williams was killed.

Guerrillas troubled Butler's troops much more than Confederate regulars did. The swamps were full of Confederate partisans who delighted in making Yankees "bite the dust," as the Vicksburg *Whig* put it.

Butler reacted vigorously to partisan attacks upon his troops. On one occasion some of his men were ambushed and two of them were killed near the town of Houma, Louisiana. He sent a colonel with four companies of infantry and two pieces of artillery to Houma with orders to seize and hang the killers if possible and to confiscate the property of every person who had been in any way an accessory before or after the deed. On reaching Houma the colonel found that most of the inhabitants had fled. Arresting all who remained in the town, he demanded to be told the names of those who had participated in the ambuscade. He threatened, unless he was given these names, to burn Houma, lay waste every plantation in the vicinity, and confiscate all of the movable property he could find. Although he got the information he wanted, he was unable to catch any of the ringleaders. He then seized five plantation owners who had sheltered the partisans, destroyed their houses, barns, and other outbuildings, and drove away their horses, mules, and cattle.

In fairness to Butler it should be noted that he was by no means the only Union commander to take reprisals upon civilians because of the acts of guerrillas. To mention only two other cases; Farragut once shelled a Mississippi River town, and when a Union steamer was set on fire at Concordia, Arkansas, a naval landing party burned 42 houses (probably all there were in the place).

★★★★★★★★★★★★

12

The "Woman Order"

Three things about which Butler was gravely concerned at New Orleans were the danger of a yellow fever epidemic, the behavior of some of the women of the city, and his inability to obtain reinforcements for the Army of the Gulf. He dealt effectively with each of these matters.

Because his father's early death from yellow fever had made an indelible impression on Butler he had investigated the epidemiology of that disease to the fullest extent a northern lawyer could. Thus he was unpleasantly aware that New Orleans had been scourged by "yellow jack" on an average of once every three years during the preceding half century and that by 1862 another epidemic was overdue. Before he went to New Orleans he agreed with the opinion held by most medical men that yellow fever, a summer time disease, was not indigenous to countries where frost occurs annually, as it does in all parts of the United States. Assuming, as many doctors did, that yellow fever was an imported disease he was inclined to believe, again in common with many doctors, that any community could protect itself completely by establishing a sufficiently rigid quarantine to shipping from tropical ports. (Some doctors argued that effective protection could not be had unless vessels in quarantine were anchored far enough away to prevent the wind from carrying the disease ashore.) Butler did not think, as some experts did, that yellow fever could be transmitted over long distances by means of inanimate objects, such as clothing, lumps of coal, etc. At New Orleans he learned from a book and a map published after the epidemic of 1853 where yellow fever usually first appeared in the city and where it had raged the worst. An inspection of these areas revealed one common factor—all of them were extremely malodorous. One of the places was a market, where, as Butler said, for almost a century the stallkeepers had been in the habit of dropping "all the refuse made in cleaning their birds, fish, and meat" on the ground "to be trodden in and in." Another spot where there was a horribly noxious odor, to Butler's way of thinking, was a turning basin at the end of a canal running from Lake Ponchartrain to the city. When he first saw the basin and the canal their surfaces were covered "with a thick growth of green vegetable scum, variegated with dead cats and dogs or the remains of dead mules on the banking." The "enormous stink" which he immediately noticed did not seem at all unusual to the city's superintendent of streets; it had always existed in hot weather. Other sources of effluvia that brought themselves to Butler's notice were the ditches that served the city as open sewers. Heavy rains occasionally flushed these ditches and they emptied themselves whenever the river fell far enough, but they were filled with stagnant, smelly water most of the time.[1]

At this time Butler began to wonder if yellow fever might not be a product of bad air, similar to malaria, which was then (and for a long while afterward) believed to be caused by miasmas arising from swamps. He decided that getting rid of the sort of atmosphere that was widely supposed to cause ship's fever, jail fever, typhoid fever, and typhus would at least help to prevent an epidemic of yellow fever. Therefore, he ordered the streets to be cleaned and the drainage ditches to be flushed daily. As an added precaution he ordered the occupants of all dwellings and places of business in New Orleans to tidy up their premises. Unpainted outside walls, whether of wood or stone, were to be whitewashed with a solution containing lime, alum, and salt. Refuse of every sort was to be deposited in covered re-

---

[1] Benjamin F. Butler, *Butler's Book* (A. M. Thayer & Co., [Boston, 1892]), pp. 395–401, passim.

ceptacles, not thrown into the streets or anywhere else. These containers were to be emptied and disinfected with cloride of lime by the street cleaners twice a week. Infractions of these sanitary regulations were made punishable by a term in the parish (county) jail. The citizenry soon learned that Butler intended to have his orders obeyed to the letter. One man vaingloriously provided a test case by throwing a piece of clean white paper onto the sidewalk at a policeman's feet. Butler sentenced him to six months in jail.

Because he did not wholly abandon the hypothesis that yellow fever was an imported disease Butler established a quarantine station in the Mississippi below Plaquemine Bend. Every vessel bound for New Orleans from any port whatsoever had to stop there to be inspected by a health officer who reported on the condition of the crew, passengers, and cargo to Butler by telegraph. No vessel was allowed to pass Fort St. Philip without the General's permission, delivered by telegraph or in writing and permission was not granted until the health officer had reported an absolutely clean bill of health. Vessels with sick persons on board, and any coming from infected ports even if all on board were well, were literally quarantined—they had to wait for 40 days, then be reinspected before being allowed to proceed to New Orleans.

As a fortuitous result of the steps Butler took to eliminate the sources of bad air the breeding places of the yellow fever-transmitting *Aëdes aegypti* mosquito were destroyed. Because the right thing was done (even though it was done for the wrong reason) there were only two cases of yellow fever in New Orleans in 1862. There would have been no cases if a vessel which had shipped two infected men at Nassau, the Bahamas, had been held a few days in quarantine. This was not done because she was loaded with urgently needed supplies and her captain swore that he had stopped at Nassau only to take on coal.

The moment the men's illness was diagnosed as yellow fever the building in which they were housed was cleared of all inmates except them and one attendant; the block in which the building was located was surrounded by sentries who allowed only the few persons who had official business there to enter or leave the area; and large fires were kept burning at the four corners of the block in order, as Butler explained, "always to keep an upward draft of air."[2] When the men died their bodies were cremated, every article in their room was buried or burned, their attendant was quarantined, and the house was thoroughly fumigated—in short every precaution suggested by medical lore or Butler's imagination was taken.

Many of the women of New Orleans, particularly those with aristocratic pretensions, missed few opportunities to be annoying, or even grossly insulting to Union officers. Unpleasant remarks were commonly made about officers in their hearing. Some "ladies" threw garbage, including rotten eggs, at officers; some spat in officers' faces; one woman emptied the contents of a chamber pot upon the heads of Captain Farragut and an Army officer as they walked past her house.

Occasionally, though amazingly rarely, such actions provoked verbal retaliation. Once, as a woman ostentatiously prepared to leave an omnibus an officer had just boarded he said to her, "Sit still old girl. You needn't rise on my account."[3] Another time five or six women on a balcony whirled around with something between a shriek and a sneer as Butler rode past a house. Turning to his aide the General loudly commented: "Those women evidently know which end of them looks best."[4]

The women's conduct would have been no more than annoying if Butler had not feared what it might eventually entail for the people of New Orleans. With his troops outnumbered six to one by a "hostile, bitter, defiant" populace he felt as if he were sitting "in a magazine [with] a spark only needed for destruction." Eventually some officer would yield to the temptation to arrest an

[2] Ibid., p. 409.
[3] John William De Forest, *A Volunteer's Adventures* (Yale University Press [New Haven, 1946]), p. 45. (Quoted with the publisher's permission.)
[4] Butler, op. cit., p. 416.

insulting woman. An attempt to rescue her would certainly be made. This would spark a riot. It would then become necessary to use every means, including artillery fire, to restore order. As a humane man he wanted to avoid such an eventuality if he could.[5]

For two weeks he tried to think of how to word a self-enforcing order capable of causing the women to modify their behavior. Finally he recollected something he had once seen by chance while doing research in connection with a revision of Lowell's municipal ordinances. Substituting suitable place names for those in the original statute, he issued General Order No. 28, reading:

> As the officers and soldiers of the United States have been subject to repeated insults from the women (calling themselves ladies) of New Orleans, in return for the most scrupulous non-interference and courtesy on our part, it is ordered that hereafter when any female shall, by word, gesture, or movement, insult or show contempt for any officer or soldier of the U.S., she shall be regarded and held liable to be treated as a woman of the town plying her avocation.[6]

The behavior which evoked this order ended within 24 hours of its issuance. Its effectiveness may be the reason why, after sober consideration at Washington, it was allowed to stand, although it was not formally approved.

Most southerners, of course, greeted the "woman order" with screams of unrestrained fury. Mary B. Chestnut, of Richmond, wrote in her diary:

> There is said to be an order from Butler turning over the women of New Orleans to his soldiers. Thus is the measure of his iniquities filled. We thought that generals always restrained, by shot or sword if need be, the brutality of soldiers. This

---

[5] Butler to J. G. Carney, July 2, 1862, as quoted in Jesse Ames Marshall (compiler), *Private and Official Correspondence of Gen. Benjamin F. Butler* (privately issued [Boston, 1917]), II, 35. (Hereafter cited as *POC*)

[6] General Order No. 28, dated May 15, 1862; *POC,* I, 490.

hideous, cross-eyed beast orders his men to treat the ladies of New Orleans as women of the town—to punish them, he says, for their insolence. . . . His amazing order . . . and comments on it are in everybody's mouth. We hardly expected from Massachusetts behavior to shame a Comanche.[7]

Actually nothing unpleasant occurred to any woman in New Orleans as a result of General Order No. 28. General M. Jeff Thompson, of the Confederate Army, whose testimony is certainly significant, wrote to Butler in October, 1863: "Nearly all of the many persons who passed through my lines, to and from New Orleans during . . . August and September 1862 spoke favorably of the treatment they had received from you, and with all my enquiries, which were constant, I did not hear of one single instance of a lady being insulted by [any of] your command."[8] Even James Ford Rhodes had to admit that all of the evidence he had been able to find (in what one may be sure was a diligent search) indicated that no woman was ever insulted in New Orleans by Butler or any of his subordinates.[9]

Mayor Monroe angrily told Butler that with the passions of the people of New Orleans already aroused, General Order No. 28 would exasperate them beyond control and he would not be responsible for the peace of the city if it was not rescinded. Butler advised Monroe that if he could not control the populace he would have to be put in jail for his own safety. At the same time the General explained to the mayor why the order was necessary and pointed out that it permitted the female portion of the populace to classify themselves as ladies or common women. Those who made themselves conspicuous by their actions toward men would be considered strumpets; quietly behaved women would be regarded and treated as ladies. The mayor thereupon withdrew his communication. Then, egged on by Soulé and other

---

[7] Mary Boykin Chestnut, *A Diary from Dixie* (D. Appleton and Company [New York, 1905]), pp. 164–65, 183.

[8] M. Jeff Thompson to Butler, October 12, 1863; *POC*, III, 130.

[9] James Ford Rhodes, *History of the United States* (The Macmillan Co., [New York, 1904]), IV, 93 ftn.

fire-eaters, he attempted to withdraw his withdrawal. At this point Butler lost his temper. He ordered the mayor, the mayor's secretary, the chief of police, a police lieutenant, the mayor's brother-in-law, and a municipal court judge to be brought before him. The judge refused to say whether he did or did not sustain the mayor's recalcitrance, the police chief supported the mayor, the secretary admitted having helped to draft the mayor's letters, the others claimed to know little or nothing about the affair. Butler committed the mayor, his secretary, the judge, and the chief of police to Fort Jackson and let the others go free.

When news of General Order No. 28 reached Great Britain in June, 1862, "nearly all of the British papers assumed, as a matter of historic certainty, that General Butler had consigned the 'pure and modest maidens and matrons' of New Orleans to the 'brutal licentiousness of a northern soldiery.' "[10] A member of the House of Commons said that if the British government had official knowledge of the order a protest ought to be made to the United States. In the House of Lords the Earl of Carnarvon called the order something without parallel or precedent. The Prime Minister, Lord Palmerston, wrote to Charles Francis Adams, American minister to Great Britain, saying that he found it "difficult, if not impossible, to express adequately the disgust which must be excited in the mind of every honorable man" by General Butler's order as it was quoted in the *London Times.*

Even when a town is taken by assault [Palmerston added] it is the practice of the commander of the conquering army to protect to the utmost the inhabitants and especially the female part of them, and I will venture to say that no example can be found in the history of civilized nations, till the publication of this order, of a general guilty in cold blood of so infamous an act as deliberately to hand over the female inhabitants of a conquered city to the unbridled license of an unrestrained soldiery. If the Federal government chooses to be served by men capable of such revolting outrages, they [the federal govern-

10 *Harper's Weekly,* August 16, 1862, p. 514.

ment] must submit to abide by the deserved opinion which mankind will form of their conduct.[11]

When these comments came to Butler's attention he gleefully told the world that his "woman order" was almost a verbatim copy of a London ordinance.

Before Butler left for New Orleans, Lincoln warned him that the Administration was not ready to announce a Negro policy so it was hoped he would avoid raising any insoluble problems or sharply defined issues. In view of these virtual orders he conducted himself circumspectly, but he managed to do much to improve the lot of Negroes in the Department of the Gulf. The mere fact that he allowed them to testify in courts-martial tended substantially to minimize their ill treatment by white men. He abolished the whipping houses to which owners too feeble (women, for instance) or too squeamish to flog their slaves sent them to have it done for a fee. An order he issued that no slaves, except convicted criminals, were to be held in jail unless their owners paid their expenses brought freedom to many Negroes who had been locked up for safekeeping while their masters were serving with the Confederate armed forces. Some planters sought to save their property by sending their slaves behind the Union lines, to be recovered when the war ended—victoriously for the South as they supposed it would. Butler announced that anyone who told his slaves "to go to the Yankees" would be considered voluntarily to have emancipated them.

Butler's practice of confiscating slaves, thus effectively freeing them, was well-known among the Negroes of Louisiana before he reached New Orleans and thousands of fugitives quickly sought refuge with the Army of the Gulf. He soon found that New Orleans could not absorb the hordes descending upon it, especially since most of them were field hands for whom there was

---

[11] Quoted in Charles Francis Adams, Jr., *Charles Francis Adams* (Houghton, Mifflin and Company [Boston, 1900]), pp. 248–49.

no possible employment away from the sugar plantations. With the permission of the War Department and under the authority of the Confiscation Acts he organized colonies of fugitive slaves who were put to work on confiscated or abandoned plantations under the direction of federal agents or loyal citizens. (Federal agents operated the abandoned places; citizens were allowed to buy the confiscated ones.) He also persuaded many Negroes to return to work for masters who had, or claimed they had, remained loyal to the Union. At first most Negroes were unwilling to do this. On being assured by Butler that they would not lose any rights or benefits that might be created in the future many of them resumed their old occupations.

A highly important thing Butler did on behalf of the Negroes in the Department of the Gulf was to promulgate a standard labor contract governing their employment. This contract provided for the payment of wages of $10 a month. It placed responsibility for the care (including medical attention when necessary) and the feeding of Negroes upon their employers. It provided for the subsistence, at the employer's expense, of the relatives of any laborer who could not work because of illness or age. It expressly forbade corporal punishment. Complaints about insubordination or other misdeeds had to be made to the nearest provost marshal who would investigate the charges and inflict punishment if it were found to be warranted. Although some planters, including loyalists, refused to hire Negroes unless they could be whipped at their employer's will, Butler did not modify this provision of the labor contract. He felt that he had no right to send Negroes back "to be scourged by their former, and in some cases, infuriated masters."[12]

Among southerners it was an article of faith that sugar and cotton could not be cultivated without slave labor. Andrew J. Butler, the General's brother, was the first to defy this superstition. He bought the standing crop of sugar cane on an abandoned plantation and hired a crew of Negroes to harvest it. As

---

[12] Butler to the Secretary of War, November 14, 1862, Butler to President Lincoln, November 28, 1862; *POC,* II, 448, 475.

soon as it became evident that he was going to turn a handsome profit others followed his example.

Probably his brother's experience was in Butler's mind when he replied to President Lincoln's request for information about the production of sugar by free laborers. The experiment was succeeding admirably, said Butler. He had been told that on one plantation the same Negroes who had been slaves there, but were now working for wages, had made a hogshead and a half more sugar a day than they had ever done before.

Although Butler's way of dealing with the Negro problem pleased Washington, it fell far short of satisfying General Phelps. As far as he was concerned the chief purpose of the war was the abolition of slavery. To further that cause he welcomed large numbers of fugitive slaves to his camp at Carrollton. This gave rise to complaints that he was harboring slaves belonging to good Union men, as he undoubtedly was in at least some cases. Butler ordered Phelps to exclude all unemployed persons, white or black, from his camp. Phelps replied, in a letter which he asked to have forwarded to the President, protesting against Butler's order and avowing his intention of recruiting as many Negro soldiers as he could. In forwarding Phelps's letter Butler said,

> Gen. Phelps, I believe, intends making this a test case for the policy of the Government. I wish it might be so, for the difference of our action upon this subject is a source of trouble. I respect his honest sincerity, but I am a soldier bound to carry out the wishes of the Government so long as I hold its commission, and I understand that policy to be the one I am pursuing.
>
> If the policy of the Government is . . . [what] I have ordered in this department, then the services of Gen. Phelps are worse than useless here. If the views set forth in his report are to obtain, then he is invaluable, for his whole soul is in it, and he is a good soldier of large experience, and no braver man lives.[13]

---

[13] Butler to the Secretary of War, June 18, *POC,* I, 614–15.

Without waiting for a reply to his letter about Negro soldiers Phelps sent a requisition to the headquarters of the Army of the Gulf for arms and equipment for five companies (approximately 300 men) he had already enlisted and for others he expected would join the regiments he planned to organize. Butler refused to honor this requisition because he regarded Phelps's action as plainly contrary to the government's policy. Butler suggested that the Negroes in and around Carrollton be employed cutting down trees, strengthening fortifications, etc., according to plans agreed upon by Phelps and Weitzel some time earlier. Probably in the hope of making it easier for Phelps to swallow what was bound to be a bitter pill Butler added that whatever wood was not needed at Phelps's Camp Parapet could be used in New Orleans.

Phelps answered Butler's diplomatic suggestion:

> While I am willing to prepare African regiments for the defense of the Government against its assailants, I am not willing to become the mere slave-driver which you propose, having no qualifications in that way. I am, therefore, . . . tendering the resignation of my commission . . . [and asking for a leave of absence pending its acceptance].[14]

Butler (who wrote many years later: "I loved General Phelps very much; he was a crank upon the slavery question, . . . otherwise he was as good a soldier and commander as ever mounted a horse")[15] tried to knock some sense into his subordinate's head. He refused officially to accept Phelps's resignation or to grant him a leave of absence and unofficially pleaded with him not to persist in his foolish course. Phelps remained adamant so Butler had to forward his resignation to the War Department which accepted it. When Phelps left the Department of the Gulf he gave his horse, epaulets, sash, and spurs to Weitzel who had been promoted to the rank of brigadier general on Butler's recommendation.

---

14 Phelps to Capt. R. S. Davis, July 31, 1862; *POC,* II, 126–27.
15 Butler, op. cit., p. 488.

A short time after Phelps resigned because he was not allowed to enlist Negroes, Butler organized several colored regiments. Before he did so he tried to find out from the War Department what chance he had of getting reinforcements. Failing to obtain any information, he sent a confidential message to Washington that if no troops could be spared to him he would "call upon Africa for assistance."

When he made this call he shrewdly did so in a manner that did not embarrasss the Administration. Early in the war the governor of Louisiana had raised one or more regiments of free Negroes, known as the Louisiana Native Guard, to help defend New Orleans. Butler located some of the former members of the Native Guard and asked them if they would be willing to serve the federal government as soldiers. All of them said they would. On August 24, 1862 Butler organized the First Regiment of the Free Colored Brigade. (This was the first body of Negro troops mustered into the federal service, although the formation of a colored regiment had begun in Rhode Island three weeks earlier.) Subsequently Butler organized a full Negro brigade— three regiments of infantry and a battery of artillery. Years later he said of them, "Better soldiers never shouldered a musket. They were intelligent, obedient, highly appreciative of their position, and fully maintained its dignity."[16]

Since Butler had followed a precedent set by a southern governor the Confederate government could not logically object to his use of Negro troops. His own government never formally approved his action, but did not interfere with it.

Nominally only free Negroes were allowed to enlist in Butler's colored brigade. However, nobody inquired closely into a recruit's background and a considerable number of self-emancipated slaves joined the brigade.

The officers of the Confederate Native Guard had been Negroes up to and including the rank of captain. In the first of the regiments organized by Butler the field officers were white, the line officers colored. The only white officers of the second regi-

[16] Ibid., p. 493.

ment were the colonel and lieutenant colonel. Both white and Negro officers were chosen, on the basis of merit alone, for the third regiment. The battery had to be officered by white men because there were no qualified Negroes available.

Butler's example of informally enlisting Negroes was quickly followed by other commanding officers "and by the time the Emancipation Proclamation was issued there were not less than 10,000 Negroes armed and equipped along the Mississippi."[17]

Many of the members of Butler's *Corps d'Afrique* were, as the General commented, actually of about the same complexion as Vice-President Hannibal Hamlin of Maine or the godlike Daniel Webster. Nevertheless, there was a great deal of prejudice among white soldiers, especially the officers, against Negro troops. Weitzel asked to be relieved of duty in the Department of the Gulf when two regiments of the Free Colored Brigade were assigned to his command. Butler persuaded him to withdraw his request.

[17] Joseph T. Wilson, *The Black Phalanx* (American Publishing Co. [Hartford, Conn., 1889]), p. 199.

★★★★★★★★★★★★

13

Butler versus Rhodes

Throughout the summer of 1862 it was rumored in New Orleans that the Department of the Gulf was soon going to have a new commanding officer. When the story finally broke into print Butler wrote to Halleck, who was now general in chief of the Union Armies: "I learn from the secession newspapers that I am to be relieved of my command. If that be so, might I ask that my successor be sent as soon as possible, as my health is not of the strongest [he lived only 31 more years], and it would seem fair that he should take some part of the yellow fever season."[1]

Halleck's reply, dated September 14, characterized the rumor that Butler was to be superseded as a mere newspaper story, without any foundation. If this statement was sincerely made Halleck soon changed his mind, or, as it was widely believed at the time, had his mind changed for him as a rssult of Secretary of State William H. Seward's machinations. In any case, on November 9 Major General Banks was ordered to proceed to New Orleans and take command of the Department of the Gulf. (Banks had not solicited this appointment and was surprised at receiving it.)

About the time Banks was given his orders in Washington, Butler emphatically informed his superiors that sickness had depleted his effective force to such an extent that he had to have reinforcements. Halleck replied with a promise that more troops

---

[1] Butler to Halleck, September 1, 1862, as quoted in Jesse Ames Marshall (compiler), *Private and Official Correspondence of Gen. Benjamin F. Butler* (Privately issued [Boston, 1917]), II, 243. (Hereafter cited as *POC*)

would soon reach New Orleans, but he did not tell Butler that he would be relieved by their commanding officer.

The fact that Butler was to be replaced was also kept a dark secret from most of the Cabinet. Five days after Banks had received his orders the Secretary of the Treasury wrote to Butler: "Gen. Banks goes to New Orleans, not, as I understand, to supersede you; but to conduct an expedition to Texas while you are engaged nearer your present headquarters."[2]

The Secretary of the Navy did not learn that Banks was to relieve Butler until late in December.

Butler did not officially know that he was to be replaced until Banks reached New Orleans. However, Butler had been unofficially advised by a trustworthy friend in Washington of what was afoot so he was not really surprised.

Farragut, who had not been forewarned of the change in any way, was both surprised and disturbed when he heard of it. His official and personal relations with Butler had been of the friendliest sort. He had always been certain of Butler's hearty co-operation, as he had given his own, but he was not sure how he would get along with the new man. (As things turned out Banks egregiously failed to co-operate with Farragut.)

In this connection it is worth emphasizing that Farragut did his part in maintaining good relations with Butler. The military and naval men who did not get along well with Butler, and there were more than a few of them, were in all cases at least as much at fault as he was for he was always as ready to be cordial and helpful as he was quick to repay discourtesy or disparagement in kind.

Banks took command of the Department of the Gulf at noon, December 16, 1862. Butler left New Orleans, Christmas Eve in an unarmed transport. Before his departure he issued a farewell address to the citizens of New Orleans (and for perusal by northerners, historians, and biographers) in which he reviewed his eight months in the Department of the Gulf. If he praised

---

[2] Chase to Butler, November 14, 1862; *POC,* II, 469.

himself somewhat lavishly he really deserved much praise. Since he received mail from the North only once in every four to six weeks he had to act largely on his own responsibility at New Orleans. While he was there he controlled, with few troops, a large area, inhabited for the most part by a bitterly hostile populace. His rule was firm, as indeed it had to be, but it was not marked by any unnecessary, much less by any wanton, severity. He compelled a decent respect toward himself and his subordinates by dealing swiftly and sternly with offenses against him and his people. At the same time he dealt equally promptly and firmly with misdeeds committed by his own men. He fed the hungry of all races and treated Negroes so well that blacks and whites of the poorer classes spoke highly of him for many years after the Civil War ended. His sanitary regulations kept New Orleans in the healthiest state it had ever known. For these reasons his administration of the Department of the Gulf was praised by most northerners, including men who admitted their dislike of him because of his political views and men who disliked him without admitting it.

Many upper class southerners, of course, adversely criticized his conduct. However, most of the things such people said about him—that he was a tyrant, a sadist, a rapist, etc.—can be dismissed, as they were by his northern contemporaries, as on a par with a story that fright occasioned by seeing him caused some women to bear cross-eyed babies.

The worst thing said by northerners during the Civil War about Butler's conduct in New Orleans was that he unduly favored his brother Andrew in connection with profit making opportunities in the Department of the Gulf. On the only occasion the General took any notice of this sort of thing (in a letter to the Secretary of the Treasury) he characterized his critics as slanderers who were seeking revenge because he had not allowed them to plunder the government.

My brother [he wrote] has indeed been engaged in commercial adventures in New Orleans, and has been successful, . . . [but] no more successful than many others. [His profits were, in

General Butler's estimation, $800,000.] I believe [his] every transaction has been legitimate. . . . I have aided him in no way officially. . . . I have aided him to [obtain] capital and credit by the use of my name at the North, and drawing on my bankers. [As a Californian, A. J. Butler would have needed a guarantor for any borrowing he did in the East.] . . . . I have aided him in no other way. I believe this is a legitimate course toward a brother.

Saying that, to avoid even the appearance of evil, he had asked his brother to close out his business affairs and leave New Orleans, the General expressed a desire to have all of A. J. Butler's doings in the Department of the Gulf thoroughly investigated.[3]

No official investigation, thorough or superficial, of Andrew Butler's conduct was made during General Butler's lifetime and the whole matter was soon forgotten. However, in 1904 (more than ten years after Butler died) James Ford Rhodes alleged that the General, concealing himself behind his brother, had corruptly traded with the Confederates in the Department of the Gulf. Rhodes was regarded by his generation as *the* authority on the history of the Civil War and many authors have uncritically accepted and echoed his assertion that Butler was a rascal. In view of these facts Rhodes's story demands careful consideration.

In connection with an examination of Rhodes's charge it is proper to note that trading between northerners and southerners during the Civil War did not necessarily involve corruption on anybody's part. The federal government permitted, not to say encouraged, the purchase of cotton almost from the beginning of the war until just before its end. There were two reasons for this policy: northern textile manufacturers were avid to obtain cotton from any source whatsoever and the Administration wanted England, despite the blockade, to get enough cotton to minimize the likelihood of British intervention on behalf of the Confederacy. At first the Confederate government did everything it could to prevent any cotton from getting into northern hands, although seeking to ship it overseas. Later, as the blockade became more

[3] Butler to Chase, November 14, 1862; *POC,* II, 423.

effective, the Confederate authorities succumbed to their country's need for certain supplies—particularly medicines and salt—and allowed trading with the enemy.

At one time or another many Union officers (including General Grant)[4] were said illicitly to have engaged in and profited by this commerce. Rhodes himself mentioned "suspicions officially entertained of two brigadier-generals, a newspaper charge against one major-general, and [was] aware of current talk which would implicate two others." However, the only "evidence of corruption in the trade with the Confederacy" that he thought was properly to be considered by a historian was that concerning Butler.[5]

The evidence considered by Rhodes consists chiefly of a series of letters sent by George S. Denison, acting collector of the port of New Orleans, to the Secretary of the Treasury in 1862 and 1863.[6]

Denison said in the most damaging of these letters (dated October 10, 1862), that ever since the capture of New Orleans a brisk exchange of salt for cotton had been carried on with the Confederates

> by a few persons, under military permits, frequently with military assistance and much to the benefit of some of the principal military officers in this department. . . . Government officers, citizens, and rebels, generally believe [A. J. Butler] to be the partner or agent of Gen'l. Butler. He does a heavy business and by various practices has made between one and two million dollars since the capture of the city. . . . Gen'l. Butler, who knows everything, controls everything, . . . should be held responsible for everything. . . . Gen. Butler has always been kind to me, and our personal relations are upon the most pleasant

---

[4] W. E. Woodward, *Meet General Grant* (Horace Liveright, Inc. [New York, 1928]), p. 266.

[5] James Ford Rhodes, *History of the United States* (The Macmillan Co. [New York, 1904]), V, 303.

[6] Rhodes, op. cit., V, 303–13, passim. Denison's letters were published, under the title "Diary and Correspondence of Salmon P. Chase," in Vol. II of the *Annual Report of the American Historical Association for the Year 1902* (Government Printing Office [Washington, D.C., 1903]). (Hereafter cited as Chase, *Diary.*)

footing. He has great ability, great energy, great shrewdness, . . . activity, and industry, but he can never acquire a character for disinterestedness.[7]

Although Denison apparently did not know it, the commerce he mentioned had been authorized and even heartily encouraged by Reverdy Johnson, a special agent of the State Department who had been sent to New Orleans to investigate complaints that had been made by various consuls about Butler's conduct. Late in July, 1862 an English cotton dealer in Mobile sent word to Butler that the Confederates would be willing to exchange cotton for salt and other noncontraband commodities they urgently needed provided a pledge was given that the cotton would be shipped to England. Because this offer posed a question of civil, rather than military, policy Butler asked Johnson for advice about it. Johnson immediately replied: "I would consent to the shipment mentioned. . . . I am sure that in doing so you will carry out the policy of the government and subserve the interests of the country." A day later, as if afraid his advice might not be followed, Johnson wrote to Butler:

I think you should not hesitate to accept [the Englishman's proposition]. The shipment of cotton, . . . to Europe or to the loyal States, from such ports as are in [our] possession, . . . is, I know, much desired by our government. It was one of the principal advantages they expected to be the immediate result of the capture of this city. So anxious are they to obtain [this] object that I am satisfied they would readily sanction such an arrangement as your note mentions. The question is as you state "rather a civil than a military one," but in either case my opinion is that you should answer it affirmatively.[8]

The fact that Butler began dealing with the Confederates at Johnson's urging was known to Rhodes.[9] Nevertheless, he implied that the General initiated the business, knowing it to be

[7] Chase, *Diary*, pp. 321–25, passim.
[8] Butler to Johnson, July 28, 1962, Johnson to Butler, July 28, 1862, Johnson to Butler, July 29, 1862. *POC*, II, 120–21.
[9] Rhodes, op. cit., V, 278.

wrong, and said, "The evidence furnishes a strong presumption of Butler's guilt: I purposely avoid the word proof."[10]

To support this weak conclusion Rhodes accepted hearsay and unsworn statements as valid evidence and cited or relied upon only those parts of Denison's letters derogatory to Butler and disregarded such comments of Denison's as: "I have closely observed [A. J. Butler's] course. I do not believe the General is interested in his speculations;" "I have never been able to find any good proof that General Butler has improperly done or permitted anything to be done for his own pecuniary advantage;" "Four-fifths of the accusations against him are false."[11]

Even if Rhodes's "evidence" against Butler were to be accepted without questioning its validity (something no court of law would, and no historian should, do) the worst anyone could possibly say is that Butler never fully proved that he did not grant more favors to his brother than he did to others at New Orleans. And this negative verdict, if sustained, would suffice only to convict him of nepotism, which is not a crime whatever else is true of it.

[10] Ibid., V, 308.
[11] Chase, *Diary*, pp. 312, 313, 355.

14

★★★★★★★★★★★★

The Army of the James

Because Butler was relieved as commanding officer of the Department of the Gulf without being reassigned he left New Orleans with the intention of returning directly to Lowell. His homeward journey was without incident, except for some rather rough weather off Cape Hatteras, until his ship was intercepted in New York harbor by a revenue cutter which delivered him a letter asking him to call at the White House as soon as possible.

On seeing the President, Butler sought to learn why he had been recalled from New Orleans. Lincoln advised him to direct his questions to the Secretary of War. The Secretary told Butler that he had not been removed because of any want of confidence in his honor as a man or his capacity as a military commander. Butler remarked: "You have told me what I was *not* recalled for. Now I ask you what I *was* recalled for." Stanton answered, with a laugh: "You and I are both lawyers and there is no use your filing a bill of discovery upon me, for I shan't tell you." Butler next saw the Secretary of State and said to him, "I have asked the President why I was relieved of command and he declines giving me reason, and I have come to you, believing you can give them if you will." Seward replied: "I do not know what you were recalled for, I assure you, but Halleck knows all about it. He is general in chief and had everything to do with it." Butler then saw Halleck, to whom he said, "I have come to ask you, as my superior officer, the reasons for my being relieved from command in New Orleans and on what account it was done." Halleck claimed to know nothing about the reason Butler had been

178

relieved, but said, unequivocally, "It was done solely under the direction of the Secretary of State." This answer confirmed Butler's suspicions and he accepted it as truthful.[1]

After his interview with Halleck, Butler dined with Seward, at the latter's invitation. As he bade his host goodnight Butler said to him, "What an infernal liar your man Halleck is! He told me that he did not know anything about the reasons I was relieved; that it was done solely upon your advice."[2]

Although Butler may never have known it, Gideon Welles also thought Seward was responsible for Butler's recall and that its purpose was to ease foreign relations.[3]

Probably the conclusion reached by Butler and Welles was correct. New Orleans had a large alien population, composed chiefly of Frenchmen and Britishers, and as a result of what one of Seward's biographers called Butler's "arbitrary proceedings" complaints from foreign ministers came so thick and fast they engrossed half of Seward's time during most of 1862.[4]

However, there were others who thought Banks had been sent to New Orleans because it was feared in Washington that Butler would enforce the (soon to be issued) Emancipation Proclamation too vigorously.[5]

The most widely held belief was that the Administration wanted southern Louisiana to be governed more mildly than it had been by Butler.

Banks' behavior at New Orleans lends some color to this theory. Either acting on his own initiative or under more or less specific orders he conducted himself altogether differently than

---

[1] Benjamin F. Butler, *Butler's Book* (A. M. Thayer & Co. [Boston, 1892]), pp. 533–34 Original italics.

[2] Ibid., p. 534.

[3] Gideon Welles, *Diary of Gideon Welles* (Houghton Mifflin Company [Boston, 1911]), I, 210.

[4] Thornton Lothrop, *William Henry Seward* (Houghton, Mifflin and Company [Boston, 1899]), pp. 342–43.

[5] Moncure D. Conway, *Autobiography of Moncure D. Conway* (Houghton, Mifflin and Company [Boston, 1904]), I, 376–77. See also John S. C. Abbott, *History of the Civil War in America* (Henry Bill [New York, 1867]), II, 304.

Butler had. And, if Denison's opinion is to be trusted, the results of the change were bad. He wrote to Chase on February 12, 1863:

> Affairs [in New Orleans] are not in a prosperous condition. Great dissatisfaction exists in at least some portions of the army. Even Gen. Banks' new troops to some extent—and Butler's old troops to a man, would hail Butler's return with enthusiasm. Banks' policy seems to be conciliatory and hesitating. He seems to be afraid of responsibility. Gen. Butler is absolutely fearless. . . . The nine months men [i.e. those who had enlisted for a period of nine months] are dissatisfied and demoralized. I think Butler could not only remove such feelings, but make most of them reenlist. Whatever Butler did pleased and satisfied the army because they had confidence in him. This is not at all true of Gen. Banks. The sooner Gen. Butler comes back the better it will be.[6]

About six weeks later Denison again compared Butler and Banks, saying:

> In my letters to you written soon after Gen. Banks assumed command, I stated that Banks had already virtually failed. I now regard his failure as complete and impossible to be relieved by [him]. . . . With an army three times as large as Gen. Butler's we hold the same amount of territory [as was] held by him. . . . Butler left New Orleans really and truly a Union City. Day by day have appearances of loyalty diminished. It is now a secession city, and matters are growing worse. . . . Slavery has been re-established, and slave labor restored; and local police regulations regarding slaves enforced by New England bayonets. . . . Time has been wasted, lives lost, money spent, . . . the well wishers of the Government discouraged and disheartened. But the large slave owners are partially satisfied and unrelenting secessionists make no complaint. [Butler could straighten things out in less than two weeks, Denison thought. But, he added] I do not suppose he will be sent here for he is too earnest a man to suit Mr. Seward, and if placed in a high position, he might possibly become dangerous as a candidate for the Presidency.[7]

---

[6] Salmon P. Chase, "Diary and Correspondence of Salmon P. Chase," *Annual Report of the American Historical Association for the Year 1902* (Government Printing Office [Washington, D.C., 1903]), II, 358–59.

[7] Ibid., pp. 372–74.

Denison also believed that there was now a great deal more corruption in New Orleans than there ever had been in Butler's day and was certain that there was "more interference with, and annoyance to, civil officers and business men in one week . . . than there was during the whole time Gen. Butler was here."[8]

En route from Washington to Lowell, Butler narrowly missed being killed in a train wreck near Bridgeport, Connecticut. Such a death in peaceful New England would have been an ironic fate for a man who had escaped assassination and yellow fever in New Orleans.

At Springfield, his train's first stop in Massachusetts, Butler was given a tumultuous welcome. As New Englanders often do he expressed his pleasure in a negative way, saying that as long as his home state so heartily commended him he could feel satisfied that his course had not been altogether wrong. At Lowell he was greeted with cannon fire and a speech by the mayor before being escorted to his home by a large crowd. The following day he went, by special train, to Boston where, on 24 hours notice, a reception in his honor had been arranged at Faneuil Hall. The Hall was completely filled almost as soon as its doors opened. The mayor made a flattering address of welcome to which Butler replied with good taste.

Less than a month after Butler left New Orleans, Lincoln began to regret his recall. Toward the end of January, 1863 the President wrote to the Secretary of War:

> I think Gen. Butler should go to New Orleans again. He is unwilling to go, unless he is restored to the command of the Department. He should start by the first of February and should take some force with him. The whole thing must be so managed as not to wrong or wound the feelings of Gen. Banks. . . . I think we can no longer dispense with Gen. Butler's services.[9]

---

[8] Ibid., p. 374.

[9] Roy Basler, *Collected Works of Abraham Lincoln* (Rutgers University Press [New Brunswick, N.J., 1955]), VI, 76–77.

An order for Butler's return to New Orleans was prepared, but he declined further service in the Department of the Gulf, chiefly because he did not like the conditions and limitations that would have been imposed upon him. Other motives for his refusal were the fact that the enlistments of many men would expire about the time he would have reached New Orleans and his belief that Banks had done irreparable harm to the relations between whites and Negroes.

While Lincoln was still considering Butler's future the General was interviewed, on behalf of the Committee on the Conduct of the War, by Stephen M. Allen. The Committee, usurping the functions of the War Department, suggested to Butler that he take 50,000 men from the Army of the Potomac, march them overland to the Ohio River, and move by boat down the Ohio and Mississippi Rivers. Hardly taking time for breath he told Allen he would have nothing to do with such an expedition. Apparently he was not at all concerned about the fact that a congressional committee had no constitutional right to offer him any sort of assignment. He simply regarded the plan outlined by Allen as unworkable because boats travelling downstream would, if crippled, drift into the Confederates hands, easily to be captured or destroyed.

A short time later Lincoln asked Butler to visit the Mississippi River below St. Louis and report upon the civil administration of the several military departments. This seemed too much like detective work to Butler so he refused to do it.

Lincoln then suggested that all of the Negro troops—by now a considerable number—be placed under Butler's command and used to reinforce the Army of the Potomac. Butler did not care to serve with the Army of the Potomac, chiefly because it contained too many West Point men to suit his taste. He disliked West Pointers as a class because he thought they discriminated against volunteer officers and were contemptuous of those with less education (professionally speaking) than they had.

As an alternative to the suggestion about serving with the Army of the Potomac, Butler asked to be allowed to land on a southern coast with an army of white men and to start marching through the Confederacy, gathering up Negroes and arming them with spears, clubs, and revolvers. Such a force, he said, would terrify the whole South. Needless to say, this idea was not adopted.

The fact that Butler's services were not being used in any way seemed regrettable to many persons, ranging from Republican members of Congress and editors to ordinary citizens. Denison, who wrote to Chase that Butler's presence would be worth 10,000 men, urged the General to come back to New Orleans. A committee of New Yorkers wanted Butler to be appointed Secretary of War in place of Stanton. Halleck suggested having Butler put in command of all of the troops in North Carolina. After the New York draft riots in July, 1863 David Dudley Field, George Opdyke, William Cullen Bryant, and Henry J. Raymond earnestly recommended to President Lincoln that Butler be sent to New York with a large enough force to keep order there. In August, 1863 Wendell Phillips proposed that Butler, or somebody else friendly to, and understanding of, Negroes be chosen as general in chief of the Union Armies. Some time later a delegation of citizens from Kansas and Missouri asked the President to appoint Butler commanding officer of the Department of Missouri in place of Major General John M. Schofield. Lincoln declined to remove Schofield, without, as he said, thereby deciding anything against Butler.

In the end Butler was recalled to active duty in November, 1863 as commanding officer of the Department of Virginia and North Carolina and the Army of the James.

By this time the Union had gained control of somewhat more of the area nominally included in the Department of Virginia and North Carolina than had been the case when Butler commanded it in 1861. In the interval Norfolk, Virginia, several islands off the coast of North Carolina, and a few of that state's coastal towns had been occupied by federal troops. The Army of the James comprised the Tenth Corps, commanded by Major General Quincy A. Gillmore; the Eighteenth Corps, Major General William F. Smith; and a cavalry division under Brigadier General August V. Kautz. Its strength was between 33,000 and 35,000 officers and men.

Soon after Butler returned to Fortress Monroe he took official notice of the fact that the recruitment of Negroes had become a settled policy of the federal government and issued a general order concerning the treatment of colored troops in his department. His aims were to prevent as many Negroes as possible from becoming charges upon either the bounty of the government or the charity of benevolent individuals; to do justice to those who should enlist; to encourage enlistments; and to cause all who were capable of working to become employed, under arms or otherwise, so that they could support themselves and their families. His order provided that Negroes enlisting for three years or the duration of the war were to be paid a bounty of $10 each to enable them to supply their own and their families' immediate needs and their families were to be furnished subsistence. At the moment Negro soldiers were being given the same uniforms, arms, equipment, rations, medical care, and hospital treatment as white men were, but the Negro soldiers' pay (set by an act of Congress) was $10 a month as compared with $13 a month for white men. Butler said he hoped and believed Congress would, as a matter of simple justice, bring the pay of Negroes up to the amount paid other troops. He could see no reason why a Negro soldier, who filled an equal space in the ranks and an equal grave if killed, should be paid less than others received. To prevent governmental agencies from competing with each other Butler ordered wages to be regulated so that unskilled Negroes could not earn more as laborers than they could as soldiers. Having heard that white officers and soldiers had compelled Negroes to work, often without imperative need and sometimes for private purposes, Butler ordered that no Negro should be impressed for any service except by a draft applying equally to white men. He noted that able-bodied Negroes were being allowed to come behind the Union lines as a means of depriving the Confederates of their labor. Women and children were also being received because it would be manifestly wrong to take husbands and fathers while leaving wives and children to be mistreated. Therefore, he ordered all officers and soldiers under his command to use every means in their power to encourage Negroes to come within his lines. He added that anyone in his department hindering Negroes who wanted to take refuge with his troops and anyone who insulted, abused, or ridiculed Negro soldiers because of their color would be punished for obstructing recruiting. Inasmuch as it seemed necessary for the government to exercise more care over Negroes "than over its white citizens, accustomed to self-control and self-support," Butler appointed a superintendent of Negro affairs to whom instructions were given for dealing with matters placed under his jurisdiction.[10]

This order was widely praised by northerners; most southerners, of course, regarded it as another example of "Beast" Butler's utter depravity. They professed to (and in some cases probably did) believe his way of treating Negroes would lead them to make war upon defenseless women and children. Butler told one man who expressed such fears that if he did not die until a Negro hurt him he would live forever.

However, one man did die as a result of Butler's policy of treating Negroes as equals of white men. According to a southern historian Dr. Wright, "a brave and chivalrous citizen of Norfolk" was "outrageously" executed "simply because he dared to shoot down an insolent officer of a negro company who had grossly insulted him."[11]

Another of Butler's "outrages" was the seizure of the privately owned Norfolk Gas Company's plant. For several months before Butler arrived at Fortress Monroe the company had refused to supply gas for lighting the city's streets. The General took over the establishment and ordered it to be "carried on efficiently and

---

[10] General Order No. 46, December 5, 1863, as quoted in Jesse Ames Marshall (compiler), *Private and Official Correspondence of Gen. Benjamin F. Butler* (Privately issued [Boston, 1917]), III, 183–90. (Hereafter cited as *POC*)

[11] H. W. Burton, *The History of Norfolk, Virginia* (Norfolk Virginia Job Print [Norfolk, 1877]), pp. 86–87.

economically" so that Norfolk might be fully lighted and its peace and quiet assured in spite of the darkness of night.[12]

At Norfolk, Butler applied, with great success, the same methods he had used to prevent yellow fever in New Orleans. Norfolk was, he said, the filthiest place he had ever seen where there were human beings of a civilized order. He changed this condition by setting some 250 military prisoners—deserters, thieves, etc., not prisoners of war—at work cleaning the streets. Volunteers for this task were secured by providing that for every 30 days a man spent at it ten days would be taken from his sentence.

While riding around Norfolk one day Butler found that certain citizens seemed to have little to do except to chaff the street cleaners. This discovery prompted him to issue an order to the officer in charge of prisoners to put any man loitering on the streets and talking to, or interfering with, the clean-up squad to work with the squad. The sidewalk committee immediately adjourned sine die.

Butler's sanitary regulations kept Norfolk in a healthy state, but at Newbern, North Carolina, yellow fever, as he supposed, was taking a dreadful toll of lives. Newbern had been held alternately by Confederate and Union troops for nearly three years. None of the commanding officers on either side knew anything about military sanitation because no such science then existed. Lacking such knowledge the various commanders had permitted open ditches to be used as latrines. When a particular camp ground became intolerably malodorous a new one was established somewhere else. Butler had the ditches in the old camp grounds filled and ordered the new grounds to be kept in a sanitary condition. The disease rate began to decline nearly as soon as the "awful stench," which had been noticeable fully two miles from Newbern began to subside.

On this occasion Butler almost certainly mistook typhoid fever for yellow fever. (The symptoms of these diseases are much alike, especially in their early stages.) However, in doing his best to

---

[12] Butler to James Barnes, December 29, 1863; *POC*, III, 264.

combat yellow fever he was fortunately led, albeit for the wrong reason, to do the right thing to prevent typhoid fever.

As a result of his experiences at New Orleans and Newbern, Butler remained satisfied to the end of his life that he had proved that filth caused yellow fever. Many medical men shared this belief until the commission headed by Dr. Walter Reed proved it wrong in 1901.

In December, 1863 Butler learned that a number of Union soldiers held by Confederates as prisoners of war were suffering from smallpox. Never one to wait for red tape to be unwound, he immediately sent the Confederate commissioner of exchange, Judge Robert Ould, enough vaccine for 6,000 innoculations and informed the War Department of what he had done. His action was approved.

A short time later Butler was named commissioner for the exchange of all Union prisoners east of the Alleghenies. He was quite unnecessarily told to protect Negro soldiers equally with white ones in making exchanges.

At first the Confederates loudly refused to recognize Butler as exchange commissioner because he had been outlawed by President Davis's proclamation. Butler informed Ould that the federal government claimed, and intended to exercise, the power of choosing its own agents without regard to any supposed sanction by Confederate authorities. As the "balance of trade" began to run against the Confederates they became more anxious to exchange prisoners than the Union was, so Ould quietly climbed down from his high horse and dealt with Butler.

Publicly Butler and Ould abused each other mightily; privately they got along remarkably well. Whenever Ould visited Fortress Monroe on exchange business Butler would have him stay for a meal. Once, after Ould had spent a night at Fortress Monroe, he ate a breakfast which he said would have cost $2,000 in Confederate money.

For the sake of the days when they had met as friends at Democratic party gatherings Butler and Ould agreed that each of them would effect the exchange of any prisoner specially requested by the other. Acting under this arrangement Ould asked to have Henry Kyd Douglas exchanged. For some reason the general commanding the prison camp where Douglas was confined did not want to release him. By the time Butler discovered this fact and overruled the order to hold Douglas the exchange boat had left Fortress Monroe. Douglas was put on board Butler's official steamer, the *Greyhound,* and her captain was instructed to overtake the exchange boat. Needless to say Butler made a friend that day. Another Confederate who came to know, and almost to like, Butler after meeting him as a prisoner of war, was Major General William F. Lee, son of General Robert E. Lee. Young Lee said that Butler had treated him with the utmost courtesy, even returning his privately owned horse and equipment to him.[13]

Early in February, 1864 Butler learned that the Confederates, relying on the almost impassable condition of the roads in the area, had left Richmond only lightly defended. He detailed Brigadier General Isaac Wistar to attempt a surprise attack with a force of about 3,000 troops. Wistar's orders were to release the Union prisoners at Richmond, to destroy public buildings, arsenals, railroad equipment, and the Tredegar Iron Works. If possible he was also "to capture some of the leaders of the rebellion." Butler promised to rush more troops to Richmond if Wistar could hold the city even briefly.[14]

Wistar conducted a skillful operation. His infantry made a forced march of 80 miles in 56 hours while his cavalry covered 150 miles in the same time. However, a deserter betrayed him at the last moment and the Confederates checkmated him.

Butler unsuccessfully offered to exchange any prisoner the Con-

---

[13] Henry Kyd Douglas, *I Rode with Stonewall* (University of North Carolina Press [Chapel Hill, 1940]), pp. 268–70; Douglas Southall Freeman, *R. E. Lee* (Charles Scribner's Sons [New York, 1935]), II, 211; Alfred Hoyt Bill, *The Beleaguered City* (Alfred A. Knopf [New York, 1946]), p. 210; Mary B. Chestnut, *A Diary from Dixie* (D. Appleton and Company [New York, 1905]), p. 300.

[14] Butler to Wistar, February 4, 1863; *POC,* III, 373–74.

federates chose to name for the deserter. He also informed the President that the traitor was an enlisted man who had been sentenced to die for killing an officer, but had been reprieved by Lincoln. Lincoln's well-known leniency toward military offenders was something of which Butler strongly disapproved, as he did not hesitate to tell the President more than once.

There were many who thought that Butler would have been elected President in 1864 if Wistar's expedition had resulted in the capture of Richmond.

15

★★★★★★★★★★★★

Bottled up at Bermuda Hundred

In March, 1864 Ulysses S. Grant was promoted to the rank of lieutenant general and put in command of all of the Union Armies. As an indirect result of this event Butler saw more front line service during the ensuing nine months than he did in all the rest of the war together.

Grant had concluded, long before he became general in chief, "that active and continuous operations of all the troops that could be brought into the field, regardless of the season and the weather, were necessary to a speedy termination of the war." In the past the Union Armies in both the East and West had, as he put it,

> acted independently and without concert, like a balky team [of horses], no two ever pulling together; enabling the enemy to use to great advantage his interior lines of communication, . . . reinforcing the army most vigorously pressed, and . . . furloughing large numbers during the season of inactivity on [the Union Armies'] part, to go to their homes and do the work of producing for the support of their armies.[1]

A similar thought had occurred to Butler. He could not see any use in having five or six Union armies, each acting without regard to what the others were doing, although none of them was big enough to accomplish much by itself. Therefore, he had suggested (in a letter sent to the Secretary of the Treasury in April, 1863) the formation of two amphibious armies, each commanded by a single officer (unification, no less), with which to strike at

---

[1] U. S. Grant, *Personal Memoirs of U. S. Grant* (Charles L. Webster & Company [New York, 1885–86]), II, 555–56.

190

the South. Above all, he urged that a pitched battle be sought
by the Union in order to end the war.[2]

On becoming general in chief Grant planned simultaneous campaigns by all of the Union Armies against the Confederate Armies
commanded by General Robert E. Lee and J. E. Johnston. In
the movement against Lee's Army of Northern Virginia—the one
of interest to us—Grant regarded the Army of the Potomac, with
which he made his headquarters, as his center, all the troops to
the westward as his right wing, and Butler's Army of the James
as his left wing.

Grant, of course, had not chosen Butler for the position the
latter was occupying in the spring of 1864. When they first met,
on April 1, Grant decided that Butler was an excellent executive
who ought to be left at Fortress Monroe as administrator of the
Department of Virginia and North Carolina with General Smith
(a particular pet of Grant's), assisted by General Gillmore, commanding in the field. Butler was unwilling to stay tied to a desk
at headquarters and a department commander could not easily be
relegated to a duty he did not care to perform so Grant yielded
to his desire for field service, hoping he would allow himself to be
guided by his West Point-educated subordinates, Smith and Gillmore.

Before giving Butler any orders concerning the part he was to
play in the forthcoming campaign Grant asked for his views as
to how the Army of the James could most usefully co-operate with
the Army of the Potomac. Butler had long thought it would be
best to advance from Fortress Monroe upon Richmond via the
James River. He was sure this would be far easier to do than
to march an army 150 miles overland with five rivers to cross on
the way. So he suggested that the Army of the James swoop upon
City Point in transports convoyed by some naval vessels. (City
Point, at the confluence of the James and Appomatox Rivers, had

[2] Butler to the Secretary of the Treasury, April 27, 1863, as quoted in
Jesse Ames Marshall (compiler), *Private and Official Correspondence
of Gen. Benjamin F. Butler* (Privately issued [Boston, 1917]), III, 61–64.
(Hereafter cited as *POC*)

for some time been the meeting place for flag of truce boats used in the exchange of prisoners. Thus the Yankees had been able to study it to some extent.)

Grant liked this idea because, as he wrote after the war, it was similar to his own view of the best way to use the Army of the James. Since Grant (like Butler and Porter) was not above giving himself more credit than was his proper due it is not improbable that Butler's suggestion influenced him more than he admitted, or perhaps even realized. According to one high ranking officer of the Army of the Potomac, Grant completely changed his mind about the sort of campaign to be waged against Lee after interviewing Lincoln, Stanton, General George G. Meade (commanding officer of the Army of the Potomac), and Butler.[3]

In any case, on April 2 Grant issued an order to Butler, reading in its significant parts:

> In the Spring campaign, which it is desirable shall commence at as early a date as practicable, . . . the Army of the Potomac will act from its present base [at Culpeper Court House, Virginia, between the Rappahannock and James Rivers]—Lee's Army being its objective point. You will collect all the forces from your command that can be spared from garrison duty, I should say not less than twenty thousand effective men, to operate on the South side of the James River, Richmond being your objective point. . . . When you are notified to move, take City Point with as much force as possible. Fortify, or rather intrench, at once, and concentrate all your troops for the field there as rapidly as you can. From City Point directions cannot be given you at this time for your further movements. The fact . . . that Richmond is to be your objective point, and that there is to be co-operation between your force and the Army of the Potomac must be your guide. This indicates the necessity of your holding close to the South bank of the James River as you advance. . . . All the main details of your advance are left to your direction.[4]

On April 19 Grant advised Butler that he would be expected

---

[3] James Harrison Wilson, *Life and Services of W. F. Smith* (The John M. Rogers Press [Wilmington, Delaware, 1904]), p. 82.

[4] Grant to Butler, April 2, 1864; *POC,* IV, 7–9.

to move from Fortress Monroe at the same time the Army of the Potomac left Culpeper Court House, on a date yet to be determined. Grant intended, as he told Butler, to fight Lee wherever he made a stand. In case the Confederates fell back to Richmond, Grant said he would follow them and if Butler's army could invest the south side of the city, with its left resting on the James, Grant would form a junction between the Armies of the James and the Potomac. Butler was, in any event, to secure a foothold as far up the south side of the James as he could and if he were unable to carry Richmond he was at least to detain as large a Confederate force as possible.

Although the possession of Petersburgh (ten miles southwest of City Point) was essential to the security of any Union force operating along the south side of the James, Grant's orders did not mention any movement against that city. If Grant thought such a movement necessary he ought to have said so in words that could not have been misunderstood, particularly in view of his distrust of Butler's military ability. However, as Theodore A. Dodge, historian and military critic, said,

> Grant's orders to Butler were very vague, and he could scarcely have supposed that Butler would look upon Petersburg as a *sine qua non* in his problem, even if the same orders to a more skilled soldier could be twisted into meaning so much. The same uncertainty as to what his eventual operations would be appeared here, as was seen in the Vicksburg campaign. If Grant really expected to use the James River route, he should definitely have ordered the capture of Petersburg.[5]

Commenting on the same subject, General Smith said,

> It is remarkable that [Grant] did not in his written instructions mention Petersburg as the first point to be taken. To anyone with the eye of a soldier it was obvious, on even a slight examination, that no movement from City Point, or even Bermuda Hundred [a neck of land across the James from City

[5] Theodore F. Dwight (editor), *Some Federal and Confederate Commanders* (Published for the Military Historical Society of Massachusetts by Houghton, Mifflin and Company [Boston, 1895]), pp. 38–39.

Point] could safely be made against Richmond, except by a very large force, without first capturing Petersburg. While Petersburg remained in the hands of the enemy, a large force would be necessary to protect the flank and rear of an army moving from Bermuda Hundred to Richmond. The force under General Butler was not equal to this.[6]

Grant telegraphed Butler on April 28: "If no unforeseen accident prevents, I will move from here Wednesday, the 4th of May. Start your forces on the night of the 4th so as to be as far up the James as you can get by daylight . . . of the 5th, and push from that time with all your might for the accomplishment of the object before you."[7]

On receiving this message Butler assembled a fleet of transports, tugs, canalboats, etc. Just before nightfall, May 4, these craft sailed into Chesapeake Bay, apparently bound for Gloucester Point on the York River where a brigade had been building a wharf suitable for the landing of an army. Confederate sympathizers and spies in the vicinity of Fortress Monroe logically concluded that the Army of the James was going to follow McClellan's old route up the peninsula toward Richmond. As soon as they had had time enough to send word to this effect where they, and Butler, thought it would do the most good, the fleet returned to Hampton Roads. A detachment of gunboats immediately sped up the James and captured every Confederate signal station along the river; the rest of the vessels lay at anchor until five o'clock the following morning.

Everything went well at the expedition's starting time, except that the transports carrying General Gillmore's Tenth Corps did not get under way when they should have. Butler had every reason to suppose his sailing orders had been fully understood and would be implicitly obeyed. He was visibly upset as the *Greyhound* left her place in the vanguard to enable him to find out what was causing the delay. Having received a satisfactory ex-

---

[6] William F. Smith, *From Chattanooga to Petersburg* (Houghton, Mifflin and Company [Boston, 1893]), p. 117.

[7] Grant to Butler, April 28, 1864; *POC,* IV, 140.

planation from Gillmore, Butler started up the river. The *Greyhound,* weaving her way through the traffic, was slowed as she came abreast of each vessel in the convoy long enough for Butler to shout: "Give her all the steam you can, captain!" An hour after she turned upstream the well-named *Greyhound* caught up with Admiral S. P. Lee's monitors, which had had a three hour headstart.

The monitors ran a couple of miles above City Point to protect the troops as they landed. However, this precaution proved to be unnecessary for the Confederates offered no opposition; they had been taken completely by surprise. Such trouble as was experienced was caused by the magnitude of the operation. Landing the men was easy; they jumped ashore as the transports pulled up to the wharf. The artillery, baggage wagons, and other impedimenta could not do the same and shipping began to pile up. However, a signal station was quickly set up, order was brought out of the initial chaos, and by the morning of May 6 the entire army had been landed, most of it at Bermuda Hundred, the rest at City Point.

Three days later Butler optimistically telegraphed to the Secretary of War:

> Our operations may be summed up in a few words. . . . We have landed, . . . intrenched ourselves, destroyed many miles of railroad, and got a position which, with proper supplies, we can hold against the whole of Lee's army. I have ordered up the supplies. . . . General Grant will not be troubled with any reinforcements to Lee from Beauregard's force.[8]

He wrote to his wife on May 11: "We shall demonstrate toward Richmond tomorrow. I have now done all I agreed to do with Grant."[9]

When Butler reached City Point, and for some time afterward, Petersburg was practically undefended. If he had thought it worthwhile he could easily have taken the place. He made no attempt

---

[8] Butler to the Secretary of War, May 9, 1864; *POC,* IV, 181–82.
[9] Butler to Mrs. Butler, May 11, 1864; *POC,* IV, 192.

to do so because he understood that Richmond, not Petersburg, was his objective. He even refused to heed a suggestion made by Generals Gillmore and Smith that they be allowed to move against Petersburg. This refusal, for which Butler has often been adversely criticized, was not illogical in view of the emphasis his orders put upon staying close to the south bank of the James and their failure even to mention Petersburg.

After four days of steady rain and hard fighting the Army of the James reached Fort Darling, a series of earthworks at Drury's (sometimes spelled Drewry's) Bluff on the James River six or eight miles below Richmond. During Friday and Saturday, May 13 and 14, Gillmore took several miles of trenches at one end of the Confederate lines and earnestly requested permission to dig in where he was. Butler refused to hear of this because it would be a defensive tactic and his movement was an offensive one. (He seems to have had an odd sort of fear that the offensive nature of his operation might somehow be compromised by stooping to defensive measures. Probably this attitude was a product of his militia training for he knew that the worst thing troops can do in the face of a civilian mob is to go, or even to seem to go, on the defensive; to do so invites trouble if it does not assure it.

Toward nightfall Sunday the rains stopped. A few hours later a thick fog settled over the area. Early Monday morning a Confederate force came out of the fog and fell upon the Army of the James like an avalanche. The battle thus unceremoniously begun continued briskly for several hours, with participants from both sides wandering out of the fog to fall into each others' hands. By the time the fog lifted (about 9 A.M.) Butler's troops had been driven back nearly a mile. After they had regained most of the ground they had lost Butler learned that a large number of Confederates from Petersburg was approaching his rear. Caught between two fires, he had no choice except to withdraw to Bermuda Hundred.

Although the Confederate commander admitted after the war that he ought to have captured Butler's entire force,[10] the Army

---

[10] G. T. Beauregard, "Drury's Bluff and Petersburg," *North American Review,* March 1887, CLXIV, 258.

of the James retreated in good order, even bringing its wounded and its supplies from the field.

Speaking of the events just described Grant said in a post war report that the time lost by Butler between May 6 and 16 cost the Union "the benefit of surprise and the capture of Richmond and Petersburg."[11] It was unfair of Grant, considering that his orders to Butler had not mentioned Petersburg, to criticize Butler for not taking that place. And, without implying that Grant was not a far abler soldier than Butler, it may be remarked that it took Grant 40 days to get from the Rapidan to the James across terrain similar to that west of Bermuda Hundred. If one must agree with A. W. Alexander that "Butler's campaign was an utter failure," one also agrees with Alexander that "it was a failure not merely because of Butler's military incapacity, but because the plan was essentially bad; the failure was Grant's more than Butler's."[12]

After the battle of Drury's Bluff, Grant sent his chief engineer, General Barnard, to inspect Butler's position at Bermuda Hundred. Barnard reported that it was defensively strong, but, he added, it was "like a bottle with Butler corked up inside of it." This phraseology caught Grant's fancy and he used it in a report as though it were his own.

Butler was by no means hermetically sealed up at Bermuda Hundred. His troops could come and go almost at will in any direction except to the west. This being so, he decided to attack Petersburg with a force of infantry moving along City Point Road and of cavalry along the Jerusalem Plank Road. Gillmore was given command of the infantry, at his own request; Kautz commanded the cavalry. Soon after Gillmore left Bermuda Hundred he complained, in a message sent back to Butler, that the pontoon bridge across the Appomatox had not been properly muffled and he feared that the noise made by the cavalry as it followed him would put the Confederates on the alert. Despite his apprehension he nearly reached the city before he met any resistance; then he

---

[11] Grant, op. cit., pp. 567–68.

[12] Augustus W. Alexander, *Grant as a Soldier* (Published by the author [St. Louis, 1887]), p. 191.

halted, decided his force was too weak to perform the mission he had assumed, and retired without even attempting an assault. Actually he could almost have walked into Petersburg for his troops outnumbered the city's defenders by at least two to one. The cavalry did, in fact, take the works on the south side of Petersburg, but lacking infantry support, was driven away from them. General Beauregard commented later that if Gillmore had been enterprising and bold enough "the 'entrance gate to Richmond' would necessarily have been lost to the Confederacy without the firing of a single gun by the Army of the Potomac."[13]

Butler relieved Gillmore upon his return to Bermuda Hundred and ordered him to wait at Fortress Monroe for a court of inquiry concerning his failure to capture Petersburg after he had volunteered for the duty.

Before there was time for the court to meet Grant wrote to Butler:

> If you have no objection to withdrawing your order relieving General Gillmore, I will relieve him at his own request. The way the matter now stands it is a severe punishment to General Gillmore, even if a court of inquiry should hereafter acquit him. I think the course here suggested is advisable, and would be pleased if you agree to it, though I do not order or insist upon it.[14]

Butler promptly acceded to this request. If he had not done so Grant might have found himself embarrassed by seeing one of the professional soldiers he had expected to guide Butler cashiered for incompetence or, perhaps, for cowardice.

Because Bermuda Hundred could be defended by a small force Grant transferred Smith's corps to the Army of the Potomac. Soon after this occurred Grant decided to move the Army of the Potomac south of the James River. Butler's experience had taught Grant the strategic importance of Petersburg so he made

---

[13] P. G. T. Beauregard, "The Battle of Petersburg," *North American Review,* October, 1887, CXLV, 367–68.

[14] Grant to Butler, June 17, 1864; *POC,* IV, 401.

plans to take the place before the Confederates could reinforce it. And, as Grant's aide-de-campe, Brigadier General Horace Porter, stated in a magazine article: "Instead of letting Butler, the actual commander of the forces [nearest Petersburg], take charge of the operation, the commander in chief . . . especially delegated Smith for it, as he was an educated soldier [who] by his intelligence had commended himself to General Grant as an officer well fitted for the task."[15]

This educated, intelligent soldier made an even worse botch of things than Gillmore did. Grant was much disturbed about Smith's failure, but he took no disciplinary action in the matter— a fact that lends at least some support to Butler's belief that the old school tie was a valuable asset.

One of Grant's biographers who blamed Butler for "assigning" the second Petersburg movement to Smith instead of making it himself[16] may have overlooked Porter's statement. However, Rhodes, who cited Porter's article in another connection, can hardly have erred unknowingly when he wrote: "If Butler had been a soldier, he would have led all his available force and captured Petersburg. . . ."[17]

A short time after Smith's fiasco at Petersburg he engaged in such a violent quarrel with Butler that Grant found it necessary to get rid of one of the pair. The issue resulted indirectly from Butler's thoughtfulness for the welfare of men in the ranks. At 9 A.M., June 21 he sent word to Smith:

> . . . I think duty requires that I should call your attention to the fact that your column, which was ordered to move at day-light in the cool of the morning, is just now passing my head

---

[15] Horace Porter, "Campaigning with Grant," *The Century,* April, 1897, LIII, 827.

[16] Louis A. Coolidge, *Ulysses S. Grant* (Houghton Mifflin Company [Boston, 1917]), p. 171.

[17] James Ford Rhodes, *History of the United States* (The Macmillan Co. [New York, 1899]), IV, 489, 493 ftn.

Qrs. in the heat of the day for a ten mile march. The great fault in our movements is dilatoriness, and if this is the fault of your division commanders let them be very seriously reprimanded therefore. I have found it necessary to relieve one general for this, among other causes, where it took place in a movement of vital importance, and in justice to him you will hardly expect me to pass in silence a like fault of less moment.[18]

As harsh as this message was, Butler was fully justified in calling Smith's attention to the fact that his troops were marching during a warmer part of the day than was necessary. On another day, when the heat was not much greater, a division commander reported that three of his men had died of sunstroke and 30 ambulances had been needed to carry those who had been overcome by the heat.

If Smith had a reasonable explanation for the delay in starting his march, as he long afterward claimed he did,[19] he should have offered it to Butler then and there. Instead of doing so he telegraphed to Butler at 3:40 P.M.:

I . . . acknowledge . . . your extraordinary note of 9 A.M. In giving your rank and position all the respect which is their due, I must call your attention to the fact that a reprimand can come only from the sentence of a court martial & I shall accept nothing else as such. You will also pardon me for observing that I have some years been engaged in moving troops, and I think in experience of that kind, at least, I am your superior.

Your accusation of dilatoriness on my part this morning, or at any other time since I have been under your orders, is not founded on fact, & your threat of relieving me does not frighten me in the least.[20]

Butler answered, with remarkable restraint:

If you will look at my note you will find it contains no threat; on the contrary, there are some words interlined [i. e. scratched

[18] Butler to Smith, June 21, 1864; *POC,* IV, 426.
[19] William F. Smith, *From Chattanooga to Petersburg* (Houghton, Mifflin and Company [Boston, 1893]), p. 160.
[20] Smith to Butler, June 21, 1864; *POC,* IV, 427.

out], lest upon reading it over it might possibly be so construed. Please read the note again and see if you cannot wish
the reply was not sent. . . . I never thought you at fault as to
the movement.[21]

At 5:45 P.M., Butler sent Smith an unofficial message, saying
in part: "No accusation is made, but the fact [that a delay had
occurred] stated, and a suggestion that if the fault was where
I supposed it might be . . . that it should be corrected."[22]

Far from being mollified, Smith forwarded copies of the first
two of the three messages to Grant and asked to be relieved from
duty in the Department.

Grant did not miss the implication that he would have to
choose between Smith and Butler. Saying that Butler was clearly
in the wrong, Grant promptly decided to keep Smith and asked
the Secretary of War to put Butler in charge of a department
where there would be no great battles to be fought, but there
would be a dissatisfied element to control. On learning that no
such department existed or could be created Grant telegraphed
to Halleck in Washington to have Butler ordered to repair to
Fortress Monroe and the troops in the field put under Smith's
command.

Orders complying with Grant's request were issued on July 7.
Two days later Butler called upon Grant at his headquarters.
Immediately after Butler's visit the order suspending him as field
commander was rescinded. On July 19 Smith was relieved of duty
in Butler's department and directed to wait at New York for
further orders (which he never received).

Why Grant changed his mind in this matter is one of history's
minor mysteries. The fact that he never admitted having changed
his mind adds to the mystery. An explanation he caused to be
quite widely circulated is that Smith was so quarrelsome that if
he had been retained several other prominent officers, including
Meade, would have had to go. Smith was told, at Grant's direc-

[21] Butler to Smith, June 21, 1864; *POC,* IV, 427.
[22] Butler to Smith, June 21, 1864; *POC,* IV, 427.

tion, that he was relieved because of his inability to get along with Butler, who was the senior.

These stories are simply beyond belief. If they had any factual basis Grant would not have tried to have Butler relegated to Fortress Monroe.

According to a charge made by Smith, first in a letter to Senator Solomon Foote of Vermont (Smith's birthplace), later repeated in a book Smith wrote, Grant became intoxicated (on two drinks of whiskey, spaced an hour apart) in Butler's presence and Butler blackmailed Grant into relieving Smith instead of Butler.[23]

This tale is patently absurd. If Grant got drunk enough to have feared exposure on the amount of liquor he was said to have consumed in the time mentioned he was certainly the world's most economical sot. Moreover, there is good reason to doubt that Grant did any heavy drinking during the Civil War. The Reverend John Eaton, who saw much of Grant in 1864, emphatically stated his "belief that after Grant's return to the army all reports of his drunkenness were wholly unsupported by the facts."[24]

Eaton's testimony is entirely credible in the light of modern knowledge of alcoholism. None of the factors that lead men to drink to excess—lack of prestige, psychological insecurity, etc.— was present in Grant's case in 1864, if at any time in the war.

Probably the decision in Butler's favor was made by President Lincoln for an urgent political reason. It was hardly a secret in 1864 and it became widely known afterward that Lincoln had asked Butler to accept the Union party's vice presidential nomination before Andrew Johnson was considered for the place.[25] At

23 Smith, op. cit., pp. 52–55; 174–80.

24 John Eaton, *Grant, Lincoln and the Freedmen* (Longmans, Green, and Company [New York, 1907]), pp. 304–5.

25 Boston *Post,* August 10, 1893; Anna L. Dawes, *Charles Sumner* (Dodd, Mead and Company [New York, 1892]), p. 200; Joseph M. Rogers, "Men Who Might have been President," *Review of Reviews,* May, 1896, CLXII, 567; George O. Seilhamer, *History of the Republican Party* (Judge Publishing Co. [New York, 1898]), I, 134–35; Ellis P. Oberholtzer, *Abraham Lincoln* (George W. Jacobs & Company [Philadelphia, 1904]), p. 310.

the least it would have been embarrassing to Lincoln for Butler effectively to have been demoted on the eve of the nominating convention. At the worst an offense to Butler at this time might have cost the President the renomination he ardently desired. The Radical element of the Republican party thoroughly disapproved of Lincoln's cautious and moderate policy and more or less openly insisted upon his either adopting sterner measures or giving way to someone who would meet this demand. Such men as Benjamin F. Wade, Lyman Trumbull, Zachariah Chandler, Salmon P. Chase, Henry Winter Davis, Horace Greeley, E. R. Hoar, Parke Godwin, J. Murray Forbes, William Curtis Noyes, Wendell Phillips, Governor Andrew, and Thaddeus Stevens made little or no effort to conceal their hostility to Lincoln and their desire to see the White House occupied by a more resolute man, by somebody like Grant, Frémont, or Butler.

Chase was interested only in his own chances of being nominated for the presidency, although he, too, wanted Butler for his running mate. Forbes preferred Lincoln to Butler. Andrew and Hoar, undoubtedly, and one or two of the others mentioned, probably, felt the same way Forbes did. The rest of the anti-Lincoln Republicans would have been satisfied with Butler's nomination. Butler was not indifferent to the possibility of his nomination for the vice presidency—no American could be indifferent to such a possibility—but he did nothing vigorously to further his chances. However, if he had been put aside in favor of Smith he could well have been provoked into active opposition to Lincoln.

Incidentally, the fact that Butler was Lincoln's first choice for the vice presidency in 1864 would afford sufficient grounds, even if no others existed, for acquitting the General of charges of corruption at New Orleans or elsewhere during the Civil War. Lincoln felt it necessary to balance the Union party ticket with a war Democrat as vice presidential candidate, but the war Democrat did not have to be Butler and Lincoln, who was in a position to know the truth about Butler's conduct, would not have chosen a corrupt man for his running mate.

16

★★★★★★★★★★★★

Fort Fisher

During the late summer and early fall of 1864 it was rumored that the Copperheads intended to make trouble in New York on election day. Senator Edwin D. Morgan of New York took this talk seriously enough to ask the Secretary of War to send some troops to preserve order there. Stanton wrote to Grant about the matter without directly instructing him to do anything concerning it. When Grant disregarded this broad hint the Secretary specifically ordered that Butler be sent to New York to keep order there. On being given this assignment Butler asked Grant to let him have 5,000 men and at least two batteries of Napoleons (smoothbore brass cannon of approximately 4½ inch bore, firing 12 pound shot.) "A show of force," he said, harking back to his militia days, "might prevent trouble."

Butler arrived in New York a week before election day and established his headquarters at the Hoffman House in Madison Square. Within the next few days he made himself thoroughly familiar with the geography of the city and decided where to station his troops. The plan he adopted was determined partly by political considerations, partly by the fact that New York was on an island and had nine ferryboat landings on one side, ten on the other. (New York then comprised only the present borough of Manhattan and there were no bridges across, much less tunnels under, either the East River or the Hudson River.) He requisitioned four ferryboats, each capable of carrying more than a regiment of infantry and four pieces of artillery and stationed them on the New Jersey side of the Hudson River. Tactically it would have been better to have had at least one of these craft on the Brooklyn side of the East River; their actual placement was determined because under the law permitting soldiers to vote a man in the field could use an absentee ballot, but anyone who might be in his own state on election day had to go to his home town to vote. If it could be prevented Butler did not want Lincoln to lose the votes of any of the large number of New Yorkers among his force, so the troops were stationed in New Jersey, to remain there unless they were needed in New York.

In addition to his improvised troopships Butler arranged to have gunboats anchored off Mackerelville (an area bounded on the north and south by Eleventh and Thirteenth Streets, on the east and west by First Avenue and Avenue A) which was supposed to contain the toughest element in the city; off Wall Street, to cover the subtreasury building and the customs house; and off the High Bridge in case any attempt was made to sabotage the aqueduct there. Four tugboats were kept ready for general use, with two of them on each side of Manhattan. All of these craft kept up full steam on election day and Butler's headquarters was able to communicate with them quickly by telegraph and wigwag. More than 50 other stations, including one near every polling place, manned by army officers wearing civilian clothes, also had telegraphic connections with the Hoffman House. Thus Butler was in a position quickly to move a large military force into any part of the city, but without a single soldier visible nobody, including angry Democrats, could allege coercion.

At Grant's request the troops were returned to the front immediately after election day. However, Butler was given permission to remain briefly in New York to attend a reception arranged by a committee of prominent citizens who desired an opportunity to express their gratitude for his influence "in preserving the peace of the city during the recent election."[1] One of the high-

---

[1] Loyal Citizens of New York to Butler, November 10, 1864, as quoted in Jesse Ames Marshall (compiler) *Private and Official Correspondence of Gen. Benjamin F. Butler* (Privately issued [Boston, 1917]), V, 337. (Hereafter cited as *POC*).

lights of this affair was a speech in which the Reverend Henry Ward Beecher proposed Butler's nomination for the presidency in 1868.

For some time before Butler was sent to New York the Navy Department had been trying to persuade the War Department to furnish troops for a joint expedition against Fort Fisher (near the southern tip of Federal Point, between the Atlantic Ocean and the Cape Fear River) which commanded the approach to Wilmington, North Carolina. Since this was the only major port still available to blockade runners it seemed to the Secretary of the Navy that to close it, "and thus terminate the intercourse of the [Confederate States] with the outside world, would be like severing the jugular vein in the human system."[2]

At the urging of the Navy Department, Grant had Fort Fisher reconnoitered in September, 1864. Because the report he received convinced him that an attack by ordinary means could not succeed he was unwilling to furnish any troops for an expedition against it.

The Navy Department had almost forgotten about Fort Fisher when an extraordinary method of attacking it, suggested by Butler, revived interest in the matter.

Butler had read that an accidental explosion of 1,000 barrels of gunpowder in a canalboat in England had wrought great destruction for many miles around. With this event in mind he proposed that a cargo of gunpowder, stowed in a shallow draught ship in such a manner that all of it could be detonated at once, by electricity or some other means, be exploded after the vessel had been beached close aboard Fort Fisher.

A group of experts considered this idea and concluded "that the explosion [of 300 tons of gunpowder] would injure the earthworks to a very great extent, render the guns unserviceable for a time, and probably affect the garrison to such a degree as to deprive them of power to resist the passage of naval vessels by

---

[2] Gideon Welles, "Lincoln's Triumph in 1864," *Atlantic Monthly*, April, 1878, XLI, 459.

the fort and the carrying of those works by immediate assault."[3]
Butler was as optimistic about the thing as the experts were. He
believed the gasses generated by the burning gunpowder might
make it impossible for the men in the fort to breathe and that
enough damage would be done to permit even a small force to take
the place if the explosion were followed by an immediate assault.

There were some men, including Lincoln and Grant, who had
little or no faith in Butler's scheme. However, it had to be tried
because if it worked it would make all coast defense fortifications
useless.

An obsolete gunboat, the U.S.S. *Louisiana,* was selected for
conversion into a water-borne bomb, or torpedo as it was called.
The experts who prepared her regarded electricity as too un-
reliable an agent for firing such a large mass of gunpowder as a
ship's cargo. They decided to use three separate clockworks to
drop weights upon a number of percussion caps in a tub filled
with gunpowder from which Gomez fuses (rubber tubes containing fulminating powder) were to run throughout the ship. As
a precaution, in case these devices did not work, a slow match
led to the tub of gunpowder. Finally, to prevent the cargo from
falling into the Confederates' hands if nothing else caused it to
explode, the ship was to be set on fire by the men who beached
her just before she was abandoned.

Porter, who was put in command of the naval part of the Fort
Fisher expedition, gathered a huge fleet at Hampton Roads in
mid-November. Late in the same month Grant directed Butler
to assign 6,500 men from the Army of the James to the expedition. Although Butler's troops were to attack a position in Butler's
department, Porter asked Grant not to let Butler accompany the
expedition. Perhaps, but not probably, influenced by Porter's request, Grant decided to have Weitzel command the troops. This

[3] *Official Records of the Union and Confederate Navies in the War
of the Rebellion* (Government Printing Office [Washington, D.C., 1894–
1922]), Ser. 1, XI, 216. (Hereafter cited as *ORN*)

choice did not please Porter at all for he hated Weitzel only a
little less bitterly than he did Butler, and for the same reason—
because of their reports about the trifling results of his bombardment of the forts below New Orleans. On learning of Weitzel's
assignment Porter forehandedly wrote to the Assistant Secretary
of the Navy (who was Porter's brother-in-law) that the Fort
Fisher expedition seemed likely to fail because Grant had not
furnished enough troops for it. Porter also said that if *he* should
be successful *he* would be more fortunate than the present prospect
indicated.[4] Fox showed this letter widely enough to make sure
that if things did go wrong the Navy would not be held to
blame.[5]

Butler, who was keenly interested in the powder boat experiment, and, of course, wanted to witness its trial, apparently remained unaware that Grant did not expect him personally to
command the troops until he received the following message from
Grant on December 6:

> The first object of the expedition under Gen. Weitzel is to
> close . . . the port of Wilmington. If successful in this, the
> second will be to capture Wilmington itself. . . . The object
> of the expedition will be gained on effecting a landing on the
> main land. . . . Should such a landing be effected, . . . the
> troops should intrench themselves, and by co-operating with
> the Navy effect the reduction and capture of [Fort Fisher]. . . .
> Should Fort Fisher and the point of land on which it is built
> fall into the hands of our troops immediately on landing, . . .
> it will be worth the attempt to capture Wilmington by a forced
> march and surprise. . . . The details for the execution are en-
> trusted to you and the officer immediately in command of the
> troops.
>
>   P. S. Should the troops under General Weitzel fail to effect
> a landing at or near Fort Fisher, they will be returned to the
> army operating against Richmond without delay.[6]

---

[4] Mrs. Butler to Butler, December 24, 1864; *POC*, V, 436.
[5] George H. Gordon, *A War Diary of Events in the Great Rebellion*
(James R. Osgood and Company [Boston, 1882]), p. 368.
[6] Grant to Butler, December 6, 1864; *POC*, V, 380–81.

To his great surprise Grant was quickly told by Butler of his intention of personally commanding the troops. Since the general of an army from which an expeditionary force was being drawn could not be denied the right to command his own men in his own department Grant either had to relieve Butler from all duty or let him go to Fort Fisher. Comforting himself with the thought that Weitzel would be in charge of the landing party, Grant did not forbid Butler to go.[7]

From conversations with Grant and from Grant's written orders Butler gathered that he was to stay with the Fort Fisher expedition until a landing had been made, then he was to decide whether or not a dash should be made toward Wilmington. If necessary he was, he understood, to go as far as Wilmington with the troops before returning to the Army of the James near Petersburg. Weitzel was never shown Grant's orders of December 6 so he knew only whatever Butler told him about the aims of the expedition and what the troops were expected to do.

Porter's conduct at this time clearly indicates a subconscious, if not a conscious, desire on his part to see the Fort Fisher expedition fail. He sailed December 13 for Beaufort, North Carolina, to load the *Louisiana* with gunpowder and to supply his other vessels with ammunition. To his way of thinking the expedition had already been delayed for two months so he did not feel there was any need for him to hurry. His fleet and Butler's transports were scheduled to meet off New Inlet, North Carolina, after nightfall, Thursday, December 15. Butler reached the rendezvous at the appointed time; Porter got there just before dark, Sunday, December 18. Thus three days of ideal weather were wasted, except by some of the soldiers who improved their enforced leisure by swimming and fishing.

When Porter finally did arrive he decided, *without consulting Butler at all,* to commence operations immediately. About 8 P.M.,

[7] Horace Porter, "Campaigning with Grant," *The Century,* July, 1897, LIV, 539; see also Adam Badeau, *Military History of Ulysses S. Grant* (D. Appleton and Company [New York, 1881]), II, 236.

he notified Butler, in writing, that the powder boat was on its way toward shore to be exploded less than an hour and a half later. Butler, Weitzel, and Colonel Cyrus B. Comstock (of Grant's staff who was present as an observer) protested vigorously to Porter that the Confederates would have a whole night's time to repair any damage done to the fort. Porter was persuaded to recall the *Louisiana* and by luck a fast tug was able to over-haul her before it was too late.

Monday morning's weather was so stormy as to make it obvious that no landing could possibly be attempted for several days. Acting on Porter's advice, Butler directed his transports to put into Beaufort until the gale subsided. On December 23 Butler sent word that he and his troops would rejoin Porter at sunset the following day. *After receiving this message* Porter decided to explode the powder boat at 1:20 A.M., December 24, a good 15 hours before the return of the troops was promised. His official explanation to his superiors for his action in the matter was that he felt that he could not afford to lose the spell of good weather following the three days' storm "and the transports with the troops not making their appearance [he] determined to attack Fort Fisher and its outworks."[8]

While the *Louisiana* was being loaded with gunpowder Porter had expressed an opinion that the explosion would "wind up Fort Fisher and the works along the beach."[9] In view of this forecast Porter may very well have expected, as a contemporary suggested he did, that a few marines could step ashore at day-break and accept the surrender of Fort Fisher's survivors, if there were any, thus gaining great kudos for himself and the Navy at the expense of Butler and the Army.[10]

Porter's hopes, whatever they may have been, and the great expectations of the other ordnance experts exploded along with the *Louisiana*. She blew up noisily enough to waken men asleep

---

[8] *ORN,* Series 1, XI, 247.

[9] Ibid., p. 217.

[10] H. C. Lockwood, "The Capture of Fort Fisher," *The Atlantic Monthly,* May, 1871, XXVII, 627.

in Fort Fisher, but there was absolutely no damage done to the place.

Before Butler's "torpedo" was tested everybody in the Navy, from Porter down, confidently expected the explosion to level Fort Fisher's walls; when the experiment failed everybody in the Navy denied ever having had any faith in it. However, Butler, who never disavowed his brain child, argued to the end of his life that the thing he proposed had not actually been tried. In a very real sense he was right. Although he had emphasized the need to run the powder boat hard aground in order to cause the shock wave to be reflected from a solid surface, the *Louisiana* was not beached. Instead she was anchored between 200 yards (Porter's estimate) and 1,200 yards offshore. Butler had stressed the importance of as nearly instantaneous as possible a detonation of all of the gunpowder in the ship to prevent the initial burst from scattering the rest of it to the four winds. Either because the fuses were not laid in the matter Butler suggested they should have been (as he said happened), because the clockworks and the slow match all failed to work, or for some other reason there were several small explosions as the ship burned instead of one big one.

By the time Butler learned of Porter's plans the *Louisiana* had already been exploded 70 miles from Beaufort. Ordering the transports to sail as soon as they could finish loading provisions and water, Butler departed for Fort Fisher. When he arrived there at sunset, December 24, he sent a staff officer to the flagship to arrange for a conference with Porter. The Admiral "returned word that he was too much fatigued to give them an audience, but would receive General Weitzel and Colonel Comstock early in the morning."[11]

In the morning Porter agreed to bombard the fort, even though he was perfectly confident he had already silenced it, and to provide a covering fire for a landing of the troops about five

---

[11] Ibid., p. 630.

miles north of the fort. He then called his ships' captains to the flagship to receive their orders for the day. While they were there he asked what they thought of the Navy's gunnery so far. When one of them "replied that it was fair; [Porter] said he considered it first rate."[12] Others have called it poor. Grant said the bombardment did little damage to the fort.[13] Colonel William Lamb, the fort's commanding officer, described the Union vessel's gunnery as "diffuse, not calculated to effect any particular damage, and so wild that at least one-third of the missiles fell in the river beyond the fort or in the bordering marshes."[14]

Because Porter's conferences kept him busy all morning it was noontime before his ships went into action. When they finally did so they fired a great deal more slowly "than on the day before which had witnessed the expenditure of nearly half their ammunition."[15]

The first troops landed at about 1 P.M. and some 2,500 of them made their way ashore without much trouble. However, in midafternoon the sea became too rough for small boats to be safe and no more landings could be made.

Weitzel pushed toward the fort with the first 500 men who got ashore. On the way he captured a few Confederates in an outlying earthwork. To his surprise they were from a division which he knew had been defending Richmond only a few days earlier. A little later he bagged some men who said they had been sent outside of the fort because there was no room for them in it. These things convinced him that the place had been strongly reinforced. Surveying the fort through a telescope from a distance of 150 yards he saw that its grass covered walls were intact and he counted 16 apparently undamaged cannons facing the direction from which the troops would have to advance. In

---

12 Daniel Ammen, *The Old Navy and the New* (J. B. Lippincott Company [Philadelphia, 1891]), p. 404.

13 U. S. Grant, *Personal Memoirs of U. S. Grant* (Charles L. Webster & Company [New York, 1885–86]), II, 392.

14 Robert U. Johnson and Clarence C. Clough (editors), *Battles and Leaders of the Civil War* (The Century Co. [New York, 1884–88]), IV, 647.

15 Lockwood, loc cit., pp. 629–30.

view of these things he advised Butler that it would be suicidal to make an assault with the force available. About the time Butler received this word he learned that the warships were nearly out of ammunition and that a rapidly falling barometer indicated an approaching storm. Before deciding what to do he took a good look at Fort Fisher from the deck of a steamer small enough to run close in with the shore. Having satisfied himself that the condition of the fort had been correctly described by Weitzel, Butler wrote to Porter: "I see nothing further that can be done by the land forces. I shall, therefore, sail for Hampton Roads as soon as the transport fleet can be got in order."[16]

Porter, always sanguine about the results of his own activities, protested this decision, mildly in a note to Butler, violently in a report to the Secretary of the Navy. He wrote to Butler:

> I think they [the troops] would have found it an easier conquest than is supposed. I do not, however, pretend to place my opinion in opposition to General Weitzel, whom I know to be an accomplished soldier and engineer . . . whose opinion has great weight with me.[17]

He told the Secretary the fort had been "so blown up, burst up, and torn up that the people in it had no intention of fighting any longer" and "there never was a fort that invited soldiers to walk in and take possession more plainly than Fort Fisher."[18]

Actually Fort Fisher's condition was correctly described by Weitzel. The only significant damage the naval bombardment did was to dismount one cannon on the landward side of the works. The commanding officer of the fort said later the other guns were silent only because he had ordered their fire held in the hope of catching the Yankees in a trap. "If they had attacked," he added, "I could have opened a fire of grape canister on the narrow beach which no troops could have survived."[19]

However, as Admiral Daniel Ammen once commented, if

[16] *ORN,* Series 1, XI, 251.
[17] Ibid., p. 252.
[18] Ibid., pp. 261–62.
[19] *Battles and Leaders of the Civil War,* IV, 646.

Porter believed anything he "never thought it worth while to inquire as to the facts."[20]

Leaving Fort Fisher early December 27, Butler was back at Fortress Monroe by eight o'clock that night. He promptly telegraphed a preliminary report to Grant at City Point, saying he had found an assault to be utterly impracticable and had withdrawn his troops. The following morning he went to Grant's headquarters to explain personally why he had returned without having accomplished his mission. Grant was not at all satisfied with the explanation offered to him. He "considered the whole affair a gross and culpable failure" and said "he proposed to make it his business to ascertain who was to blame." Because he had not positively ordered an assault on Fort Fisher he was not concerned over the fact that none had been made, "but he was exceedingly dissatisfied that the important part of his instruction as to gaining and holding an intrenched position had been disobeyed, . . . the troops withdrawn, and all further efforts abandoned." He became highly incensed on learning that Weitzel had never been shown the orders of December 6 issued for his special guidance.[21]

Butler sought to justify his conduct by arguing that he had not effected a landing within the purview of his orders because scarcely more than a third of his men, with only 40 rounds of ammunition each, and no artillery had been able to get ashore; that the naval vessels had exhausted their ammunition and would have to return to port for several days, leaving the troops unprotected; and that a large force detached from the army of Northern Virginia was approaching his rear.

These claims did not impress Grant. He soon decided that Butler had flagrantly disregarded his nondiscretionary orders to hold any beach-head he might gain and asked to have him removed from command of the Army of the James.

On January 7, 1865 Butler was relieved and directed to repair to Lowell. The next day he published a farewell address to the

---

20 Ammen, op. cit., pp. 461–62.
21 Porter, loc cit., p. 368.

Army of the James in which he praised the Army's conduct and said,

> Knowing your willing obedience to orders, witnessing your ready devotion of your blood to your country's cause, I have been chary of the precious charge confided to me. I have refused to order the useless sacrifice of the lives of such soldiers, and I am relieved from your command. The wasted blood of my men does not stain my garments. For my action I am responsible to God and my country.[22]

Although this language was highly insubordinate, Grant, to whom it obviously referred, took no notice of it except that he opposed Butler's reassignment to any sort of duty.

Butler's dismissal evoked widespread discussion and as the full story of the Fort Fisher expedition unfolded there were many who came to believe the General had been unfairly treated because Porter should have been held equally responsible for the debacle.

Although Porter was not even reprimanded, it may be inferred that the Navy Department considered him blameworthy at least to some extent. When plans were being made for a second Fort Fisher expedition the Assistant Secretary of the Navy informed the Admiral that the country would not forgive another failure. Interestingly, too, the naval force, again commanded by Porter, did much better shooting in its second attack than in its first one.

Soon after Butler left Virginia the Commerce Committee of the House of Representatives decided to investigate a report that he had given G. W. Lane of Baltimore permission to trade with the Confederates in North Carolina. When General O. C. Ord, Butler's successor as commanding officer of the Army of the James, heard of this he wrote to Grant:

> I propose . . . to order a military commission with power [to investigate rumors of extensive and corrupt trade with the

---

[22] *POC,* V, 475–76.

Confederates in the vicinity of Norfolk]. General [George H.] Gordon, shrewd and fond of such hunting, . . . Colonel [probably Robert B.] Potter, . . . and Major [probably S. Tyler] Read, . . . I propose as members. I think this report . . . is a sword with two edges, and . . . may be used by politicians. . . . If we can fasten the matter upon either the Treasury or Benjamin F's agents, and clap them in the guard house, . . . the politicians will find they have started the wrong rabbit, with a bushy tail. . . . I write you . . . rather than telegraph, for all our telegrams are viséd in Washington. . . . If you can suggest a better man than Gordon for the leader, please do.[23]

Apparently Grant was unable to think of a better man than Gordon so he headed the commission which tried long and hard to pin something on Butler. When a friend called Butler's attention to the committee's activities he wrote: "Conscious that in nothing I have done there [in the Department of Virginia and North Carolina] I can have deserved any reproach, I am entirely indifferent as to what investigations or inquiries are set afoot."[24]

His confidence was well-founded. Gordon discovered only that Butler had recommended to the President that Lane be allowed to trade with the Confederates in Chowan County and this recommendation had been accepted just as hundreds like it made by various officers had been.

The Commerce Committee, which broadened its investigation to cover all of the facts connected with commerce between the North and South from the beginning of the war, found there had been much trading done, apparently under the sanction of law, and that such trade had been extremely harmful to the Union cause, but that no individual could be blamed for these things.

---

[23] Ord to Grant, January 19, 1865, *POC,* V, 503–4.
[24] Butler to Major W. P. Webster, March 20, 1865; *POC,* V, 565.

17

Home From the Wars

Butler was given a hero's welcome on his return to Lowell. The biggest crowd the city had ever seen met his train. At a reception in Huntington Hall the mayor expressed the very real feelings of the General's neighbors and friends, saying:

> On behalf of this committee [which had arranged the affair] and this vast assemblage of your fellow-citizens, I bid you a cordial welcome to your home, assuring you, sir, that to whatever circumstances we are indebted for your visit, our confidence in your patriotism, integrity, and ability is unimpaired.[1]

Responding to the mayor, Butler gave a lengthy account of his entire course of action since his return to active duty 13 months earlier. Among other things he described his efforts to further and speed the exchange of prisoners of war, said his attack on Petersburg had failed because Gillmore had disobeyed orders, gave his views about the Fort Fisher affair, said he had not meant adversely to criticize anyone in his farewell address to the Army of the James, and emphatically asserted that Negroes had demonstrated their ability and willingness to fight. He seemed particularly proud of what he had done for the freedmen in his department. In this connection he claimed, with some little justification, to have brought order out of chaos in Negro affairs in Virginia and to have made it possible for many former slaves to become self-supporting.

In view of Butler's really praiseworthy handling of Negro affairs it was natural for President Lincoln to turn to him, among

---

[1] *General Butler at Home,* 1.

others, for advice about the future of the many thousands of Negro soldiers. Lincoln gravely doubted that Negro veterans could live peaceably in the United States. He even believed, as he told Butler, that it would be best for everybody if all of the Negroes in the country could be shipped to some fertile place, with a pleasant climate, which they could have for their own. The President asked Butler if he thought it would be too difficult for the Navy to carry out such an evacuation. Calling at the White House two days later, Butler said he thought "exporting" the Negro population would not be possible. Even if every seaworthy naval and merchant vessel owned by the United States were used for the purpose he did not think Negroes could be transported to the nearest place he thought fit for their habitation—the island of Santo Domingo—as rapidly as colored children would be born. Lincoln admitted that this estimate was probably correct and asked Butler if he had any other idea of what could be done with Negro soldiers. He did. He would like to take them to the Isthmus of Darien (Panama) and dig the ship canal the United States had long wanted to construct there. The men in question had enlisted for three years or the duration of the war. Nearly all of them owed the government at least another year of service, many of them two years or more, and until the war officially ended all soldiers could be sent wherever the commander in chief might direct. If, said Butler, he were put in command of the Negro troops, whose confidence he believed he had (as he certainly did) he would engage himself to take them to the Isthmus and build the canal. One-third of his force would be employed as excavators, another third at erecting buildings, the rest at planting vegetables and raising animals for the subsistence of all of them. In his view the project would cost the government no more than the men's pay because the clothing they would need would otherwise be eaten by moths while the Army was so well supplied with arms, wagons, shovels, etc., that the amount of such property they would have to take would not be missed. After his labor force had established itself a petition would be sent to Congress, under the President's recommendation, for the transportation at government expense of his and his men's families to the Isthmus. At best the canal would be dug and a colony able to defend it would be established; at least Lincoln's fear of an immediate race war would be alleviated.

Disregarding any technical difficulties this plan might have involved, one cannot help wondering what Butler would have done to protect his people against yellow fever—the real reason Ferdinand de Lesseps was unable to build a Panama Canal in the 1880's. None of the theories about the epidemiology of yellow fever that Butler held to the end of his life was correct; yet, being a thoughtful man and not without considerable scientific ability, he might have recognized the connection between the presence of mosquitoes and *el vomito*—if he had not died too soon of yellow fever.

Lincoln thought rather well of Butler's idea—there was meat in it, he said—but he was not willing to act on it at once. Before he reached a decision, or at least before he communicated any decision he may have made to Butler, the President was assassinated.

Butler was in New Jersey on his way from Washington to Lowell when he learned of Lincoln's death. He immediately returned to the capital.

A short time after Andrew Johnson succeeded to the presidency he asked Butler for advice about the best procedure for trying Jefferson Davis if he should be captured. Butler said Davis ought to be tried by a military commission if he were arrested in a locality where there was no civil government recognized by the United States; if he were taken at a place where a recognized civil government existed he would have to be tried in the regular courts. Johnson then asked Butler to draft a plan for the trial of the (as yet uncaught) Confederate President. Several weeks later Butler presented to Johnson an elaborate memorandum suggesting a trial by a military commission of 13 ranking Army officers, with a right of appeal to the Supreme Court of the United States reserved to Davis in the event of his conviction.

Since Butler's resignation of his commission, submitted on April 14, 1865 (four days less than four years after he had gone off to the wars) was not accepted until November 30, 1865 he would have been available for employment by the prosecution if Davis had been brought before a military commission. It was suggested at a Cabinet meeting that Butler be so employed. All agreed that he would be suitable in most respects, but some thought he might be an unpleasant associate and foresaw a danger of his thinking more of himself than of the case at bar. Gideon Welles believed, nonetheless, that Butler ought to be of counsel for the prosecution. Welles did not have unreserved confidence in Butler as a politician, but did esteem his great ability, courage, strength, and audacity as a lawyer. Welles thought, too, that personal feelings ought not to be allowed to control so important a matter as choosing counsel to prosecute such a criminal as Welles considered Davis to be.[2]

Within a month of his accession to the presidency Johnson adopted and set in motion a modified version of Lincoln's Reconstruction policy. Thankful that he would be free from legislative interference for more than six months (until the opening of the Thirty-ninth Congress in December, 1865) Johnson issued a series of executive orders removing restrictions on commercial intercourse with the southern states, ending the blockade, amnestying many former Confederates, etc. Following Lincoln's example, Johnson appointed provisional governors for a number of southern states. (Lincoln had already appointed such governors for Tennessee, Louisiana, Arkansas, and Virginia.) These governors were to preside over conventions which were expected to repeal their states' ordinances of secession and their slave laws, to repudiate the Confederate war debt, and to arrange for the election of United States senators and representatives, state legislators, etc. Johnson suggested to the governors he named that it would be wise for their states to enfranchise all Negroes who could read

---

[2] Gideon Welles, *Diary of Gideon Welles* (Houghton Mifflin Company [Boston, 1911]), II, 365–68, passim.

and write or who paid taxes on real estate worth $250 or more. This would place the freedmen in the South upon a footing similar to that occupied by Negroes in the North, and, as Johnson said to the provisional governor of Mississippi, it would completely foil the Radical Republicans, who (it seemed to Johnson) were "wild upon Negro franchise," in their scheme "to keep the southern States from renewing their relations with the Union by not accepting their senators and representatives."[3]

Because Johnson was a Jeffersonian Democrat, albeit a war Democrat, he firmly believed the states alone could determine who were their citizens and what the qualifications of their voters should be; consequently he did not make even limited Negro suffrage a basic part of his Reconstruction policy.

Johnson's recommendation about Negro suffrage could have been adopted, as he remarked, "with perfect safety,"[4] from the southern whites' point of view since it would have created too few Negro voters to have been an important factor in any state or even in any community. Instead of accepting Johnson's well meant, if somewhat cynical, advice the conventions called by the provisional governors more or less grudgingly abolished slavery and reluctantly repudiated the Confederate war debt. Then, as if determined to alienate northern Moderates, the southern states' legislatures enacted various laws, which came to be known as "black codes." These measures conferred upon Negroes the right to sue and be sued and to marry and have legitimate children, but they also prohibited Negroes from possessing firearms or other weapons and provided that colored orphans or colored children whose parents could not or would not support them were to be apprenticed to suitable white persons, preferably their former owners; that in the management and control of such apprentices their "masters and mistresses" were to have the right to inflict moderate, but not cruel or inhuman punishment (with the dis-

---

[3] Edward McPherson, *Political History of the United States . . . during . . . Reconstruction* (Philp & Solomons [Washington, D.C., 1871]), pp. 19–20.

[4] *Ibid.*, p. 19.

tinction to be made by the white master or mistress); that farm laborers must make yearly contracts with employers in January and that if a contract were not fulfilled the laborer was to forfeit all wages earned up to the time the contract was broken.

Southerners insisted in the 1860's, southern apologists have insisted since then, that the black codes were no harsher than were the laws dealing with free Negroes in most northern states. This thesis may be entirely valid, but if the southern leaders had deliberately undertaken to furnish ammunition to the Radicals nothing could have served the purpose better than the black codes did. Differing widely among themselves as to what might be the best Reconstruction policy, most northerners agreed wholeheartedly that former slave masters could not be trusted to treat Negroes fairly and decently. Southerners said the black codes conferred upon the freedmen rights they had not enjoyed as slaves. However, these laws also (and hardly accidentally) made white persons the sole judges of the conduct of their black employees (a privilege certain to be abused); they made it nearly impossible for Negroes to secure a just return for their labor and punished them for being poor; they were designed to force Negroes to work when their services were urgently needed and to permit them to be dismissed and neglected at other seasons. The enactment of such laws could do nothing but support the claim advanced by the Radicals that the South would substitute peonage for chattel slavery if steps were not taken to prevent it.

As if the actions of the conventions and the adoption of the black codes had not done enough to flaunt their intransigence the former Confederate states elected as their delegates to the Thirty-ninth Congress four Confederate generals, five colonels, six members of Jefferson Davis's Cabinet, and 58 Confederate senators or congressmen. Plainly the South expected to be allowed to return to "the Union as it was," except for the purely nominal abolition of slavery.

For a while Butler was more puzzled about Johnson's Reconstruction policy than opposed to it. In September, 1865 the General spoke approvingly of the President's policy, so far as he understood it. As time clarified Johnson's policy Butler came, in common with most northerners, to dislike it. Not satisfied with being merely an adverse critic, Butler offered for the country's consideration a plan less easy on the South than Johnson's, but much milder than the proposals being made by the Radical Republicans. He thought there should be legislation to forestall compensation by the federal government for emancipated slaves, to disfranchise the leading Confederates (who had been, after all, rebels against the United States), and to prevent the South from benefiting from a representation in Congress based in part on its nonvoting Negro population. The South's arrogant rejection of all such relatively moderate programs as Butler's drove him and many other northerners into the Radicals' camp and brought on Radical Reconstruction with all of its mistakes and horrors, real or alleged.

A battle between President Johnson and the Radicals began as soon as the Thirty-ninth Congress opened its first session. The Congress would neither admit the legitimacy of the governors the President had appointed nor seat the senators and representatives the southern states had elected; the President refused to budge from the position he had taken. When the session ended Johnson and the Radicals carried their cases to the people, each appealing for the election of a friendly Fortieth Congress.

The Johnsonites took the initiative by holding a convention on August 14, 1866 at Philadelphia in a "wigwam" built for the occasion. The call for this gathering, issued by the National Union Club, urged the choice of delegates who agreed

that the maintenance inviolate of the rights of the States, and especially of each State to order and control its own domestic concerns, according to its own judgment exclusively, subject only to the Constitution of the United States, is essential to that balance of power on which the perfection and endurance of our political fabric depends, and the overthrow of that system by the usurpation and centralization of power in Congress would be a revolution, dangerous to republican government and destructive of liberty.[5]

(The fact that the Johnsonites and the Radicals both called themselves National Unionists introduces an element of confusion for anyone who attempts to follow the course of the 1866 campaign through contemporaneous newspapers. Both groups thought there was a magic quality attached to the word Union, so each sought to appropriate it. Really the Radicals had a somewhat better claim to it since the Republicans had been the dominant element in the original National Union party, the coalition of Republicans and war Democrats, which nominated Lincoln to succeed himself in 1864.)

To the Johnsonites' great satisfaction their convention was attended by men from every state and territory, hence it could be called a national gathering. Significantly, however, there were far more Democrats than Republicans among those present. In the caustic language of the New York *Tribune* 90 per cent of the delegates were "Rebels and Copperheads." Of course, the *Tribune*'s Radical bias colored its estimate, but many of the delegates were former Confederates and some few of them were notorious Copperheads. Two of the latter, Clement L. Vallandigham of Ohio and Fernando Wood of New York, underwent some vigorous arm twisting before they decided not to occupy the seats to which they had been elected.

As the convention was called to order General Darius N. Couch of Massachusetts, who had commanded a corps in the Army of the Potomac, and Governor James L. Orr of South Carolina, walking arm in arm, led the delegates from their states, arm in arm, into the hall.

This bathetic performance led the Radicals, citing Genesis, VII, 2 and 8, to describe the wigwam as a political Noah's ark into which there entered two by two beasts that are not clean, fowls, and everything that creeps upon the earth.

The "arm in arm" convention, of course, lauded President

---

[5] Ibid., pp. 118–19.

Johnson and everything he had proposed or done, called for the election of Conservatives to the next Congress, and asserted that the Radicals were subverting the Union by opposing Johnson's Reconstruction policy.

Immediately after the convention adjourned a committee of two men from each state hastened to Washington to present an official copy of its proceedings to the President. In delivering his thanks to the committee Johnson emotionally referred to the entrance, "arm in arm," of the delegates from South Carolina and Massachusetts. Excited by the applause this remark evoked, he continued:

The nation is in peril. We have just passed through a mighty, a bloody, a momentous ordeal; and yet we do not find ourselves free from the difficulties and dangers that first surrounded us. While our brave soldiers, both officers and men, have by their heroism won laurels imperishable, there are still greater and more important duties to perform; and while we have had their co-operation in the field, now that they have returned to civil pursuits, we need their support in our efforts to restore the Government and perpetuate peace.[6]

This speech furnished the Radicals with fresh ammunition for use against Johnson. For several months past some southern newspapers had been urging the President to call together the southern men who had been elected to Congress (but not allowed to take their seats) and their northern "fellow travelers," to recognize them as the legitimate members of Congress and to order the Army to evict the Radical usurpers from the capitol. This advice had been echoed by a Democratic senator from Kentucky and by the (Democratic) Chicago *Times*. In Virginia a prominent Democrat had told an audience that the country was on the brink of a bloody revolution. A New York Democrat had asserted that unless moderate and judicious statesmanship intervened (by which he meant unless the members elected to Congress by the southern states were promptly admitted) there would be a civil war more terrible than the one just ended. In the light of these and similar

[6] Ibid., p. 127.

events many of those who heard or read the President's speech inferred that he was contemplating a *coup d'etat.* Today nobody imagines that Johnson entertained any idea of trying to establish a dictatorship, but many of his contemporaries thought he did; the Radicals felt certain of it.

Early in the spring of 1866 Johnson was invited to attend the laying of the cornerstone of a monument to the memory of the late Senator Stephen A. Douglas of Illinois. This invitation afforded him an opportunity, as he put it, to make "a swing around the circle of the Union" and personally explain his Reconstruction policy to the people. He was supremely confident that his policy was being misrepresented by the press and would be heartily approved if it were more clearly understood. Between August 28 and September 10 he spoke at Baltimore, Philadelphia, West Point, Albany, Auburn, New York, Niagara Falls, Buffalo, Cleveland, Toledo, Ohio, Detroit, Chicago (where the monument was being erected), Springfield and Alton, Illinois, St. Louis, Indianapolis, Louisville, Cincinnati, Columbus, Ohio, Pittsburgh and Harrisburg, Pennsylvania. Addressing audiences containing Democrats, Conservative Republicans, and Radical Republicans in various proportions, he defended his policy at great length and scathingly denounced his congressional opponents. Throughout the trip he conducted himself as though he were stumping rural Tennessee in a hotly contested canvass, always speaking aggressively and disputatiously. On several occasions he threw dignity to the winds and bandied insults with Radical hecklers.

A couple of weeks after Johnson's tour ended the Radicals held a soldiers and sailors convention at Pittsburgh. For the sake of appearance this gathering had a former private soldier, L. Edwin Dudley, for its temporary chairman and many of its officials had been privates, seamen, or noncommissioned officers. However, it was actually managed by high ranking ex-officers, with Butler prominent among them. Besides leading the grand procession he made a number of impromptu speeches and a prepared address.

All of them were delivered in his usual pungent style, in all of them he paid his sarcastic respects to Jefferson Davis and General Robert E. Lee, both of whom he linked to Johnson. He also introduced a series of resolutions which were enthusiastically adopted. One of them commended the Thirty-ninth Congress for its wisdom, prudence, and justness in having submitted the fourteenth amendment to the federal Constitution to the states for ratification. That amendment, said Butler, clearly defined American citizenship and guaranteed all of his rights to every citizen; placed the right of representation in Congress on a just and equal basis, making the vote of a man in one state equally potent with the vote of a man in another state; righteously excluded from positions of honor and trust the chief conspirators and guiltiest rebels, whose crimes had drenched the land in blood; and put into the very frame of government the inviolability of the national debt and the nullity forever of all obligations in support of the Rebellion. A second resolution read: "It is unfortunate for the country that these propositions have not been received in the spirit of conciliation, clemency, and fraternal feeling in which they were offered, as they are the mildest terms ever granted to subdued rebels." Two other resolutions set forth the Radicals' theses that, as an executive officer, the President had no right to differ with the legislative branch of the government about policies; that his attempt to fasten his "scheme of reconstruction" upon the country was dangerous and unwise; that his efforts to maintain his policy had retarded the restoration of peace and unity and had converted "conquered rebels into impudent claimants" of rights they had forfeited and places they had desecrated; that the President's plan, if consummated, would render the nation's sacrifice useless and would make the Civil War truly the failure that Johnson's "present friends" (the Democratic party) had, in 1864, declared it to be; and that for the good of the country Congress had the "undoubted right to establish measures for the conduct of the revolted States and to pass all acts of legislation . . . necessary for the complete restoration of the Union."[7]

---

[7] *Ibid.,* pp. 242–43.

After the Pittsburgh convention adjourned Butler appeared before various state legislatures and spoke at a number of political rallies, always urging the choice of Radical senators and congressmen in the forthcoming election. His tour resembled a triumphal procession. He was received with wild enthusiasm everywhere he went except in New York. That city gave him a wild, but not a friendly, reception. At City Hall Park a hostile crowd tried to prevent him from speaking by shouting and throwing things at him. At first he remained as cool as the proverbial cucumber. He caught an apple as if it were a baseball and munched it while waiting for quiet. However, he soon lost his patience and began trying to outshout the crowd. His remarks, audible only to persons near at hand, were more interesting than persuasive. Among other things he told the crowd he had hanged better men than any of them were. Finally the police secured order enough to permit him to be heard, although it is to be doubted that he made many converts to his cause.

At Cincinnati, early in October, Butler suggested for the first time, that Johnson ought to be impeached. On this occasion he argued, as he was to do again and again, that the President deserved impeachment because he had corruptly appointed and removed federal officeholders; because he had not enforced various laws passed over his veto; because he had corruptly used his power to grant pardons; because he had usurped a prerogative of Congress by ending the Civil War by means of executive orders instead of by means of a treaty adopted with the advice and consent of the Senate; and because he had ridiculed Congress and sought to bring it into contempt by the speeches he had delivered while making his swing around the circle. Each of these actions, Butler declared, was a high crime and misdemeanor within the meaning of the federal Constitution. Therefore, he asserted, the President ought to be brought personally before the Senate to be dismissed from office if he pleaded guilty or, unless he could furnish bail, to be committed to jail while awaiting trial if he pleaded not guilty.

The Radicals naturally wanted such an ardent supporter of

their views as Butler in the Fortieth Congress, but he did not want to oppose his old friend George S. Boutwell, who represented the district in which Lowell was located (contiguous with Middlesex County). In these circumstances Butler became a "carpetbagger" candidate from the Fifth District (Essex County) wherein he had a summer home. At the Republican convention held in Salem 166 delegates voted for Butler's nomination; two other men got one vote each.

William Schouler, an old Whig and one of Butler's opponents in the days of the ten-hour movement, now a Conservative Republican, circulated handbills and wrote open letters saying that although he had been a Republican ever since the party's beginning, he could not and would not vote for Butler. Schouler argued that because Butler did not live in the Fifth District he was ineligible to represent it in Congress. To this Butler correctly replied that no constitutional provision, federal or state, barred anyone from representing a district in which he did not reside. Schouler also charged that Butler favored impeaching President Johnson. This, Butler bragged, was quite true.

Butler was elected to the House of Representatives by a substantial majority.

★★★★★★★★★★★★

18

Impeachment Manager

The elections of 1866 resulted in a small gain by the Democrats, but left the Republicans in overwhelming control of both Houses of the Fortieth Congress. By some peculiar logic the Radicals in the Thirty-ninth Congress (which would sit until noon of March 4, 1867) regarded the outcome of the canvass as a vote of confidence in them. In the belief that they were carrying out the expressed will of the electorate some of the more extreme Radicals undertook to impeach President Johnson soon after the lame duck session of the Thirty-ninth Congress began. Congressman-elect Butler heartily applauded these efforts.

On January 7, 1867 Congressman James M. Ashley of Ohio, echoing Butler, charged the President with having corruptly used his appointing power, having corruptly used his veto power, having corruptly interfered with various state elections, having corruptly disposed of public property (or as we should say today, of surplus war goods), and with other (unspecified) high crimes and misdemeanors. These charges were duly referred to the Judiciary Committee of the House of Representatives with authority to subpoena persons and papers and to conduct a thorough investigation. Two days before the Congress was to expire the Committee reported that its inquiry had not been completed and ought to be pursued further.

By this time the contest with the President had become so bitter that the Radicals were unwilling for Congress to take its usual vacation of nine months between March 4 and the first Monday of the following December. Accordingly the Thirty-ninth Congress passed a law providing that the Fortieth Congress should meet immediately after its predecessor adjourned sine die.

On the third day of the Fortieth Congress, Ashley presented a resolution authorizing and instructing the new Judiciary Committee to continue the inquiry begun during the previous session. Butler's maiden speech, for which the galleries had been interestedly waiting, was in favor of this resolution. When the Republicans caucused two days later he fought for the formation of a select committee to push for impeachment. The caucus voted to leave the matter in the hands of the Judiciary Committee.

The Committee had not reported when, on March 23, 1867, James G. Blaine, Speaker of the House, proposed an adjournment until the following November because he thought all of the pressing business before the Congress had been completed. Butler immediately objected on the ground that the Thirty-ninth Congress had ordered a special session of the Fortieth Congress because President Johnson was a bad man who needed to be watched. There was also the matter of impeachment to be considered, Butler reminded his colleagues. Nobody could accuse him of not living up to his campaign and postelection promises to do all he could to further the impeachment of President Johnson.

After some debate the Congress adjourned on March 30 to meet again July 3. On July 8 Butler introduced a resolution calling for the appointment of a special committee, of which he would, of course, be chairman, to examine "all the facts and circumstances connected with the assassination of the late lamented President." Remarking that suspicion existed that persons in high places (meaning Johnson) had been involved in the assassination conspiracy, Butler argued that in order to secure evidence from all possible sources the committee he proposed should be empowered to grant immunity to persons not already tried who could furnish valuable information.[1]

Butler's "Assassination Committee" accomplished nothing and the Judiciary Committee did little better in their efforts to find

---

[1] David Miller Dewitt, *Impeachment and Trial of Andrew Johnson* (The Macmillan Company [New York, 1903]), p. 237.

any evidence against Johnson. During a period of 11 months the Judiciary Committee heard almost 100 witnesses. Some of them were questioned two or three times about Johnson's personal conduct and public acts in Tennessee and Washington and his bank account was carefully studied in the hope of finding some evidence of corruption. Finally, on November 23, 1867, the chairman of the Judiciary Committee presented a resolution calling for the impeachment of the President for high crimes and misdemeanors. However, the arguments advanced in favor of this motion were so weak it was defeated by a vote of 108 nays to 57 yeas. Butler, of course, voted for it.

With that vote all hope of impeaching Johnson seemed lost. However, as an end result of a series of events dating back to the last days of the Thirty-ninth Congress the Radicals at last had their way.

Both the Conservative Republicans who opposed impeachment and the Radicals who favored it agreed wholeheartedly in their dislike of Johnson's use of patronage to gain support for his program. As David M. Dewitt aptly put it: "Of all the sins of the President, none was so unpardonable as his removal from office of tried Republican politicians to give place to supporters of his policy."[2] Even the Conservatives came to believe that every federal officeholder who was "not faithful to the principles, and did not respond to the exactions of the Administration" would be dismissed as soon as the Thirty-ninth Congress ended.[3] To protect their friends the Republicans in the Thirty-ninth Congress passed a Tenure of Office Act and sent it to the White House on March 2, 1867. The sections of the Act relevant to this biography provided (1) that without the consent of the Senate no Cabinet member could be dismissed during the term of the President by whom he was appointed and (2) that during a recess of the Senate the President could suspend any of his appointees, except federal judges, but that if the Senate failed, at its next

---

[2] Ibid., p. 180.

[3] James G. Blaine, *Twenty Years of Congress* (The Henry Bill Publishing Company [Norwich, Conn., 1886]), II, 267.

meeting, to ratify the suspension the official should be restored to his place and powers.

Johnson vetoed this act; the Congress promptly passed it, the President's objections notwithstanding.

Secretary of War Stanton was at this time, as he had long been, strongly in sympathy with the Radicals. Eventually his behavior became such that Johnson was no longer willing to have him remain a member of the Cabinet. In August, 1867, while the Fortieth Congress was enjoying a recess, the President suspended Stanton and appointed General Grant Secretary of War *ad interim*. When the Senate met again, the following November, it refused to ratify Stanton's suspension. Grant immediately surrendered the War office to Stanton. Johnson endured Stanton's presence until February 21, 1868, then ordered him to vacate his office in favor of Major General Lorenzo Thomas.

As required by the Tenure of Office Act, the President notified the Senate of Stanton's dismissal. Almost without debate and with little delay the Senate passed a resolution "that under the Constitution and laws of the United States the President has no power to remove the Secretary of War and designate any other officer to perform the duties of that office *ad interim*."[4]

On receiving a copy of this resolution Johnson sent a message to the Senate, saying, in part:

> If my successor would have the power to remove Mr. Stanton after permitting him to remain a period of two weeks, because he was not appointed by him, but by his predecessor, I, who have tolerated Mr. Stanton for more than two years, certainly have the same right to remove him, and upon the same ground, namely, that he was not appointed by me, but by my predecessor.[5]

The Senate could do nothing but fuss and fume about the "pretended removal" of Stanton; the House of Representatives could, and did, do more.

---

[4] James D. Richardson, *Messages and Papers of the Presidents* (Published by Authority of Congress [1900]), VI, 3820.

[5] Ibid., p. 3823.

In hot temper and great haste Congressman John Covode of Pennsylvania moved that the President be impeached for having committed high crimes and misdemeanors. Normally and properly a motion to impeach an official contains specific charges, known as articles of impeachment. Covode's motion contained no such specifications. An impeachment motion is ordinarily referred to the Judiciary Committee. Covode's motion was referred to the Committee on Reconstruction, headed by Thaddeus Stevens of Pennsylvania, who was unquestionably Johnson's bitterest foe in the Congress, if not in the whole country. After a single day's consideration Stevens reported the Covode resolution with a recommendation that it be passed without debate.

As eager as the Radicals were to impeach Johnson they were even more eager to talk to the galleries, and, through the *Congressional Globe* and the newspapers, to their constituents about the President's "crimes." The speeches actually delivered during the two days devoted to this pastime, and those for which leave to print was given, fill more than 200 column inches of fine print in the *Congressional Globe*. Butler said, in part,

> For a tithe to these acts of usurpation, lawlessness and tyranny [which he ascribed to the President] our fathers dissolved their connection with the government of King George; for less than this King James lost his throne, and King Charles his head; while we, the representatives of the people, adjudge only that there is probable cause shown why Andrew Johnson should be deprived of the office he has desecrated and the power he has abused, and if convicted by the court to which we shall send him, be forever incapable of filling that office—the ambition to be again nominated to which has been the moving spring of all these crimes.[6]

When the Covode motion was finally put to a vote it was passed by 126 ayes to 47 nays. Only Republicans voted for it; only Democrats voted against it; 14 Republicans and one Democrat were absent or did not vote. The House next voted (again strictly along party lines, Butler again with the majority) to have

---

[6] Quoted in Blaine, op. cit., II, 358.

the Speaker appoint a committee to appear at the bar of the Senate to impeach the President of high crimes and misdemeanors, to inform the Senate that the House of Representatives would in due time present particular articles of impeachment, and to demand that the Senate order the President to appear to answer the charges eventually to be brought against him. Another committee of seven was then named to draw up the articles of impeachment for presentation to the Senate. This topsy-turvy procedure would not have been tolerated by the Senate for a moment if that chamber had not been as hot on Johnson's trail as the House was.

Thaddeus Stevens of Pennsylvania, George S. Boutwell of Massachusetts, John A. Bingham of Ohio, John A. Logan of Illinois, George W. Julian of Indiana, Hamilton Ward of New York, and James F. Wilson of Iowa were named as members of the committee to prepare the articles of impeachment. Butler ought logically to have been on this committee. Besides being the ablest lawyer in the House, with the possible exception of Stevens, he had begun making a special study of impeachment cases and impeachment proceedings even before he was elected to Congress. He was kept off of the committee because he was believed to be at odds with General Grant whom the Republicans intended to nominate for the presidency a few months in the future.

Excluding Butler from the articles committee was one thing; keeping him quiet about a matter in which he was as much interested as he was in the impeachment of Andrew Johnson was another thing. It proved to be impossible.

The committee recommended adoption of nine articles of impeachment. Stripped of verbiage and tautology the first three articles charged Johnson with having violated the Tenure of Office Act; articles 4, 5, 6, and 7 charged him with having conspired with General Thomas to violate that Act; article 8 charged "intent unlawfully to control the disbursement of money appropriated for the military service and the Department of War;" article 9 charged an effort to induce Major General William H. Emory to violate the Army Appropriations Act of March 2, 1867.

Butler appeared before the committee to suggest the adoption of a tenth article, charging that during his "swing around the circle" the President,

> unmindful of the high duties of his office and the dignity and propriety thereof, and of the harmony and courtesies which ought to exist and be maintained between executive and legislative branches of government . . . did attempt to bring into disgrace, ridicule, hatred, and reproach the Congress, . . . to impair and destroy the regard and respect of all the good people . . . for the Congress . . . and to excite . . . odium and resentment . . . against Congress; . . . and, in pursuance of this . . . design and intent, openly and publicly, and before divers assemblages of . . . citizens . . . did, on the 18th day of August, A. D. 1866, and on . . . others days and times, . . . make and deliver with a loud voice certain intemperate, inflammatory, and scandalous harangues, and . . . loud threat and bitter menaces . . . against Congress . . . amid the cries, jeers, and laughter of the multitude then assembled and in hearing, . . . which . . . utterances, declamations, threats, and harangues, highly censurable in anyone, are particularly indecent and unbecoming in the Chief Magistrate of the United States, by means whereof said Andrew Johnson has brought the high office of President . . . into contempt, ridicule, and disgrace, to the great scandal of all good citizens; whereby said Andrew Johnson . . . did commit and was then and there guilty of a high misdemeanor in office.[7]

When the Committee rejected this article Butler presented it to the full membership of the House. Saying that it was based upon the eighth article in the impeachment (in 1805) of Justice Samuel Chase of the Supreme Court, he added: "That article obtained more votes on that trial than any other." He also claimed there was a need for an article of the sort he proposed in order to show what kind of man Johnson was.

> If [he said] we place this article side by side with the articles setting forth his technical crimes we show to all posterity the justification for our action; and they will only wonder why we bore with him so long. If we leave the articles as they now stand posterity may well wonder why we struck at him at all.

[7] *Congressional Globe,* 40th Cong., 2nd Sess., Pt. 2, p. 1615.

If we add this article they will wonder why we were so patient and long suffering.[8]

When a fellow congressman commented that Chase had been acquitted despite the eighth article Butler repeated his statement that even so it had been a good vote catcher. This cogent argument led the House to adopt the article he proposed by a vote of 88 to 44 with 57 not voting.

Subsequently an 11th article, drafted by Stevens, was adopted. It reiterated the charges of violation of the Tenure of Office Act and accused the President of having said that the Thirty-ninth Congress, in which some of the southern states had not been represented, "was not a Congress of the United States, . . . but a Congress of only part of the States," therefore, its acts were not valid or binding on him.

In some ways the charges not leveled against Johnson are as interesting as those made. The articles noticeably failed to allege inebriety, although it had been widely rumored and quite widely believed that he had been roaring drunk much of the time during his "swing around the circle" in 1866. Neither was there any allegation of corruption despite months of Herculean effort on the parts of two bitterly hostile Judiciary Committees and Butler's "Assassination Committee" to find any sort of peg on which to hang such a charge.

The board of managers (i.e. council for the prosecution of the case against the President) chosen by the House on March 2, 1868, comprised Bingham, chairman, Boutwell, Stevens, Logan, Wilson, Thomas Williams of Pennsylvania, and Butler. Butler received the votes of 108 of the 118 Republicans present. The Democrats refused to vote for or against any of the managers.

To his delight Butler was chosen to make the opening address at the President's trial. This opportunity came to him by default; none of the other managers was willing to undertake the preparatory work involved. Characteristically he proposed to outline the case against the President of the United States as though

[8] Ibid. p. 1638.

he were outlining a "horse case;" which, as he remarked, was something he knew how to do. It seemed to him that the other managers were "a good deal cut up" about his intentions because they thought so important a case as the one at hand ought to be conducted in the highest possible manner. He conceded this point, but disagreed with them as to what was the highest possible manner of conducting the case. Finding him immovable, they left him to his own devices.[9]

They also left him pretty much alone during the three days and nights he spent preparing his speech. Boutwell asked him if he would like to have the start of the trial postponed; none of the others offered him any sort of help. By limiting himself to a total of nine hours sleep in a period of 72 hours he was ready at the scheduled time.

On the day the trial opened Butler happened to enter the Senate chamber just as the sergeant at arms called: "Hear ye! Hear ye! Andrew Johnson." Butler stopped in his tracks, apparently puzzled as to why such a cry was hurled at him. Everybody else present enjoyed this bit of by-play greatly.

If Butler had had his way the President would have been brought personally to the bar of the Senate and kept standing until he was offered a chair. However, as Butler remarked: "The board of managers was too weak in the knees or back to insist upon this, and Mr. Johnson did not attend."[10]

The President appeared through counsel—Henry Stanberry of Ohio (who resigned as United States Attorney General in order to represent Johnson), Benjamin R. Curtis of Massachusetts (a former justice of the Supreme Court of the United States), Thomas A. R. Nelson of Tennessee, William S. Groesbeck of Ohio, and William M. Evarts of New York.

Jeremiah S. Black of Pennsylvania, Attorney General in President Buchanan's Cabinet, was also to have been of counsel for the President. Black was acting at this time as attorney for an

[9] Benjamin F. Butler, *Butler's Book* (A. M. Thayer & Co. [Boston, 1892]), pp. 929–30.
[10] Ibid., p. 929.

American firm which was engaged in a dispute with the Domin-
ican Republic about the right to exploit the guano deposits on
Alta Vela Island. He asked Butler, Stevens, Logan, Blaine,
James A. Garfield, and a number of other Republican leaders to
aid him in seeking to persuade the Administration to support his
client's cause. Black used the letters they wrote to him in a thinly
veiled effort to threaten Johnson. The President resentfully dis-
pensed with Black's services.

Johnson's lawyers asked for 40 days to prepare their case.
"Forty days! As long as it took God Almighty to destroy the
world," Butler shouted. One of the President's counsel protested
that railroad speed ought not to be used. Butler asked: "Why
not?" The defense could summon any witnesses it needed by
telegraph and they could come to Washington by railroad.[11]

The Senate granted the defense a postponement of ten days.
At the end of that time the President's answer to the articles of
impeachment was presented and his counsel asked to be allowed
a period of not less than 30 days to prepare for trial. They were
given a week's time.

Butler had faced, and would often again face, bigger audiences
than he did on the day he made the opening address at the trial
of President Johnson, but he never appeared before a more distinguished group. The Senate galleries were crowded with bigwigs, including the entire diplomatic corps in Washington, every
member of the House of Representatives was present, and 44 of
the 54 senators were keen, capable lawyers. It was a momentous
occasion and he made the most of it.

He began by discussing the importance of the case at bar and
the wisdom of the men who drafted the Constitution in providing
for its possible occurrence. Turning next to the question of what
constituted an impeachable act he said,

> We define . . . an impeachable high crime or misdemeanor to
> be one in its nature or consequences subversive of some funda-

---

[11] *Supplement to the Congressional Globe . . . The Trial of Andrew
Johnson* (F. & J. Rives & George A. Bailey [Washington, D. C., 1868]),
p. 8.

mental or essential principle of government or highly prejudi-
cial to the public interest, and this may consist of a violation
of the Constitution, of law, of an official oath, or of duty, by
an act committed, or, without violating a positive law, by the
abuse of discretionary powers from improper motives, or for
any improper purpose.[12]

As to the nature and functions of the Senate sitting as a high
court of impeachment, he asked,

Is this proceeding a trial, as that term is understood so far as
relates to the rights and duties of a court and jury upon an
indictment for crime? Is it not rather more in the nature of
an inquest of office?[13]

He answered himself:

The Constitution seems to have determined it to be the latter,
because, under its provisions, the right to retain and hold office
is the only subject that can be finally adjudicated; all preliminary inquiry being carried on solely to determine that question
and that alone.[14]

He went on to assert that the Senate was not sitting as a court.
This matter, he emphasized, was of much consequence for if the
Senate were sitting as a court it would have to observe the rules
and precedents of common law, the senators constituting the court
would be liable to challenge on many grounds (political prejudice suggests itself as an obvious one) and the President might
claim that he could not be convicted unless the evidence made
his guilt clear beyond a reasonable doubt instead of his being
convictible by a preponderance of evidence. In Butler's view the
fact that the Chief Justice of the United States happened to be
presiding did not convert the Senate into a court of justice because in impeachment cases not involving a President the Senate's
regular presiding officer would occupy the chair. In further sup-

---

[12] Ibid., p. 29.
[13] Ibid., p. 30.
[14] Idem.

port of his premise that the Senate was not sitting as a court of justice Butler argued that procedures in impeachment cases were in no way analagous to procedures in ordinary trials. For one thing, in impeachment proceedings, he explained, the accused is merely notified that a trial is pending, but is not required to appear personally.[15]

(The managers, of course, accepted this thesis. Throughout the trial they called Chief Justice Salmon P. Chase, "Mr. President." Johnson's counsel, equally consistently used the terms "Your Honor," or "Mr. Chief Justice.")

Summarizing the managers' position, Butler said,

[As] a constitutional tribunal solely, you are bound by no law, either statute or common, which may limit your constitutional prerogative. You consult no precedents save those of the law and custom of parliamentary bodies. You are a law unto yourselves, bound only by the natural principles of equity and justice, and that *salus populi suprema est lex* [the safety of the people is the supreme law].[16]

Turning to the articles of impeachment, Butler said the first eight "set out, in several distinct forms, the acts of the President in removing Mr. Stanton and appointing General Thomas." These acts, Butler asserted, contravened the President's oath of office and disregarded his duties. Butler also claimed that every fact charged in the first article, most of those in the next several articles, and a general intent to set aside the Tenure of Office Act had been admitted in the President's replication. Therefore, said Butler, the real question before the Senate and the American people was,

Has the President, under the Constitution, the more than kingly prerogative at will to remove . . . and suspend from office indefinitely, all executive officers of the United States, either civil, military, or naval, at any and all times, and to fill the vacancies with creatures of his own appointment, for his own purpose,

[15] Idem.
[16] Idem.

without any restraint whatever, or possibility of restraint by
the Senate or by Congress through laws duly enacted?[17]

As to the President's claim that the Tenure of Office Act did
not protect Stanton because he had been appointed by Lincoln,
Butler argued that Johnson was not serving a term of his own
but was merely an acting President until the expiration of Lincoln's second term.[18]

Dealing rather slightingly with the ninth article Butler said,
"If the transaction set forth in this article stood alone we might
well admit that doubts might arise as to the sufficiency of the
proof. But the surroundings are so pointed and significant as to
leave no doubt in the mind of an impartial man as to the intents
and purposes of the President" to induce General Emory to hin-
der the execution of the Tenure of Office Act and to prevent
Stanton from holding the office of Secretary of War.[19]

As might be expected Butler dwelt fondly on the tenth article.
First he undertook to demonstrate (what nobody questioned) that
the reports of Johnson's speeches contained in the articles of impeachment were substantially accurate. Then he asked if such
speeches were "decent and becoming in the President of the United
States, and [did they] not tend to bring the office into ridicule
and disgrace?"[20]

Butler referred briefly to the 11th article, then, after having
talked for three hours, "with the exception of a recess of ten
minutes, which was taken on the motion of Mr. Senator [Henry]
Wilson, when he had spoken about two hours," he summed up
the charges against the President, saying:

The acts set out in the first eight articles are but the culmina-
tion of a series of wrongs, malfeasances, and usurpations committed by the respondent, and, therefore, need to be examined
in the light of his precedent and concomitant acts to grasp their
scope and design. The last three articles presented show the

17 Ibid., p. 32.
18 Ibid., p. 34.
19 Ibid., p. 37.
20 Ibid., p. 38.

perversity and malignity with which he acted, so that the man as he is known may be clearly spread upon the record, to be seen and known of all men hereafter. . . . We have presented the facts in the constitutional manner; we have brought the criminal to your bar, and demand judgment for his so great crimes. . . . I speak . . . not the language of exaggeration, but the words of truth and soberness, that the future political welfare and liberties of all men hang trembling on the decision of the hour.[21]

Individual reactions to Butler's address were largely determined by the political attitudes of those who heard it delivered or read its text in the newspapers, most of which published it in full. Stanton thought it was a great argument. The House of Representatives ordered 5,000 copies of it printed for the members' use. The violently Radical *Nation* found it excellent. The (Democratic) Boston *Post* referred to it as a three hour tirade. So it went clear across the country.

Despite Bingham's titular chairmanship of the board of managers Butler was in fact the chief manager. He carried the brunt of the prosecution, presenting the managers' witnesses, cross-examining witnesses for the defense, and, more than anyone else on his side, arguing points of law. Since there were few facts at issue the trial was, much to Butler's liking, a highly legalistic affair. Early in the proceedings he engaged in an interesting tilt with Chief Justice Chase. A witness called by the managers testified that General Thomas had avowed his intention of forcibly taking possession of the War Department. The defense objected to the admission of this evidence. Chase ruled it admissible. Even though this ruling was helpful to the prosecution, Butler protested against Chase's right to rule at all on the admission of evidence. He did so because he believed, as many others did, that Chase hoped to be the Democratic party's presidential candidate in 1868, hence that he was partial to Johnson. The Senate voted to sustain the Chief Justice.

Throughout the trial Butler displayed great adroitness and

---

21 Ibid., pp. 40–41, 51.

ability. Moorfield Storey, who disliked Butler intensely, thought he completely outfenced and outsparked the President's counsel.[22]

The managers concluded their presentation of evidence Saturday, April 4. Curtis opened for the defense the following Thursday. His speech, even longer-winded than Butler's, lasted all of one day and part of another. He did not bother to reply to Butler's argument concerning the functions of the Senate sitting as a court of impeachment. Well aware that all of the Democrats would vote to acquit Johnson and all of the Radicals to convict him, Curtis addressed himself to the handful of Republicans who might consider the case on its merits. He dealt extensively with the first article, which he said substantially charged that Stanton's dismissal was, and was intended by the President to be, a violation of the Constitution. "These," Curtis asserted, "are the allegations . . . it is necessary for the honorable managers to make out to support that article." He demolished Butler's argument that Johnson was not a new President, serving in his own right, by saying that Lincoln's death had terminated his presidency. After briefly discussing each of the next eight articles Curtis dismissed the tenth (Butler's) with the simple, but unanswerable, statement that the President's speeches had not violated the Constitution or any laws existing at the time they were delivered, so they were not impeachable offenses. Remarking that the 11th article was merely a rehash of the other ten and needed no answer, Curtis concluded:

> This trial is and will be the most conspicuous instance that has ever been, or ever can be expected to be found, of American justice or of American injustice; of that justice which is the great policy of all civilized states; of that injustice which is certain to be condemned, which makes even the wisest men mad, and which, in the fixed and unalterable order of God's providence is sure to return and plague the inventor.[23]

Many years later Butler wrote that after Curtis finished speak-

---

[22] M. A. DeWolfe Howe, *Portrait of an Independent* (Houghton Mifflin Company [Boston, 1932]), pp. 92–93.

[23] *Supplement to the Congressional Globe,* pp. 123–26, passim.

ing "nothing *more* was said in [the President's] behalf, although in the five or six closing speeches presented by his other counsel much *else* was said."[24]

When the managers presented their closing arguments Stevens, who was literally on the verge of death, attempted to speak, but found himself too weak to do so for long. He handed his manuscript to Butler who read it to the Senate, probably with less emotional drive than Stevens would have done. Perhaps if Stevens had been able to speak for himself American history might have taken a different turn for the President was acquitted on each of the three articles put to a vote by a margin of only one vote.

Butler's (tenth) article was not brought to a vote. If its charges of bad manners and intemperate criticism of Congress had sufficed for Johnson's removal it might have gone hard in later years with Presidents Grover Cleveland and Harry S. Truman. Cleveland could have been found guilty on the first of these counts; Truman on both of them.

---

[24] Butler, op. cit., p. 930, Original italics.

19

****

Congressman Butler

Two questions that arose early in Butler's congressional career were should the millions of dollars of greenbacks (legal tender notes which had never attained parity with coin) issued during the Civil War be eliminated from the currency system and should the government bonds sold to help finance the war be redeemed in gold or in cheaper paper money.

These questions were answered differently by "hard money" men and "greenbackers." The first group advocated a return to the gold standard and redemption of the bonds in gold. The greenbackers argued that a return to the gold standard would ruin thousands of debtors by adding 25 per cent to the sums they owed and called the hard money men constructive cheats because they had loaned depreciated greenbacks and were seeking to be repaid in gold. The hard money men could not refute these assertions, but their wealth enabled them to control most organs of propaganda so they defended themselves by attacking the greenbackers. The greenbackers were charged with a desire to bilk their creditors, violate their contracts, and destroy the nation's honor.

Because Butler became a greenbacker and an advocate of a tax on incomes derived from government bonds many men who had lavishly praised him only a short time earlier turned savagely against him in the late 1860's. A large number of Republican newspapers executed a similar *volte face*. Most of those who made this change rationalized their new attitude by proclaiming that he had always been a demagogue and that his Army record was one of unrelieved corruption. Actually, as the tenor of the resolutions adopted at a number of Republican conventions clearly indicates Butler's financial heresy bothered far more men than his personal qualities did. A Cleveland, Ohio, clergyman who "preached a sermon . . . in which he denounced Mr. B. F. Butler for proposing in Congress 'to tax the bonds,' "[1] was either remarkably naive or intellectually honest, but he certainly typified many of Butler's postwar opponents.

The greenbackers were interested in many things besides the currency question. They were the political descendants of such reformist groups as the Liberty party of the 1830's, the Free-Soil party of the 1840's, and even the original Republican party of the 1850's and early 1860's, and the ancestors of the Populist party of the 1890's, and the Progressive party of 1924. Because Butler's district contained a large number of laborers who longed for many sorts of reforms advocated by him and the greenbackers he was nominated to succeed himself as congressman at a convention held in Salem in September, 1868. The vote was 175 in his favor to 4 for others.

Butler's renomination led *The Nation*, then as strongly partisan a Republican journal as there was in the whole country, to express a hope that if no Republican could be found willing to challenge his financial principles his Democratic opponent would win.[2]

A Republican who was more than willing to challenge Butler was nominated at a special convention held in the Fifth District on October 5. The chairman of this gathering told the self-appointed delegates that they were old time Republicans, which he said Butler was not, and that they were in sympathy with General Grant (Republican nominee for the presidency), which he said Butler was not. After applauding these remarks the convention nominated its foreordained candidate, Richard Henry Dana, Jr., of Cambridge, as an independent candidate for Butler's seat in Congress. (Dana, like Butler, had a summer home on Cape Ann in the Fifth District.)

---

[1] *The Nation,* December 24, 1868.
[2] *The Nation,* October 1, 1868.

Dana, a Federalist by heredity and a conservative by instinct, was just about the worst candidate the hard money men could have chosen to run in a largely working class district. He was known to be extremely friendly to the managers of the cotton mills of Massachusetts. His fondness for "Society," as personified by the wealthy, polished business and professional men of Boston was no secret in nearby Essex County. His frigid manners made it difficult for him to let himself down to the level of his own class, much less to mingle with the masses.

In the ensuing campaign the Democratic candidate, Judge Otis F. Lord, conducted himself unimaginatively and unaggressively but Dana and Butler fought tooth and nail. Butler brutally exploited Dana's aristocratic pretensions and the way he talked down to audiences at political rallies. The Dana crowd threw quantities of billingsgate at Butler.

A pamphlet entitled *Why I Cannot Vote for Ben. Butler, by a Carpet Bag Voter of the 5th District,* so scurrilous that nobody dared to admit its authorship, was prepared at the instigation of, and distributed by the Dana people. One of the 24 reasons why the author of this screed said he could not vote for Butler was: "Because I have known him from boyhood, and known him well." Another was: "Because his life accords precisely with his looks— very twisting."

Grant secretly endorsed Dana's campaign against Butler and Grant's managers, with the approval of the Republican National Committee, paid General Judson Kilpatrick $200 a day for speaking on Dana's behalf.[3]

Henry Adams wrote from Washington, offering to assist Dana's campaign in any way possible. Adams also expressed a hope that the much discussed reports about Butler's misdeeds would be brought out of their pigeon-holes.[4]

If Dana's friends searched Butler's dossier, as President John-

---

[3] William B. Hesseltine, *Ulysses S. Grant* (Dodd, Mead & Company [New York 1935]), p. 135.

[4] Worthington C. Ford (editor), *Letters of Henry Adams* (Houghton Mifflin Company [Boston, 1930]), p. 147.

son's supporters had already done, they found nothing harmful to the General. However, they trotted out General George H. Gordon, who had headed the military commission that had investigated allegations of corruption brought against Butler early in 1865. Gordon's evidence had not impressed the Commerce Committee, but it sufficed virtually to convince a hard money Republican (who, of course, wanted to be persuaded) that Butler had been personally interested, "at an enormous profit," in furnishing provisions to Lee's army near Petersburg at a moment when the outcome of the Civil War hinged upon cutting off Lee's supplies.[5]

Butler ignored Gordon's allegations, as he did all others like them throughout his political career. It seemed to him that if he ever answered any such charge he would have to waste time answering all of them or be taken, by his silence, to have confessed guilt in connection with something of which he might not even have heard.

The hard money men did not really expect Dana to be elected; they did confidently believe he would take enough votes away from Butler to cause his defeat. The editors of the *Atlantic Monthly* recalled, long after the event, "the profound dinner-table harangues" to the effect that the Fifth District was "no other place than Essex County. Old Essex—the place of all the world where the most pure blooded Americans were to be found, . . . a country rich with memories of devotion to duty, and to religion," hence a place where a greenback sympathizer could not possibly be elected.[6]

The dinner table analysts turned out to be badly mistaken. Butler got 13,000 votes, Lord nearly 5,000, and Dana less than 2,000.

Although the hard money men were disappointed at their failure to prevent Butler's reelection, they optimistically assured them-

---

[5] George S. Merriam, *The Life and Times of Samuel Bowles* (The Century Co. [New York, 1885]), II, 92.

[6] *Atlantic Monthly,* August 1873, XXXII, 254.

selves that he would be rendered harmless because they believed
he would not be able to get along with President Grant. However, George Wilkes, a Radical editor with whom Butler was
associated in a speculative business venture, urged Grant to seek
a reconciliation with Butler. At first Grant flatly rejected this
suggestion. Wilkes pressed the matter, pointing out as he did
so that Butler's chief grievances were Grant's statement that
Butler had been "bottled up" at Bermuda Hundred and the
unduly late delivery of an invitation to a reception given by the
Grants in 1866. Without offering to apologize for either of these
things Grant told Wilkes that no offense had been meant by
them. Wilkes relayed this word to Butler and took him to call
on Grant at the White House. The two men smoothed out their
differences and from then on they worked so closely that many of
their contemporaries believed Butler had more influence with
Grant than any other member of Congress. (They disagreed
only about financial legislation, with Grant following the dictates
of the hard money men.)

Butler's Republican opponents were puzzled about, and disturbed by, his postwar relations with Grant. Apparently it never
occurred to them that Grant may have found Butler politically
compatible and personally likeable so they fell back upon a simple,
and to them a satisfactory explanation—blackmail.

Senator George Frisbee Hoar and his brother Judge Ebenezer
Rockwood Hoar spread, if they did not originate, a tale of Butler's
having bragged openly that Grant would not refuse anything he
demanded because he could prove that Grant had been drunk on
seven different occasions during the Civil War.[7]

Judge Hoar's biographers, Moorfield Storey and Edward W.
Emerson (both Butlerphobes) happily accepted this allegation
at face value, although no evidence in support of it was cited by
them or the Hoars.

[7] Moorfield Storey and Edward W. Emerson, *Ebenezer Rockwood Hoar*
(Houghton Mifflin Company [Boston, 1911]), pp. 255–56; George F.
Hoar, Autobiography of Seventy Years (Charles Scribner's Sons [New
York, 1903]), I, 361–62.

The Hoar brothers, it is perhaps worth noting, had a reason in addition to their class bias for hostility toward Butler. Grant, who was a most inept politician, began his first term with two Massachusetts men in his Cabinet—Judge Hoar as Attorney General and George S. Boutwell as Secretary of the Treasury. When the death of a Supreme Court justice offered Grant an opportunity to kick one of this pair upstairs he nominated Hoar for the judgeship. The Senate tabled the nomination. Butler loudly, and quite plausibly, claimed that his influence was responsible for Hoar's rejection.

According to another blackmail story told by General William F. Smith, Butler prepared a pamphlet attacking Grant's Civil War record and caused short excerpts from it to be published in various newspapers. (They must have been remarkably brief excerpts for a diligent search by the writer failed to discover anything answering their description in any Boston paper or several New York ones.) A synopsis of this pamphlet was made ready for transmission by the Associated Press. Grant heard of this plan, sent for Butler, "peace was made, the pamphlet was not published, and General Butler became one of General Grant's most earnest supporters and is said to have controlled the distribution of federal offices in Massachusetts; and General Grant thereafter spoke more mildly of General Butler's faults."[8]

Only a person who thought Butler was at least slightly mad at the time these events are supposed to have occurred could accept Smith's story, for Grant's popularity was so great that no one except a lunatic would have belittled his military record without expecting to be laughed at for doing so.

Soon after the last session of the Fortieth Congress began Butler introduced a bill authorizing and directing the Secretary of the Treasury to issue a minimum of $300,000,000 worth of treasury certificates (greenbacks) which should be legal tender for all debts, public or private, except where contracts specifically

[8] William F. Smith, *From Chattanooga to Petersburg* (Houghton, Mifflin and Company [Boston, 1893]), pp. 85–86.

called for the payment of coin. Speaking in support of his bill he said the desirable features of a currency were uniformity, soundness, cheapness of manufacture, stability, and elasticity. All of these virtues, he claimed, could be found in paper money of the sort he proposed. Calling the gold standard an instrument of tyranny, he argued that a return to it would be equivalent to confiscation, by act of Congress, of one-third of all wages and other incomes except those of recipients of interest and that it would depreciate by a third the value of all property in the United States except bonds and promissory notes. Resumption, he concluded, was a scheme designed to enrich a few financiers at the expense of everybody else.

Needless to say this speech did nothing to win friends for Butler or to influence people in the financial community in his favor. However, many farmers and laborers thought he had spoken the truth.

Almost literally as soon as the Forty-first Congress met Butler introduced a bill, two lines long, unconditionally repealing the Tenure of Office Act. Grant had given the Republican members of the Congress clearly to understand that he would make no appointments while the Act remained on the books except in cases where flagrant misconduct necessitated the removal of an incumbent. The patronage-hungry Republicans passed Butler's bill by an overwhelming majority (138 to 16, with 39 not voting) even before the House was organized. In due course the Senate amended the House bill in such a manner as effectively to repeal the Act without doing so in specific terms. The conferees on the part of the House, headed by Butler, refused to accept a measure retaining any shadow of congressional control over presidential appointments except for confirmation by the Senate. The Senate, therefore, enacted a bill different from, and wordier than Butler's, but which he was satisfied left the President's power to remove officeholders exactly as though the Tenure of Office Act had never existed.

While the Senate was hemming and hawing about repealing
the Tenure of Office Act the House considered a bill "to
strenghten the public credit." The hard money men in and out
of the Congress highly approved of this bill. Butler, who led
the fight against it, said he opposed it both on principle and because he estimated that 90 per cent of the bondholders whom it
would benefit lived east of a line drawn through Lake Ontario
whereas three-quarters of the votes a Republican presidential
candidate needed to be elected were to be found west of there.
Despite Butler's efforts to block it this measure was passed in
time for it to be the first law signed by President Grant.

In 1870 and 1872 Butler was allowed to run for reelection to
Congress without opposition from any member of the Republican party.

Immediately after Butler returned to Washington in December,
1872 the House of Representatives investigated one of the worst
scandals in the history of American politics. This inquiry resulted
from allegations made during the previous fall's campaign by
the (Democratic) New York *Sun* that in 1867 a bill to regulate
rates chargeable by the Union Pacific Railroad had been defeated
as a consequence of bribery by Congressman Oakes Ames of
Massachusetts. On the first day of the second session of the Forty-
second Congress (December 2, 1872) Speaker Blaine called a
Democratic member to the chair and moved appointment of a
special committee to look into the *Sun's* charges, which had been
repeated by other newspapers as well as by many Democratic
orators. Blaine's motion called for an investigation of the possibility of bribery by Ames. Butler suspected that plans had been
made for Ames dramatically to be found guilty of bribery in order
to distract attention from those mentioned as having been bribed.
An amendment he offered to Blaine's motion led to a broader inquiry than was first intended.

A committee headed by Luke P. Poland, a Vermont Republican, discovered that Ames had sold stock in the Credit Mobilier

Corporation (which had built the railroad) to Vice President Schuyler Colfax of Indiana, Vice President-elect Henry Wilson of Massachusetts, Congressmen Bingham and Garfield of Ohio, James Brooks of New York (a government director of the Union Pacific), and many other members of both major parties. Ames had not only sold these shares at par, far less than their market price, but had also let anyone who chose to do so pay for them out of dividends which had been ranging from 80 to 90 per cent and had reached 300 per cent in 1868. The Poland Committee whitewashed everybody concerned except Ames and Brooks. Ames was declared guilty of bribery, Brooks of having accepted a bribe intended to influence him in matters brought before him both as congressman and as government director of the railroad. The Committee recommended that they be expelled from Congress.

This drastic penalty probably would have been imposed upon the pair if Butler had not spoken forthrightly in defense of Ames. Saying that Ames had been made a scapegoat by men who did not dare to disclose the truth about their dealings with him, Butler strongly intimated that Blaine had instigated the investigation in an attempt to blacken Ames's reputation. (If Butler were right about Blaine's animus Blaine could have been projecting his own guilt for it was subsequently discovered that he had solicited and accepted bribes from the Union Pacific and other railroads in the late 1860's.) Butler's speech forced the House to face the fact that bribery involved at least two persons so if Ames were found guilty it might become necessary to name those who had been bribed. In these cricumstances the House voted to condemn the conduct of the two men, but not to expel them.

Incidentally, Butler's powerful defense of Ames was not merely rhetorical. In 1880, when the Credit Mobilier affair had been largely forgotten, he stated publicly that he had never been able to see the least thing wrong with Ames's sale of stock to his colleagues.

About a month before the Forty-second Congress was destined to expire Butler introduced a bill providing for a retroactive 50 per cent increase (from $5,000 to $7,500) in congressmen's salaries. He emphatically said he was presenting the bill at the instruction of the Judiciary Committee and that he had not written the report on it, although he concurred with it. Personally, he said he did not care how the bill might fare because his law practice netted him much more than his congressional salary did. In one fee alone, he told his colleagues, he had collected the equivalent of a congressman's yearly salary. He favored the measure because he believed public servants ought to be paid well enough not to need private resources.

When the question of raising their own salaries was put to a vote Republicans and Democrats in both Houses voted "Aye" with equal vehemence.

Members of several previous Congresses—the Thirty-ninth which had adjourned sine die on March 4, 1872 being the most recent one—had increased their salaries without having heard any loud public protest. No outcry was expected by the members of the Forty-second Congress. Probably none would have been made if it had not been for the panic of 1873. With many men unemployed and others having to take drastic pay cuts much was said and written about the "salary grab."

The members of the Forty-third Congress cut their salaries back to $5,000 a year almost immediately after they met for their first session. Many of the same men who had enthusiastically voted for an increase less than a year earlier now vied with each other to announce their repentance. Butler did not do so. He argued that the $7,500 salary ought to be retained because a man needed that much to support himself and his family in Washington.

In February, 1874 Butler asked President Grant to appoint William A. Simmons collector of the port of Boston. Grant sent Simmons's name to the Senate for confirmation without having consulted any member of either House except Butler. The "better element" in Massachusetts immediately lined up against Simmons, apparently simply because he was known to be one of Butler's intimate friends. Governor William B. Washburn, Senator Charles Sumner, the Hoar brothers, Henry L. Pierce, J. Murray Forbes, Dr. Oliver Wendell Holmes, John G. Whittier, the merchants of Boston, and others of the same social status opposed the appointment of Simmons. Despite the protests of this galaxy of Republicans Grant flatly refused to withdraw the nomination unless it could be shown that Simmons was unfit for the office. Since this was not done his name remained before the Senate and his nomination was confirmed.

Rhodes asserted that Simmons was finally confirmed only because of Butler's hold over Grant.[9] It would be interesting to know by what logic Rhodes reasoned that Butler's hold over Grant (assuming it really existed) led the Senate to confirm the appointment of Simmons.

After Simmons had been in office for a couple of years Judge Hoar alleged publicly that employees of the customs house ran errands for Butler and attended to many details of his political campaigns. Butler said, in an open letter to Hoar,

> Men do kindly things for me from motives . . . you cannot possibly appreciate and can hardly understand, because you never did a service to any man without pay down that I ever heard of; therefore, you never knew what it was to have men grateful enough to you, . . . of their own free will and friendliness [to] do everything they can do for you. I would advise you to try to act kindly towards somebody once, and get somebody to feel in that way towards yourself. It would be a new sensation, and it would please you with its novelty, if it did not touch your heart.[10]

In 1874 Mayor William Cogswell of Salem offered himself as a hard money, anti-Butler candidate for the Republican nomination for congressman from the Fifth District. Butler was renominated without any difficulty, but he was defeated in the

---

[9] James Ford Rhodes, *History of the United States* (The Macmillan Co. [New York, 1920]), VII, 24.

[10] Benjamin F. Butler, *Letter of General Benj. F. Butler to Hon. E. R. Hoar,* October, 1876 (Published by request [Lowell, 1876]).

subsequent election. His Democratic opponent, Charles P. Thompson got 8,700 votes to his 7,700. When Thompson died 17 years later the Boston press heavily stressed the fact that he had once bested Butler in a political contest.

There was a tendency in some quarters to attribute Butler's defeat to his presumed connection with the salary grab. He claimed he lost because the Republican State Committee betrayed him while he was speaking in the West at the behest of the National Committee. It is true that Blaine worked *sub rosa* against Butler,[11] but being a Republican was enough to have beaten him in 1874. A Democrat was even elected governor of Massachusetts that year, a most unusual event in those days.

The Nation profoundly congratulated the country on Butler's elimination, but it soon became evident that he still had much political influence. In March, 1876 President Grant nominated Richard Henry Dana, Jr., to succeed General Robert C. Schenck as American minister to Great Britain. Dana's close friend and biographer, Charles Francis Adams, believed "there was no position in the gift of the President or the people of the United States which would have been so agreeable to Mr. Dana as the English mission." To be sent to London to represent his country would have gratified his Anglomania; it would have afforded vindication from the charges of plagiarism brought against him in connection with his editing of the eighth edition of Henry Wheaton's *Elements of International Law;* and, not least in importance, it would have furnished "balm to the wound inflicted on his pride by the outcome of his contest with Butler" seven and a half years earlier.[12] Chiefly at Butler's instigation, the Senate Foreign Relations Committee made an adverse report on Dana and his appointment was not confirmed.

During the summer of 1876 Butler was invited to come home,

[11] Boston *Herald* January 24, 1894; Springfield, Massachusetts, *Republican,* January 29, 1894.
[12] Charles Francis Adams, *Richard Henry Dana* (Houghton, Mifflin and Company [Boston, 1890]), II, 362.

politically speaking. In August more than 2,000 Republicans in the district in which Lowell was located asked him to become a candidate for their party's nomination for congressman. He accepted this call and was nominated at a convention held in Lowell on September 13. Eighty-four votes were cast for him, 22 votes went to two other men. However, a motion to make the nomination unanimous was not carried.

The business class of the entire country regarded Butler's nomination as a distaster, but took some comfort from a report published by *The Nation* that there was talk of a bolt in his district.[13]

The Nation was well informed. Early in October a group of hard money Republicans met at Young's Hotel in Boston, far outside of the Lowell congressional district. This gathering was attended by the Hoar brothers; John Fallon, manager of the Pacific Mills Corporation of Lawrence; George Dove, of Smith and Dove, an Andover manufacturing concern; Professor J. Wesley Churchill, of the Andover Newton Theological Seminary, and other members or representatives of the business class, but not by any rank and file Republicans. Judge Hoar spoke of the need to name an independent (he did not need to say financially orthodox) Republican candidate to run against Butler. The Judge was, of course, promptly chosen to make the race. He professed to be reluctant to run, but said he would do so from a sense of duty.

Butler never believed that Hoar's reluctance was genuine.

[After] I was regularly nominated . . . by a fairly counted majority of votes [Butler said in his autobiography] . . . up started the Hon. Ebenezer Rockwood Hoar, who had been an office-holder nearly all his life and wanted to be [one] the rest of his life by getting Grant to appoint him as associate justice of the Supreme Court of the United States, but whose confirmation for reasons affected by public policy and private wishes I had caused to be rejected by the Senate. Mr. Hoar thought this would be a good time to revenge himself upon me.

13 *The Nation*, October 5, 1876.

. . . So [he] called together some of his friends in a Boston hotel and had himself nominated as the bolting candidate of the Republican party.[14]

Butler was stumping Ohio at the request of the Republican National Committee when he heard of Hoar's bolt. He publicly dared the Judge to call another convention of Republicans *in the Lowell district* at which he and Hoar could start fresh as candidates for the nomination if Hoar would promise to abide by the result should he lose. Hoar ignored this challenge; he knew too well what the outcome would be.

On election day it was demonstrated once again that Butler could not be beaten in a congressional race by another Republican. He polled more than 11,500 votes, the Democratic candidate got nearly 10,000, Hoar got less than 2,000.

Having proved his ability to be elected from his home district, Butler chose not to run again for Congress.

During his eight years in Congress, Butler made his voice heard and his influence felt in connection with many matters besides those already mentioned.

In view of his Civil War service he considered himself something of an expert on military affairs. Today, with billions being spent for defense, it is wryly amusing to note that he once proposed a reduction of the standing army from 39,000 to 25,000 men as a means of saving from $13,000,000 to $15,000,000 a year. He thought, too, that the existence of the Military Academy at West Point should obviate the need for a large peace time army by creating a cadre of professional officers who could assume command of the militia in the event of war. Another of his ideas was that ironclad floating batteries such as the U.S.S. *Monitor* would be more effective for harbor defenses than stone forts. (He was probably mistaken about the uitility of monitors; he was certainly right about the uselessness of stone forts.)

---

[14] Benjamin F. Butler, *Butlers Book* (A. M. Thayer & Co. [Boston, 1892]) p. 925.

Partly because of his dislike of all things British, partly because "twisting the lion's tail" was a popular sport with politicians throughout the nineteenth century, Butler made much ado about the Treaty of Washington (signed in May, 1871). Of course, he did himself no harm with the Irish immigrants in his district by claiming the treaty was unduly advantageous to Great Britain.

Butler supported Grant's efforts to annex Santo Domingo as strongly as he opposed Secretary of State Seward's proposal to purchase Alaska from Russia.

He thought Alaska was too remote and difficult of access to be worth having and that the price asked for the area involved ($7,200,000 or about two cents an acre) was unreasonably high. When it was suggested that the purchase be made as a gesture of gratitude for Russia's friendliness to the Union during the Civil War he said it would be better to hand over the money and let Russia keep Alaska.

As shortsighted as we can now see that Butler was in the Alaska matter he was not a parochial congressman, interested only in things of direct value to his own district. For example, he supported a proposal to establish a federal bureau of education, although, as he commented, it would not benefit his state which already had an excellent school system. The fact that it would be good for the whole country was enough to cause him to favor it.

Like many Americans of his own day and afterward Butler believed in free trade among the states and protection of domestic manufacturers from foreign competition. In this he could have been motivated partly by self-interest since he was proprietor of a bunting mill. However, no such motive can be inferred in connection with his attitude about the income tax law passed as a war measure and destined to lapse in 1872 unless reenacted. He considered an income tax fairly and justly levied to be the most equitable of all taxes, but the existing one seemed to him unfair, unjust, and inquisitorial. Its chief defects were, in his view, that it taxed the product of honest labor, mental or physical; treated everybody as if he were a rogue, likely to try to evade his just obligations; and actually succeeded in compelling only conscien-

tious persons to pay their taxes. As a substitute for the existing
tax he suggested one providing for a fair tax on incomes derived
from investments, including government bonds. Since he was an
investor and a bondholder he would have been subject to such
a tax.

While he was in Congress, Butler consistently supported measures designed to protect the civil rights of Negroes. Toward
this end he introduced a so-called Ku Klux Klan bill which
would have permitted the President to use the Army and to
suspend writs of habeas corpus in order to enforce federal laws
and to remove state officials whenever there was doubt as to the
fairness of their elections. He punctuated a speech in favor of
his bill by waving a bloodstained nightshirt, taken, he informed
the House of Representatives from the back of a white teacher
in a Negro school who had been flogged by klansmen. Thus he
enriched the American language by adding to it the phrase "waving the bloody shirt," often used to characterize the sort of
oratory by which a generation of Republicans sought to keep
memory of the Civil War alive and themselves in office. When
Charles Sumner died Butler took charge of a civil rights bill
sponsored by the Senator. This measure, passed in 1875, prohibited the exclusion of Negroes from juries and granted Negroes
"the equal enjoyment of accommodations, advantages, facilities,
and privileges of inns, public conveyances on land and water,
theaters, and other places of amusement; subject only to the conditions established by law, and applicable alike to citizens of
every race and color."[15] (Eight years after its passage this act
was nullified by a decision of the Supreme Court of the United
States.[16]

Butler also appointed the first Negro, Charles Sumner Wilson
of Salem, Massachusetts, to a cadetship at West Point.

Women's rights was another cause for which Butler spoke,
voted, and worked in committee and on the floor of the House.
In January, 1872 a group of women, headed by Mrs. Belva A.

---

[15] *U. S. Statutes at large*, XVIII, 335 ff.
[16] *Civil Rights Cases, 109 U.S. 3.*

Lockwood (who was nominated for the presidency in 1884 and 1888 by the Equal Rights party) presented Butler with a bouquet as a token of their appreciation of his efforts.

A few examples, out of many that could be cited, will suffice to show why Butler had the allegiance of many laborers and the approval of most trade union leaders.

A bill introduced by Congressman James M. Garfield of Ohio (who became the 20th President of the United States) contained a provision that printers employed by the Government Printing Office should be paid the same wages as similar workmen were receiving in New York, Philadelphia, and Baltimore. Butler pointed out that wages paid in those places were lower than wages paid in Washington whereas living costs were higher in the capital than elsewhere. He said Garfield and those who supported his bill were aware of these facts and they hoped to prevent the unionization of printers in Washington. Butler thought their efforts to organize ought not to be hampered and his remarks showed a real understanding of laborers' problems.

In connection with the debate on the Army Appropriations bill of 1878 Butler spoke harshly of the use of the Army to break the railroad strikes of 1877, ill-judged though he admitted the strikers' actions to have been. He also said he had heard it argued that a large standing army was needed to suppress possible outbreaks on the part of laboring men, but if the causes of strikes were removed there would be no reason for the Army to exist except to fight Indians on the western frontier.

During the severe depression of 1873 to 1878 Butler suggested that relief could be provided for the unemployed by eliminating the expenditure of $40,000,000 for the maintenance of the Army and using the same sum to establish settlers on the frontier. Thus, he said, a self-supporting, self-recruiting army capable of adding to, not substracting from, the country's wealth would be created. This suggestion led some people to call him an anarchist.

When the Fortieth Congress passed a law reducing the workday of government employes from ten hours to eight most officials promptly cut their employees' pay by 20 per cent. The

laborers affected appealed to the Congress to order the payment
of ten hours' wages for eight hours' work. Butler, who vigorously
supported this appeal, said he had heard much talk about the
faith of the government in connection with the rights of bondholders and he thought the faith of the government was also involved in the question now under consideration.

★★★★★★★★★★★

20

Butler for Governor

In 1871 and 1873, when there were no congressional elections, and four more times after he left Washington, Butler sought to become governor of Massachusetts. Each of his "onslaughts upon the governorship" (to borrow a phrase coined by the "respectable element") threw the state into a dither. In all of his campaigns he was opposed by conservatives of both major parties and supported by Republicans, Democrats, and Greenbackers to whom his liberal record, his personality, or both appealed.

Butler's decision to seek the Republican nomination for governor in 1871 was made known to the public by the Springfield *Sunday Chronicle* in mid-July. The *Chronicle* claimed to have learned of Butler's intention by asking him what he planned to do in view of rumors that Governor William C. Claflin was not going to seek another term. Some of Butler's opponents believed he had prompted the paper's questions, but they never proved it.

Although the state's Republican newspapers differed widely about the merits of the several other aspirants for the nomination they agree unanimously in preferring anybody else to Butler. Their attitude amused the General. He had become well accustomed to being opposed by his party's press.

In the short period between the announcement of his candidacy and the opening of his campaign Butler had three narrow escapes from severe injury or death. First he barely missed drowning at Newburyport, Massachusetts. Next a horsecar in which he was a passenger tipped over in Boston, shaking him badly. Finally, while on his way to Springfield to deliver his first campaign speech, he was in a train wreck. A superstitious man might have thought the fates were against him.

During the five weeks he devoted to his preconvention campaign Butler spoke chiefly about the state's prohibition law and the sort of labor legislation he thought desirable.

There was much dissatisfaction among the "drys" about the way the prohibition law was being flouted in some places. Butler said this law, like all others on the statute books, ought to be enforced impartially. He promised that if he were elected he would cause it to be applied with equal vigor against exclusive hotels, such as the Tremont House and the Parker House, and "Bridget O'Flaherty, . . . selling liquor in a cellar to eke out her washing wages."[1]

Some men, unwilling to give Butler credit for a single decent impulse, argued that his promise to enforce the prohibition law could not be sincere because its real enforcement would lead to its repeal.

What Butler said about labor legislation actually amounted to no more than a promise to work for a law establishing a maximum workday of ten hours for persons employed in factories. This was in fact all the various labor reform associations of the time were asking any politician to do, but the business class believed the labor reformers intended "war upon the whole profit-making system,"[2] and Butler's bid for their support frightened the conservatives nearly out of their collective wits.

To make matters worse from the hard money men's point of view Butler seemed more than likely to secure the nomination and there was not much doubt that if he did he would be elected. In these circumstances Samuel Bowles of the Springfield *Republican,* D. A. Goddard of the Boston *Advertiser,* W. W. Clapp of the Boston *Journal* and a number of other conservatives desperately appealed to Senator Sumner to speak out against Butler. Sumner

---

[1] W. S. Robinson (Pseudonym, "Warrington"), "General Butler's Campaign," *Atlantic Monthly,* December 1871, XXVIII, 745.
[2] Ibid., p. 744.

had habitually refrained from participating in intraparty contests
and his personal relations with Butler had always been cordial.
With these facts in mind the conservatives shrewdly took advantage of Sumner's intense egotism by telling him he was the only
person who could save the Republican party in Massachusetts
from defeat and disaster. He was thus persuaded to issue a public
statement deploring Butler's "extraordinary" campaign and saying that his nomination would operate against the best interests
of the Commonwealth and the Republican party.[3]

Senator Wilson was delighted to be allowed to concur with
Sumner.

Immediately after reading Sumner's statement Butler called
upon the Senator with whom he happened to find Wilson. The
General pungently expressed his opinion about Sumner's action
and insulted Wilson by pointedly ignoring him.[4]

The conservative Republicans accused Butler of packing the
local caucuses, at which delegates to the state convention were
chosen, with Democrats and foreigners—using these terms synon-
ymously. An anonymous handbill charged Butler with suborna-
tion of a plan to dynamite the convention hall if he were not
nominated. Senator Hoar, who was to be chairman of the convention, theatrically proclaimed his belief that Butler would
personally lead his followers in a riot if he were denied the
nomination. Hoar agreed to preside only after the State Committee promised to put 100 trustworthy policemen under his
absolute control so that he could protect the delegates against
Butler.[5]

On the eve of the convention it was estimated that 125 delegates
would vote for Alexander H. Rice, the same number for George
B. Loring, 350 for William B. Washburn, and 500 for Butler.
After a warm debate Butler's opponents decided to unite behind

---

[3] Ibid., p. 747; Edward L. Pierce, *Memoir and Letters of Charles
Sumner* (Roberts Brothers [Boston, 1877]), IV, 194–95; Moorfield Storey,
Charles Sumner (Houghton, Mifflin and Company [Boston, 1900]), p. 400.

[4] Robinson, loc. cit., pp. 747–48.

[5] Ibid. p. 746; George F. Hoar, *Autobiography of Seventy Years*
(Charles Scribner's Sons [New York, 1903]), I, 348.

Washburn, a colorless conservative. Rice and Loring withdrew from the contest; their delegates voted for Washburn, and he was nominated with 643 votes to Butler's 464. In sharp contrast to what Hoar professed to have expected Butler to do in such circumstances he immediately promised to support Washburn while continuing to work within the Republican party for the causes he had advocated in his preconvention campaign. The business class greeted the news of Butler's defeat with deep satisfaction; the party leaders were greatly relieved at hearing that he would not bolt.

In 1872 Butler was interested only in returning to Congress. Nevertheless 259 out of 984 delegates to the Republican convention voted to nominate him as candidate for governor; the rest voted for Washburn's renomination.

Stressing much the same issues as he had two years earlier, Butler opened his 1873 campaign at a Fourth of July Temperance Alliance picnic in Framingham. A Temperance Alliance leader, named B. D. Godfrey, who spoke at considerable length and with obvious self-satisfaction, intimated that Butler had organized the picnic in order to further his own ends. According to the Boston *Journal* of July 5, "The load on [Godfrey's] mind . . . seemed to be Gen. Butler and the raid he was about to begin. [Godfrey's] views of the General were as unique as [his views] upon other topics. He thought of [Butler] as an unregenerate man and full of selfishness, but if regenerated [he] might make a valuable ally for the temperance cause." (If Godfrey had not been a temperance leader his involved language would almost lead one to suspect him of having been a bit tipsy.) Another speaker vehemently denied that Butler had played any part in arranging for the picnic.

Butler's candidacy was endorsed by a Labor Reform Association convention held in Lowell in August. The Association was not a partisan political body, but a pressure group favorable to the enactment of ten-hour laws and such other state or federal legislation as its members thought were needed to improve the lot of the working class. Thus its endorsement of Butler was in complete accord with its policies and entirely logical, considering his record and his platform.

In view of his record the conservatives' opposition to Butler was equally logical. As the Boston *Traveller* put it: "The war waged against General Butler was an expression of hostility to [his] radical ideas [as they seemed to the conservatives to be] in politics."[6]

One of the weapons used in this war was a pamphlet entitled *The Salary Grab . . . with special reference to the responsibility of Gen. B. F. Butler,* written by William S. Robinson. This screed alleged that Butler had been the chief architect of the act by which the members of the Forty-second Congress had granted themselves a retroactive pay increase. Since the issue of the *Congressional Globe* containing Butler's statement that he had not drafted the bill and did not care whether or not it passed was cited by Robinson he deliberately lied about the matter. Undoubtedly he thought the end justified the means; most of the conservatives would have agreed with him.

For some reason Butler came nearer to defending himself against Robinson's charge than he ever did against what almost everybody else would have considered far more serious ones. At a dinner in Boston he repeated what he had said in Congress about his not being author of the act. With the exception of this statement he showed no embarrassment over what Robinson had hoped would be a damaging exposé. If anything Butler glorified, rather than apologized for, his part in securing higher salaries for members of Congress.

The editors of the *Atlantic Monthly* regarded Butler's campaign and the farmers' movement (which gave rise in turn to the Grange, the Granger laws, the Greenback, Greenback-Labor, Anti-Monopoly, and the Populist parties in the 1870's, 1880's, and 1890's) as the two most important developments of the year 1873. In August the *Atlantic's* editors apprehensively asked: "Will it be possible to defeat General Butler—to defeat him, that is, if he secures the nomination?" They answered themselves: "There

---

[6] Boston *Traveller,* September 8, 1873.

is only one way in which it can be done, and that is by a union against him of the conservative forces throughout the State, . . . a union of the capital, the intelligence, the morality, and what is left of religion in the State." But they feared it might be too late for the formation of such a union. In their view Massachusetts was not the same sort of community it had been half a century earlier. The old families had lost their "proscriptive political rights." The bar had lost its influence and had almost ceased to be a political school. The Church (i.e. the Congregational denomination) no longer exercised its "old duty of supervision over the lives and morals of the people." The state's economy had shifted from an agricultural to an industrial base and town meetings had become gatherings of factory laborers. "In short," said the worried editors, Massachusetts had "become the home of a genuine prolitiariat [sic], working for wages for a few rich men, these latter not endowed with any great sense of responsibility either for the welfare of their 'hands,' or for that of the general public."[7]

The standpat element of the Massachusetts Republican party needed no prodding to arouse it against Butler and his "radical" ideas. Neither did the standpatters have to be told of the importance of a united front against him. However, with about half of the State Committee friendly to Butler and with President Grant's Administration actively supporting him the conservatives had to operate outside of the regular organization. In these circumstances Judge Hoar and a few others arranged for a meeting to be held at Hamilton Hall in Boston. The call for this gathering did not state that its purpose would be to consider what could be done to stop Butler, but its recipients fully understood this to be the fact. On July 25 Judge Hoar (in whose office plans for the meeting had been made) called Senator Hoar, J. Murray Forbes, Henry L. Dawes, Harvey Jewell, A. W. Beard, John E. Sanford, Henry D. Hyde, and about 100 other politicians and politically active businessmen to order. The Judge opened the proceedings by delivering a speech in which he said, without nam-

---

[7] *Atlantic Monthly*, August 1873, XXXII, 252–55.

ing Butler, that the people of Massachusetts would never allow a Tichborne claimant to become their governor. There was much more talk of a similar sort by other men who sedulously avoided mentioning Butler. Finally somebody bluntly said there was no point in beating around the bush any longer; the purpose of the meeting was to concert measures to prevent Butler from becoming governor and it would be a good idea to get along with that business. If a letter to the editor of the *Boston Daily Evening Traveller* (published July 30, 1873) is to be trusted, the antics the "ex-judges, ex-representatives, ex-speakers, and ex-everything else that is good" performed on hearing the General's name pronounced were enough to have caused a 3,000 year old mummy to "smile audibly."

The activities of the Hamilton Hall crowd had little visible effect on Butler's campaign. Describing him as a menace probably bored more people than it frightened. His own speeches and the efficiency of his organization gave him much strength. As the date for the Republican convention drew near he had some little reason to hope to be nominated; his opponents had as much reason to fear the same thing.

Some conservative Republicans openly threatened to bolt if they could not stop Butler. He met them with a shrewd counterattack. As soon as the convention was organized he presented a resolution providing that any action taken by a majority of the delegates should be binding on all of them. Since the party hacks, who made up a majority of the delegates (as they do at all political conventions) would have voted for this resolution the anti–Butler men did their best to sidetrack it without discussing the principle it involved. Only one conservative, the Reverend James Freeman Clarke, a politically active Unitarian minister, was intellectually honest enough to face the real issue. "Every member of the Republican party," he said, "has a right to say, 'I will not vote for a man whom I believe to be . . . dangerous . . . to his country.' I came here to give my honest vote, according to my own convictions or the convictions of those I represent; and when that vote is cast and I return to my town, then I have the right to decide, as any other independent man decides, whether I shall vote for the nominee."[8]

As always Butler acted as his own floor manager. When a test vote went against him he read the handwriting on the wall and withdrew his name from further consideration by the convention. The conservatives were elated by this development. *Harper's Weekly* regarded the "elimination" of Butler as "a cause of national congratulation."[9]

However, anyone who thought Butler had been crushed was badly mistaken. He was convinced that the Republican party would never nominate him for its candidate as governor, nothing more.

In August, 1878 Butler officially withdrew from the Republican party. Within a month he had been chosen as the Greenback-Labor party's candidate for governor and was seeking the Democratic party's nomination.

There were many Democrats who eagerly desired Butler to be their party's nominee; there were many others who, without particularly liking him, believed their party would have to nominate him unless it chose to lose the election by default; but the members of the conservative State Committee opposed him so bitterly that they threatened to bolt if he were nominated.

On the eve of the Democratic convention it was apparent that a large majority—perhaps as much as 90 per cent—of the delegates favored Butler. The State Committee, ready by fair means or foul, to prevent his nomination, issued a set of rules designed to keep the Butlerites from attending the convention. However, Butler's young and enthusiastic followers were not willing to accept defeat without making a fight. About 3 A.M. of the day the nominations were to be made some 50 pro–Butler delegates quietly entered Mechanics Hall in Worcester and rallying parties

[8] Boston *Traveller,* September 8, 1873; George S. Merriam, *The Life and Times of Samuel Bowles* (The Century Co. [New York, 1885]), II, 265.

[9] *Harper's Weekly,* September 27, 1873, p. 842.

were sent abroad to rouse others. Before the police closed the
doors of the hall at 8:30 A.M., more than 300 of the faithful had
gathered. They barred the State Committee from the building.
The Committee called upon the mayor of Worcester to use the
police reserves and, if necessary, the militia to clear the place.
The mayor did not think the circumstances justified the bloodshed
he knew would result from the use of force so he refused the
Committee's demand. However, he did try persuasion. Saying
that the hall had been rented by the State Committee, he hopefully admonished those present to relinquish the place to the Committee. A few hotheads proposed to eject the mayor; the rest of
the crowd listened to him respectfully. Some timid souls even left
the building. Most of them soon reconsidered what they had done
and returned by means of a ladder and a second story window,
thus avoiding the policemen at the doors. The mayor finally decided that he had no legal right to disturb anyone and departed
from the scene. Soon after he left Butler was nominated by
acclamation.

The State Committee, whose members never did get into the
hall, declared that Butler had been nominated by a mob, not by
a regular convention. A regular convention, called by the State
Committee, named another Democrat as candidate for governor.

The Republicans chose Thomas Talbot, a former lieutenant
governor, to run against Butler and the "regular" Democratic
nominee.

As the Springfield *Republican* said, the Republicans "blindly
assumed that the social order, the national banks, and the resumption of specie payments were in danger from the Butler party."[10]
This imaginary party was described by the Republican State Committee on its own letterhead as composed of "Repudiationists,
Greenbackers, and Communists."[11]

Since Butler was an outspoken opponent of the resumption of
specie payments he could be called a repudiationist with some
degree of logic and many of his followers were avowed green-

[10] Loc. cit., November 11, 1878.
[11] Springfield *Republican,* November 2, 1878.

backers, but calling him a communist was so utterly ridiculous that it did not disturb the Roman Catholic hierarchy of Massachusetts, a group as hostile to Communism then as it is now. The *Pilot* (a Catholic weekly) said it believed Butler had made "many and sore mistakes in judgment," but on balance he was to be preferred over his opponents."[12]

However, anyone who believed that men and women ought not to have to work more than 60 hours a week and who thought it possible that depressions such as the one that began in 1873 and lasted until 1878 might be caused by underconsumption resulting from low wages was a dangerous radical by the standards of the conservatives of both major parties.

The Republicans were not afraid that if Butler became governor of Massachusetts he would succeed in overthrowing the national banks, preventing the resumption of specie payments, and establishing Communism. They did fear that his election as governor in 1878 could lead to his becoming President in 1880, whereupon he might effect his fell purposes.

Partly because the Republicans were so frightened the Massachusetts campaign of 1878 was one of the bitterest ever seen in the state, if not in the whole country. Nearly 1,000,000 pages of anti–Butler, hard money literature was circulated by the Republicans. With the entire nation listening Butler was described as a thief, a pirate, a murderer, a forger, a trickster, a bloated monopolist, a man who sought to ruin every property owner in the state, etc. He gave back as good as he was sent in the way of vituperation.

An additional reason for the vigor of the Republicans' attack was the hope held by some of them that Butler, who would be 60 years old on election day, would retire from politics in the event of his defeat.

In the midst of the campaign Denis Kearney, a leader of the California Workingmen's party, asked Butler if, in his opinion, California had a constitutional right to exclude Chinese immigrants. Regretting the necessity of answering hastily and with-

---

[12] *Pilot*, quoted in the Boston *Globe*, September 5, 1878.

out an opportunity to consult treaties or law books, Butler said
that under a decision rendered by the United States Supreme
Court no state could bar Chinese as such. But, he added, no
state could "be made the lazar-house of the world, or even one-
third of it;" therefore, he thought California could declare the
Chinese a nuisance and banish them under its police powers.[13]

Kearney's question was wholly irrelevant to Butler's gubernatorial campaign, as he and Butler both knew, of course. However, Butler's answer could have been of considerable importance
if he had become a presidential candidate in 1880. Kearney was
looking as far ahead as the Republicans were.

The canvass of 1878 ended with Talbot's election by 126,000
votes to Butler's 105,000. The General attributed this outcome
to the lavish use of money by his opponents and the bulldozing
of laborers by their employers. There is no real reason to believe
that money played a direct part in effecting Butler's defeat. According to figures published by the Springfield *Republican* (whose
accuracy one does not doubt) the amount spent by the Republicans was not enough greater than that spent by the Butler parties
together to have made the difference between winning or losing.
But, as the same paper commented, the Republican victory was
achieved through a political machine "in the hands of men thoroughly alarmed at Butler's strength and determined to compass
his downfall."[14] In the light of this admission the charge of
coercion would seem to have considerable merit.

The Brahmins of Massachusetts and elsewhere rejoiced over
Butler's defeat, but they were less than happy about the manner
of its accomplishment. They had widely anticipated "that the
bulk of the respectable Democrats would adhere to their party
nominee [i.e., the so-called regular or anti–Butler candidate] and
that the Republican party, singlehanded, would be able to crush
Butler. These expectations were not realized. The respectable
Democrats, with comparatively few exceptions, voted for the Re-

---

13 Ellis Paxson Oberholzer, *A History of the United States since the
Civil War* (The Macmillan Co. [New York, 1931]), IV, 378.
14 Loc. cit., November 12, 1878.

publican candidate, and without their votes Mr. Talbot probably would not have obtained a plurality."[15] Neither, in all likelihood, would Talbot have won if a fair degree of recovery from the depression of the past five years had not alleviated discontent to a considerable extent. In these circumstances it was obvious that the "respectable element" could not forever prevent the election of some liberal, even if Butler really had staked and lost his all on the throw he had just made.

To the dismay of those who had counted Butler out after his defeat in 1878 he was again a candidate for governor in 1879. Before announcing his plan to seek the nomination he sought to make peace with the conservative wing of the Massachusetts Democracy. The "respectable Democrats" scornfully rejected his offer so he took their party away from them. He was nominated by the Democratic convention with only one vote cast against him.

The day after the Democratic convention adjourned 1,400 Independents, most of whom had been Republicans, unanimously named Butler as their candidate for governor. The platform they adopted clearly indicates that they were revolting against the self-styled better element and its presumption that, because of the superior virtues it attributed to itself, it had a right to rule the rest of the populace.

As always Butler conducted a whirlwind campaign, but he knew before it ended that he would be beaten. A few hours after the polls closed he estimated that he would lose by about 10,000 votes. The actual count was 123,000 votes for the Republican candidate, former Lieutenant Governor John D. Long, 111,000 for Butler.

By the summer of 1880 Butler had gained almost absolute control of the Massachusetts Democracy. The party's state convention of that year was aptly described as "his minstrel show from start to finish." If he had not resolutely prevented it he would

---

[15] Anonymous, "Limited Sovereignty in the United States," *Atlantic Monthly,* February 1879, XLIII, 184.

have been nominated for governor by acclamation. It seemed likely to be a Democratic year (as it nearly was); he intended to campaign on behalf of the Democratic presidential candidate; and he refused to stand for any office so that it could not be said he was motivated by opportunism. He consented to the nomination for governor of Charles P. Thompson, the only man who had ever defeated him in a congressional election. Apparently he regarded any man who could beat him as a good vote getter. However, Thompson was not quite strong enough to win this time.

21

★★★★★★★★★★★★

"The Stone that the Builders Rejected"

In 1881 Butler took a political holiday, but he bobbed up again as the gubernatorial candidate of the Greenback-Labor and Democratic parties the following year. He was nominated by the Greenback-Labor convention on the second ballot; the Democrats chose him by acclamation at one of the shortest, most harmonious conventions that party ever held in the Bay State.

As the newspapers commented Butler's 64 years had not lessened his physical or mental powers or his enjoyment of rough and tumble politics. He opened his campaign by making speeches at two different halls in Boston on the same night. As he stood, wearing his familiar evening clothes and boutonniere, surveying the capacity crowd in Fanueil Hall, an admirer shouted: "The same old Ben; ain't he a good boy though?" At Music Hall, where another big crowd waited for his arrival, he spoke for an hour, devoting most of the time to answering a series of "civil service" questions propounded by the (Republican) Boston *Advertiser*. One of these questions was: To how many parties had he belonged? He had belonged to three parties so far, he replied, and he would join as many more as he pleased if their principles seemed good to him. Another query was: Had he ever gone from one party to another for the sake of improving his chances of being elected to any office? To this he answered: "Never. The first time I changed my political relations was when I went to war, and I did not go to war for the sake of office. . . . When I left the Republican party it was in authority, and I went to the Democratic party when it was in the minority. Does that look as if I

277

were changing for the sake of office?" The *Advertiser* admitted somewhat ruefully the next morning: "Both the candidate and his audience seemed measurably satisfied with the way in which he passed the examination."[1]

The Republican candidate, Robert R. Bishop, president of the state Senate, found his party label a heavy load to carry. Nationally the GOP had not fully recovered from the scandals of the Grant Administration; locally the party was beset by petty squabbles and the reactionary attitude of its congressional delegation on such issues as the tariff, government spending, and civil service reform.[2]

Before the canvass ended it was practically certain that Butler's seventh attempt (including two before the Civil War) to become governor of Massachusetts would be successful. Almost as soon as the polls closed the Republican State Committee publicly conceded the defeat of its candidate. This news reached Butler at his home in Lowell about 6 P.M. A couple of hours later he decided to go to Boston. Arrangements were quickly made for a special train to leave Lowell at 9:15 P.M. Shortly before nine Butler and a dozen or so of his friends started for the railroad station. Their carriages were stopped by a large crowd gathered near the office of the Lowell *Courier*. Before the cavalcade was allowed to proceed the General had to make a speech. On the train Butler sat alone, at his own request, vigorously puffing a cigar, but showing no other signs of excitement; his friends made no effort to conceal their elation. A large crowd, having somehow learned that Butler was on his way to town, met his train at Boston. "The feelings of one delighted representative of the people boiled over," reported the next morning's Boston *Globe*, "in a series of enraptured shrieks, and in the following friendly and well-meant caution: 'For God's sake General, button up your coat, and don't take cold and ruin us all.'" Even though it was nearly 11 P.M. before Butler reached the Revere House nothing would satisfy the crowd gathered there except a speech from their

---

[1] Loc. cit., October 17, 1882.
[2] *The Nation,* November 9, 1882, p. 391.

hero. When the cheering died away he began: "Fellow citizens, to quote a few words from the scriptures, the stone that the builders rejected, the same has become the head of the column. With reverent submission I bow in grateful thanks to the Almighty Father for His blessing in this victory and triumph for the people of the Commonwealth of Massachusetts."[3]

There were many who regarded Butler's election as more of a conquest of the people of Massachusetts than a triumph for them, but nobody could deny that it was a personal triumph for the General. Except for some members of the General Court he was the only Democrat elected in the state that year.

On Inauguration Day (January 4, 1883) Butler reached the State House about 1 P.M., arrayed in evening clothes, carrying a gold headed cane, wearing a white tie, white gloves, and a boutonniere. One observer thought he seemed almost ready to shout: "Veni, vidi, vici," as he strode into the House of Representatives to deliver his address. His inaugural touched at more or less length upon a wide variety of topics, including prison reform, the conduct of the state's charitable institutions, the desirability of a single purchasing agent for all of the state's departments, secret voting, naturalization of foreigners, labor relations, poll taxes, and woman suffrage, and concluded with a statement that he did not wish or intend to be a candidate for a second term as governor.

Every newspaper in Massachusetts and many outside of the state commented extensively upon Butler's address. Most Massachusetts papers published it in full, even though its delivery had taken two and a half hours and it filled 200 column inches, using six point type. Broadly speaking, the Republican press criticized it adversely while Democratic papers praised it uncritically. Really, as the Boston *Herald* remarked, with unwonted objectivity, it deserved praise for some of its parts, criticism for other parts.

Friction between executives and legislatures, national and state, is, of course, a characteristic of American political history. With

---

[3] Boston *Globe,* November 8, 1882.

the General Court of Massachusetts controlled by his political
opponents Butler had his share of such trouble. The legislative
session of 1883 lasted from January 3 to July 27 and was the
longest ever held up to that time. (In the 1960's this would have
been considered a brief session.) According to Butler, the General Court "sat down" on every reform he proposed. Actually a
considerable amount of fairly advanced labor legislation was enacted in 1883. The Governor, on his part, vetoed an unusually
large number of bills and allowed 40 others to become laws without his signature. With 17 Democrats and 23 Republicans in the
Senate; 90 Democrats and 149 Republicans in the House, Butler's partisans could support his vetoes if they chose to do so and
they failed him only once.

Butler handed his opponents in and out of the legislature a
weapon they gladly used against him by continuing to practice
law in the federal courts while he was governor. After his third
absence from the state during his first three months in office the
Boston *Advertiser* said, under a Washington, D.C., dateline;
"People here are wondering whether General Butler has really
been elected, and is now serving as governor of Massachusetts.
He appears here so often on behalf of parties prosecuted by the
Federal government that this doubt is natural."[4] The Boston
Journal urged the Governor to do something to save his callers
from looking for him at the State House when he was in Wash-
ington, New York, Providence, or some other place. This could
be accomplished, the *Journal* suggested, by having suitable cards
printed, such as one reading "G. T. C. H.," meaning "Gone to
Court House."[5]

Butler countered these attacks by saying the nights were long
enough to enable him to make up any time he might lose from
his public duties because of his private activities. An opposition
newspaper retorted, certainly with justification; "The constitution of the State provided [the governor] a regular salary in

[4] Loc. cit., March 23, 1883.
[5] Loc. cit., March 24, 1883.

order that he may not have his attention diverted to his private concerns."[6]

Another Boston paper observed that the Governor's absences at least permitted the General Court to go on with its work unimpeded by "the fearful torrent of special messages with which he [had] threatened to vex the legislature and irritate the people."[7]

One of the first things to which Governor Butler turned his attention was the situation at the state prison in Concord, where both guards and prisoners were virtually in revolt against Warden David Earle. Butler officially ordered the warden to inform the prisoners that they could send sealed, uncensored letters to the governor. He took this step in the hope of promoting better discipline at Concord by affording the prisoners an outlet for their complaints. "Frequently," he said to a newspaper reporter, "a man is uneasy because he cannot tell his story to anybody. If he can tell his story and have a hearing he feels easier." Most of the letters the prisoners sent to Butler alleged cruelty on the part of prison officials, especially the warden. Earle's failure even to pretend to deny these accusations was widely accepted as a practical admission of his guilt. In any case, the Governor's Council voted, as Butler recommended, to dismiss Earle. Since the Council was solidly Republican there must have been substantial grounds for Earle's removal. Butler personally introduced the new warden, Roland G. Usher, to the inmates of the prison. The convicts, assembled in the chapel, greeted the Governor with salvoes of applause as cordial as it was noisy. He began a brief speech to them: "Prisoners, you are here because it has been ascertained, by the only means of ascertaining facts yet made known to the ingenuity of man, that you have broken the laws of the Commonwealth, and . . . you are sentenced by the laws of the Commonwealth to a certain term of hard labor within these walls." New rules, he continued, had been promulgated and he knew they would be justly enforced because he had appointed as warden a friend of 25 years standing in whom he had absolute confidence.

---

[6] Boston *Advertiser,* March 26, 1883.

[7] *Butler Clippings,* Boston Public Library, p. 27.

He concluded by saying; "I commend the warden to you, I commend you to the warden. Treat him as he treats you and this prison will be the model institution of its kind in the United States."[8]

Butler's belief that prison reform was something desirable was, of course, harshly criticized by hard-boiled advocates of the Mosaic law. However, some men who heartily disliked the Governor spoke favorably of his choice of Usher as warden.

Another of Butler's appointments, that of George L. Ruffin as judge of a court in Charlestown, also deserves at least passing mention. Ruffin was the first Negro appointed to an honorable and dignified position in Massachusetts. (The second Negro judge in the state's history was named and sworn in by Governor Robert F. Bradford in December, 1948.)

So far as Butler's contemporaries were concerned the most exciting episodes of his governorship were the Tewksbury investigation and Harvard University's refusal to grant him an honorary degree.

In his inaugural address Butler said the Tewksbury Almshouse, located in a town near Lowell, had been grossly mismanaged for many years. He alleged that one of the trustees of the Almshouse had openly boasted of having made large sums of money from commissions illegally paid to him by vendors of goods; that infant mortality at Tewksbury ran as high as 90 per cent of live births; that the bodies of dead infants had been sold to a single medical institution (meaning the Harvard Medical School); and that bodies of adult paupers had been unlawfully utilized at the same institution.

The law to which Butler referred permitted state and local almshouses to give unclaimed bodies of paupers to doctors and surgeons for dissection. Recipients of such bodies were required to give bond that they would be used only for scientific purposes and that after such use the remains would be decently buried.

---

[8] Boston *Herald,* February 10, 1883.

Butler claimed that students at the Harvard Medical School had
flayed a number of bodies (he did not say how many), had tanned
the hides, and had made the leather thus obtained into gloves,
pocketbooks, bookbindings, etc.

Partly, if not chiefly, because most of the managers and trustees
of the Tewksbury Almshouse were Republicans the Republican
members of the state legislature vigorously denied Butler's charges
and called upon him to prove them to the satisfaction of a special
investigating committee. He accepted this challenge.

The proceedings of the Tewksbury Investigating Committee
attracted the attention of newspapers all over the United States
and eastern Canada. Many New England papers outside of Boston thought the investigation was necessary and discussed its
progress objectively. However, as the St. Louis *Globe-Democrat*
not unfairly remarked, the predominantly Republican press of
Boston talked all around the subject, loudly denying things that
had not been alleged and undertaking to cover up what could
not be disproved.[9]

All of the committee's public sessions were attended by large
crowds. The Green Room, the biggest hearing room in the State
House, where most of the sittings were held, was always packed
almost to suffocation. Every seat was taken, the aisles and space
near the doorway were occupied by standees, even footholds on
the arms of settees were at a premium. As a rule Butler sat facing the committee; occasionally he swung toward the audience as
though he realized that many were present chiefly to see him in
the flesh. The committee, whose members had often seen him,
paid no attention to him and little to the proceedings. Usually
one or two of them listened to the testimony being presented while
the others wrote letters, read newspapers, or occupied themselves
in ways not visibly connected with the investigation they were
supposedly conducting.

After meeting 65 times between the end of March and the middle of July, 1883, a majority of the committee (composed ex-

---

[9] St. Louis *Globe-Democrat,* quoted in the Boston *Advertiser,* April 13,
1883.

clusively of Republicans) reported that the Governor had not supported the charges he had made. Despite its somewhat partisan flavor one finds it impossible to quarrel with this verdict. However, the investigation did uncover some undesirable conditions at the Tewksbury Almshouse and led to some reforms.

While the Tewksbury Investigation was in full swing the overseers (trustees) of Harvard University met to consider whether or not to confer an honorary degree of doctor of laws upon Governor Butler as Harvard had done upon every governor of Massachusetts since 1800 (except for those who had received a doctorate in the course of their academic careers).

Much unsolicited advice was given to the overseers. Some of it came privately from Harvard graduates, some of it was publicly offered by newspaper and magazine editors, not all of whom were Harvard men.

Edward Everett Hale (class of 1839) wrote home from Europe, counseling against refusing an honorary degree to Butler.[10] Many other alumni spoke to the same effect, even though few of them liked Butler personally or politically. Some of them urged that tradition be disregarded in Butler's case, but the consensus was that Harvard was under the disagreeable necessity of doing as much for him as had been done for most of his predecessors.

The newspapers commented on the subject in various ways.

The Boston *Journal* said Harvard was under no compulsion to confer a degree upon Butler; that "a bad precedent cannot be broken too soon;" and if the University proposed "to draw a line anywhere this would be a good time and place to draw it."[11]

The New York *Evening Post* remarked that Harvard did not have to, and ought not to, honor Butler with a degree.[12] *The New York Times* concurred with the *Evening Post*.[13]

The Boston *Advertiser* was satisfied that Harvard had full power to refrain from giving Butler a degree, but thought it

[10] Boston *Traveller,* June 6, 1883.
[11] Loc. cit., May 26, 1883.
[12] New York *Evening Post,* quoted in the Boston *Post,* May 26, 1883.
[13] *The New York Times,* quoted in the Boston *Advertiser,* May 26, 1883.

would be unnecessarily harsh to withhold a compliment which both giver and receiver (and by inference the world as well) knew carried no endorsement of the individual honored.[14]

The Boston *Transcript* believed that honoring Butler in accordance with tradition would be of little more significance than any other part of the ritual of commencement, but it would be a mistake for Harvard to take occasion to rebuke him inasmuch as he was entitled to all the forms of respect usually paid to a governor and "as a demagogue he could not desire a better handle than the refusal of the degree would afford him."[15]

The Lowell *Mail* cautioned Harvard to avoid a public exhibition of spite against Butler, urged that he be given a degree, and said, "If it should appear desirable to do away with the custom let it be fully discussed when there is no possibility of personal considerations influencing the decision."[16]

In the end the overseers decided not to confer an honorary degree upon Butler. The meeting at which this decision was reached was held behind closed doors on May 31, 1883. The only information officially made public was that the president and fellows of Harvard had unanimously favored conferring a degree, but the overseers had refused their concurrence by a vote of 15 nays to 11 yeas. However, the Boston press learned enough about the meeting to be able to describe much of what had happened.[17]

For various reasons a majority of the overseers at first favored conferring a degree upon Butler. Some of them thought that not doing so would furnish Butler with political capital. One man who was of this opinion argued that it would be wiser to follow routine and call it routine than to single out a particular governor in such a way as to enable him and his followers to claim he was being persecuted by Tories. Others said that long usage made it highly desirable for a degree to be conferred upon Butler no matter how much some of the overseers disliked him. This camp held that the bestowal of honorary degrees upon other governors

[14] Loc. cit., May 28, 1883.
[15] Loc. cit., May 28, 1883.
[16] Lowell *Mail*, no date, *Butler Clippings*, Boston Public Library.
[17] See the Boston *Advertiser, Globe, Herald,* or *Traveller,* of June 1, 1883.

had been clearly understood to have been complimentary to them as chief magistrates, not as individuals, and no more would be signified in Butler's case than in any other, whereas a departure from custom when Butler was governor would be construed as an act of partisanship and would hurt Harvard far more than it would the Governor. President Charles W. Eliot warned against provoking Butler's supporters because it might lead to legislation inimical to Harvard.

Fervid arguments against conferring a degree upon Butler were made by Judge Hoar, president of the Board of Overseers, Moorfield Storey, and the Reverend Freeman Clarke. Storey expressed himself as certain that few of the overseers would agree with the statement contained in the diploma accompanying the degree that the recipient was intellectually and morally deserving of it. Clarke said Harvard owed a duty to its alumni not to cheapen its degrees by bestowing them inconsiderately or indiscriminately and that honoring Butler would have a bad influence on young men by indicating, in effect, that if they succeeded, by fair means or foul, Harvard would honor them with a degree.

In the hope of mollifying the opposition Eliot offered to have the wording of the citation changed to indicate that the degree was being conferred upon the governor of the Commonwealth in conformity with an immemorial, or at least long-standing, custom. Another proposal was made to confer the degree, but to pass and publicize a resolution or several resolutions condemning Butler's political methods and certain of his actions as governor. One of these compromises (the newspapers were not quite sure which of them) was put to a vote. This test indicated a probability that a majority of the overseers would favor granting of the degree. Thereupon, Clarke reiterated the case for the negative so vigorously as to turn the scales against Butler. However, a book recently published by the Harvard University Press (Geoffrey Blodgetts's *The Gentle Reformers*), says that Butler was denied the degree because of Storey's intervention.[18]

---

[18] Geoffrey Blodgett, *The Gentle Reformers* (Harvard University Press, [Cambridge Mass., 1966]), p. 24.

The overseers decision, of course, evoked widespread comment. Butler characterized it as "a puny effort at insult from political opponents."[19] Some Harvard men were even more outspoken. Wendell Phillips (class of 1831) said rank Toryism had governed the majority of the overseers.[20] An alumnus who believed the overseers had made a grave mistake remarked that "prejudice and political hostility blinded the judgment and warped the reason of the eminent gentlemen who composed the majority."[21] Another said, "For one politician on the board of overseers [presumably Hoar] to say to the chief magistrate of Massachusetts, 'I am better than thou,' and to persuade fourteen others to join the chorus is altogether too much like the political methods these people pretend to condemn."[22] A member of the class of 1877 thought it was "an outrage for the overseers, in their desire to gratify personal and political spite, . . . to drag down the University into the political mire." Their action, he added, would cause Harvard to "be known as Unitarian in religion and bigoted in politics."[23]

Although Toryism, political hostility and personal spite certainly influenced some of the overseers, the minority included men who were equally conservative, equally ardent in their Republicanism, and equally hostile toward Butler personally. Indeed, some of those who voted "yea" had openly expressed such feelings about Butler that if the matter had been a judicial one they could not ethically have sat on the case.[24]

The news that Harvard would not give Butler an honorary degree was greeted with approval by several editors in Boston, a few in the rest of New England, and several in New York. With these exceptions the press throughout the East condemned the overseers' action as an ill-advised and unwarrantable insult. Some

---

[19] Boston *Herald,* June 1, 1883.
[20] Boston *Traveller,* June 5, 1883.
[21] Boston *Globe,* June 1, 1883.
[22] Idem.
[23] Ibid., June 2, 1883.
[24] See the Boston *Journal,* June 1, 1883. for the individual overseers' votes.

newspapers called it politically foolish as well, because it would certainly gain thousands of votes for Butler at the next election and was likely to start a boom for him as a presidential candidate. The Boston *Traveller* bluntly said the overseers could not have done a bigger favor to Butler if he had dictated their decision.[25]

One thing the overseers could not do was to interfere with the ex officio right of the governor to be present at Harvard's commencement. Butler attended the exercises in high style. He was driven from the State House to Harvard in a barouche drawn by six horses, escorted by the Lancers (a militia regiment) attired in red dress uniforms, and he and the president of the University led the academic parade. Long after the event Joseph H. Choate, president of the Alumni Association in 1883, said, "Butler appeared to great advantage and quite turned the tables upon the College overseers."[26] At the alumni dinner, to which the governor had to be invited, Butler responded to the toast, "The Commonwealth of Massachusetts," with a speech which even his bitterest opponents had to admit was in excellent taste.

[25] Loc. cit., June 1, 1883.
[26] Edward S. Martin, *The Life of Joseph Hodges Choate* (Chas. Scribner's Sons [New York]), I, 362.

22

★★★★★★★★★★★★

Butler for President

Soon after Butler was elected governor he was stung by the presidential bee. There is no clear evidence as to just when this happened. It may have been at the Jackson Day dinner in the Revere House on January 8, 1883 when several speakers "nominated" him as Democratic standard bearer for 1884. Perhaps it resulted from the considerable amount of speculation about his future among politicians and journalists caused by his "tidal wave" victory. In Washington, where political gossip was, as it still is, almost the breath of life, he was regarded as a strong contender for the next Democratic nomination. This fact led *The Nation* editorially to warn Governor Grover Cleveland of New York, if he aspired to the presidency (as he did) to watch out for Governor Butler.[1]

Butler's hopes and his stock were given a strong boost in May, 1883, when he was invited to give the "long talk," or principal speech, at Tammany Hall's Fourth of July celebration. Business arrangements he was unable to change, though he tried to do so, made it impossible for him to accept this "kind invitation."[2]

Because a reelection as governor would obviously be helpful to his efforts to secure the presidential nomination Butler quickly forgot having said he would not seek a second term. Oddly enough no Republican seems to have reminded him of it.

The Republicans, well aware that Butler would be renominated if he so desired, began looking for a gubernatorial candidate far earlier in 1883 than usual. They soon found that nobody was

---

[1] Loc. cit., November 16, 1882, p. 411.
[2] Boston *Journal,* May 28, 1883.

eager to make the race, for, as Henry Cabot Lodge, chairman of the State Committee, later commented, the prospect of a Republican victory was not bright.[3]

After several men had refused to let their names even be considered the Republican leaders decided to lay the burden of opposing Butler upon Henry L. Pierce. Suddenly, two days before the nominating convention was to be held, Pierce told the State Committee he would not run. He recommended Congressman George D. Robinson to the Committee and the convention. Having no practical alternative, the convention chose Robinson to head what the Boston *Globe* called "the Dude's ticket."

To nobody's surprise the Democrats renominated Butler.

When the Greenback-Labor convention met there was some talk about choosing a candidate other than Butler because of his association with the Democracy. However, the delegates decided that Butler was entitled to the support of every Greenbacker in the state in view "of his great efforts on behalf of the people for the last forty years," and nominated him unanimously.[4]

The Republicans outdid themselves in the ensuing campaign. Robinson spared no effort. The "strong men of Massachusetts" banded together against Butler. The "new Massachusetts Reform Club" was organized especially to oppose him. Moorfield Storey and Arlo Bates prepared a scurrilous broadside (which also was published in pamphlet form) entitled *The Record of Benjamin F. Butler*.[5]

Despite all they had done the Republicans were by no means sure of the outcome of the canvass when the polls closed November 6, 1882. However, the final returns showed 160,000 votes for Robinson to 150,000 for Butler.

Butler received the news of his defeat stoically; the Republi-

---

[3] Henry Cabot Lodge, *A Fighting Frigate and Other Essays and Addresses* (Charles Scribner's Sons [New York, 1902]), p. 169.

[4] Boston *Globe,* September 25, 1883.

[5] Lodge, op. cit., p. 172. Sarah Forbes Hughes (editor) *Letters and Recollections of John Murray Forbes* (Houghton, Mifflin and Company [Boston, 1899]), II, 204; M. A. DeWolfe Howe, *Portrait of an Independent* (Houghton, Mifflin Company [Boston, 1932]), pp. 146–47.

cans greeted it with joy and (literally) feasting.[6] The Boston
Advertiser and the Boston *Journal*, presumably by coincidence,
used identical headlines over their election stories: "Redeemed."[7]

Events soon demonstrated that Butler's defeat had not robbed
him of control of the Massachusetts Democracy or of nation-wide
popularity with an important segment of the electorate.

Late in April, 1884 he was chosen, almost unanimously, to head
his state's delegation to the Democratic party's national convention and the delegation was pledged to support him for the presidential nomination.

On May 14 the newly organized Anti-Monopoly party held its
first nominating convention. After adopting a platform denounc-
ing the existing tariff as favorable to monopolies, proposing the
equal application to all classes of just and equal laws, and opposing further land grants to corporations, the delegates nominated
Butler for the presidency. The vote on the first and only roll call
was 122 for Butler, 7 for Allen G. Thurman of Ohio, 1 for
Solon Chase of Maine.

When the Greenback-Labor convention opened in Indianapolis
two weeks later a message was sent to Butler asking him if he
would accept the party's presidential nomination upon a suitable
platform. He replied with a question of his own: "Is not my record as a greenbacker for twenty years sufficient without a formal
pledge to you which would cause me to be pointed at a man who
bids for the nomination."[8]

This response satisfied the delegates. They nominated Butler
on the first roll call with 322 votes to 99 for Jesse Harper of
Illinois, and 1 each for Edward P. Allis of Wisconsin and David
Davis of Illinois.

Somewhat to the disappointment of the leaders of the Anti-
Monopoly and Greenback-Labor parties Butler answered their

[6] Boston *Globe,* November 7, 1883.
[7] Loc. cit., November 7, 1883.
[8] Fred E. Haynes, *Third Party Movements Since the Civil War* (The
State Historical Society of Iowa [Iowa City, 1916]), p. 149.

notification committees noncommittally. He did not refuse the honor they offered him, but he did not definitely accept it. However, he undoubtedly hoped their nominations would benefit his efforts also to be chosen as the Democratic candidate.

The fact that Butler was favored by two labor oriented minor parties certainly must have influenced those present at a conference of Democratic leaders held in the Fifth Avenue Hotel in New York at some time in June, 1884. This hush hush gathering was attended by Butler and a number of other men from various parts of the country representing several aspirants for the presidential nomination (not including Cleveland). Apparently it was instigated by "Honest" John Kelly, Grand Sachem of Tammany Hall, for the purpose of procuring support for Butler against Cleveland. Tammany's ostensible reasons, and partly its real ones, for opposing Cleveland were a doubt that he would be a strong candidate in the country at large and a firm belief that he could not carry New York state. Kelly said he was certain that Cleveland's nomination would result in a state-wide Republican majority of 40,000 to 50,000 votes, with even New York City going Republican. (Another important, but unspoken, reason for Tammany's hostility toward Cleveland was a well-grounded fear that in the event of his election the Hall would not get any federal patronage.) Under Kelly's astute management the group was brought to feel that the best, if not the only, way to stop Cleveland was to support Butler. A suggestion that Butler would be weak in the South was answered by a Virginian who emphatically said that for every white man's vote the General would lose he would gain three Negro votes.[9]

The (Democratic) Boston *Globe* believed Butler would be the strongest candidate his party could name. Admitting his unpopularity "with a few nice persons who call themselves the better element of Massachusetts," the *Globe*'s editors described him as indisputably "the first choice of the 150,000 Democrats of [his] State and of the working people everywhere." The *Globe* also

---

[9] Boston *Globe,* July 1, 1884.

thought the colored men of the South had "not forgotten" his friendship "at a time when they sorely needed friends."[10]

Early in June, Butler decided to attend the convention in Chicago in order to represent the Anti-Monopoly and Greenback-Labor elements of the Democracy. As soon as his plans became known to them labor unions from Boston to Chicago made arrangements to greet him fittingly everywhere his train was scheduled to stop. At most places he could do no more than show himself; occasionally he had time for brief speeches. At Chicago 3,000 union members met him at the station and escorted him past 50,000 cheering spectators to the Palmer House. Later he was called from the hotel to address an enormous and spontaneous street gathering. (One observer estimated the size of the crowd as 20,000 persons; it was at least big enough to stop all traffic in the vicinity of the Palmer House.) He had to wait 15 minutes for the applause to subside before he could make himself heard. Willis J. Abbot, who witnessed the event, wrote long afterward that Butler's radical and ringing speech evoked more genuine enthusiasm in the working class crowd than was manufactured at the convention.[11]

As he had hoped to do, Butler secured a place on the platform committee. Displeased with the currency, labor, and tariff planks drafted by the rest of the committee, he presented a one man minority report. The currency and labor planks he proposed had the merit of using plainer language than the majority's planks did. The majority's pronouncement on currency read: "We believe in honest money, the gold and silver certificates of the Constitution, and a circulating medium convertible into such money without loss." Butler's plank stated that legal tender notes (greenbacks) had become part of the currency of the United States and neither policy nor duty called for any meddling with this arrange-

10 Ibid., July 6, 1884.
11 Willis J. Abbot, *Watching the World Go By* (Little, Brown and Company [Boston, 1933]), pp. 72–73.

ment. The majority's labor plank favored "the repeal of all laws restricting the free action of labor and the enactment of laws by which labor organizations may be incorporated and of all such legislation as will tend to enlighten the people as to the true relations of capital and labor." Butler's plank called for a promise "to provide by law that laboring men may combine and organize for their own protection as capital may be incorporated and combined for its protection, and that all devices, either by contract, terrorism, or otherwise to obstruct and set aside this right in laboring men are oppressive and in derogation of the rights of American freemen, and should be made penal by law." (Butler's shade must have hovered over the Congress that passed the National Labor Relations Act in 1935.) The majority's tariff plank and Butler's were both composed of meaningless double-talk. The majority called for a tariff for revenue only, but pledged the party "to revise the tariff in a spirit of fairness to all interests," in a manner calculated "not . . . to injure any domestic industries, but rather to promote their healthy growth," and with due regard to the effects on capital and labor of any changes made. Butler proposed a tariff for revenue only, with heavy duties levied on luxury goods, but raw materials and necessities of life not produced in the United States admitted free, with "the laws imposing duties for revenue . . . carefully adjusted to promote American enterprise and American industry, to cherish and foster American labor, [but] not to create monopolies."[12]

Butler was allowed 30 minutes at a late hour during a night session of the convention in which to present his report. In the belief that he could do justice to only one subject in so brief a time he talked chiefly about his tariff plank, which he thought dealt with a matter vital to the future of the Democracy and the country. By some strange mental process he found a radical difference between the majority's Mumbo Jumbo and his own. In his opinion the majority had written a free trade plank while his definitely promised protection to the laborers of the country. De-

---

[12] *Official Proceedings of the National Democratic Convention of 1884* (Douglas Taylor's Democratic Press [New York, 1884]), pp. 195-206.

spite his eloquence his proposals were rejected by a vote of 721½ to 96½. From the moment the vote was announced Butler ceased, as he later said, to desire the Democratic nomination because he believed the defeat of anyone advocating free trade would be inevitable, as well as desirable. Perhaps he really terminated his candidacy because of the "free trade plank," but one thinks it more likely that he realized how little chance he had of being nominated and withdrew rather than be defeated.

For some time after the convention adjourned Butler refused to say what he intended to do in the forthcoming campaign. Because of his large and devoted labor class following his silence gravely alarmed the Democratic leadership. Finally Samuel J. Randall, a former Speaker of the House of Representatives, was sent to negotiate with Butler.[13] According to Butler's autobiography he was told that if he supported the Democratic ticket he would be given grateful consideration by Cleveland in the event of his election.[14] If such an offer were made, and it or something like it probably was, Butler did not accept it. Instead he announced in a lengthy address, published August 12, 1884, that he would be an active candidate of the Anti-Monopoly and Greenback-Labor parties. He advocated a consolidation of those parties into a People's party and recommended a short, sharp, decisive campaign to begin in mid-September.

The Democratic press immediately alleged that Butler had virtually been hired by Blaine to work against Cleveland. As the story was told, Butler met William E. Chandler of New Hampshire, Blaine's confidant of 20 years standing, on board a yacht in Portsmouth, New Hampshire; accepted $25,000 for campaign expenses; was promised as much more as he wanted; and was guaranteed control of federal patronage in New England if Blaine won the election.

---

[13] M. P. Curran, *Life of Patrick A. Collins* (The Norwood Press [Norwood, Mass., 1906]), pp. 92–93.

[14] Benjamin F. Butler, *Butler's Book* (A. M. Thayer & Co., [Boston, 1892]), p. 983.

There does not seem to be any disinterested evidence to support these allegations and the fact that they were first publicized by Patrick A. Collins, chairman of the Massachusetts Democratic State Committee,[15] makes them suspect, yet they ring basically true. Blaine and his supporters certainly needed all the help they could get from anyone at all. Blaine's (well-founded) reputation as the most corrupt politician (at least of his own day, perhaps of all American history) had caused many prominent Republicans and such Republican newspapers as the *New York Times,* the New York *Telegram,* the New York *Evening Post,* the Philadelphia *Times,* the Philadelphia *Record,* the Boston *Advertiser,* the Boston *Transcript*, and the Boston *Herald* to support Cleveland. To make matters worse from the Republicans' point of view the Prohibition party's candidate, John P. St. John (a former Republican governor of Kansas) directed his fire wholly and heavily against Blaine because his party had refused to include a dry plank in its platform. Paralleling the Republicans' need for help from any quarter was Butler's ability to use more money than it is likely his two parties could have provided for him.

Whatever may have been the truth about the financing of Butler's campaign, many laborers came to believe that he and the Republicans had struck a mutually satisfactory bargain. This feeling undoubtedly cost Butler many votes, whether it was justified or not.

Butler said he took an active part in the campaign only in the hope of effecting Cleveland's defeat and avowed that his opposition to Cleveland was based on hostility toward a free trader. It is difficult to see how a President who failed to veto the Wilson-Gorman Tariff Act of 1894 could be regarded as a free trader. However, Butler was satisfied to consider Cleveland to be one. Of course, Butler would have found some ground for rationalizing his opposition to any Democrat who might have secured the nomination he desired for himself.

---

[15] Curran, op. cit., p. 92.

Because New York would obviously be the key state Butler concentrated his anti-Cleveland campaign there. The General's efforts might have cost Cleveland the election if it had not been for a labor dispute between the New York *Tribune* and Local No. 6 of the International Typographical Union. The Local, known in New York as Big Six, declared war against Blaine because the *Tribune* supported him. Throughout the canvass the members of Big Six worked vigorously for Cleveland, instead of supporting Butler as they might have done in different circumstances. With Big Six on the Democratic side the vote in New York was 563,154 for Cleveland, 562,005 for Blaine, 25,016 for St. John, and 16,994 for Butler. Cleveland's tiny plurality gave him the state and the presidency.

S'ome years after the event Butler claimed that votes actually cast for him in Brooklyn and New York City were fraudulently counted for Cleveland. Subsequently G. F. Hoar and Edward Stanwood (who was related to Blaine by marriage) echoed this charge.[16] When Stanwood reiterated it after Cleveland's death it was examined and disproved by William G. Rice and Francis L. Stetson.[17]

---

[16] Butler, op. cit., p. 983; George F. Hoar, *Autobiography of Seventy Years* (Charles Scribner's Sons [New York, 1903]), I, 408; Edward Stanwood, *James Gillespie Blaine* (Houghton Mifflin Company [Boston, 1905]), p. 294.

[17] Edward Stanwood, "Election Superstitions and Fallacies," *Atlantic Monthly*, October 1912, CX, 559; William Gorham Rice and Francis Lynde Stetson, "Was New York's Vote Stolen?" *North American Review*, January 1914, CXCIX, 79.

23

L'Envoi

After the election of 1884 Butler retired from the political arena, but he was not forgotten by his old followers or by the press.

At least once a year the newspapers mentioned him in their reports of the Butler Club dinners, held on the anniversary of the capture of New Orleans. These affairs were always attended by many well-known men, often including the governor of Massachusetts.

In October, 1887 Butler appeared in the United States Supreme Court on behalf of August Spies and Samuel Fielden, two of the so-called Chicago anarchists. Spies, Fielden, and six codefendants had been convicted of murder by means of a bomb of a policeman who had been one of a force which broke up a labor demonstration at Chicago's Haymarket Square on May 4, 1884. The anarchists' case (which attracted as much attention throughout the world as the Sacco-Vanzetti case did in the 1920's) was appealed to the federal courts on the grounds that the conduct of their trial by the Illinois courts had violated their constitutional right to the equal protection of the law. Their lawyers argued that they had been tried and convicted by a hand picked "hanging jury." Butler also held that because his particular clients were foreigners (Spies was a German, Fielden an Englishman) they enjoyed special privileges in addition to their constitutional rights. They should have been tried, he argued, in accordance with laws dealing with search for evidence, legal juries, etc., in force when certain treaties between their countries and the United States had been ratified. The justices, who were widely believed to have prejudged the case,

298

did not even pretend to pay any attention to Butler's argument. While he was speaking to them they read briefs or other papers. In the end they denied his petition for a writ of error, saying that the point he was trying to make had not been raised in any of the lower courts and it could not be raised for the first time in the Supreme Court.

In August, 1890 the Grand Army of the Republic (an organization of Union veterans similar in structure and comparable in political power to the American Legion) held its annual encampment, or national convention, in Boston. The GAR officially favored legislation to make all Union veterans eligible for pensions for service alone. Butler expressed his heartfelt approval of this idea. As he said, the men who served on the Union side in the war had entered into a contract with the federal government and in good faith the government "owed" them the difference between the amount of their pay in greenbacks and the war time gold value of the dollar. There had been, he remarked, a lot of talk about justice to bondholders, he hoped justice would be done to the veterans.

Time took its toll of Butler, as it does of all men. His voice lost much of its power, his eyesight failed to a considerable extent, and it became increasingly difficult for him to carry his bulk on his small feet and slender ankles. In his later years he practically dropped his criminal practice, but continued to handle civil cases. A case he had appealed to the United States Supreme Court kept him in Washington during much of the winter of 1892–93. On January 10, 1893 he spent part of the day in court, then visited the War Department, and returned at dinner time to the home of his niece and her husband where he stayed when he was in Washington. For some time past James G. Blaine, the Mr. Republican of his day, had been mortally ill, with the newspapers issuing press time bulletins about his condition. At dinner Butler said, "Mark me, Blaine will outlive all of us yet." He also remarked that when his allotted time came to its end he hoped he would die suddenly, not lingeringly as Blaine was doing. After chatting with his niece and her family until about 11 P.M., Butler went to bed, apparently in normal health. A couple of hours later he was seized with a coughing spell so violent it woke his Negro valet. The valet stayed with the General until he seemed relieved and said nothing more needed to be done for him. At 1:30 A.M., he began coughing again and died before a hastily summoned doctor could reach his bedside.

The Lowell Post of the GAR, of which Butler had been a member, took charge of arrangements to give him a major general's funeral. His body lay in state in Huntington Hall in Lowell for several days and was viewed by thousands. His burial was delayed to permit distant GAR posts to be represented. He was finally buried on a stormy, bitterly cold day.

The rule of *nil nisi bonum* was not observed in regard to Butler. Eighteen years after he died the Massachusetts legislature considered erecting a statue on the State House grounds as a memorial to him. Led by Moorfield Storey, those of Butler's enemies who were still alive rallied in opposition to this proposal and rehashed all of the ugly things they had ever said about him.

In a very real sense Butler had three different careers—legal, military, and political. In the first he was eminently successful. In the second he did as well as his background and training permitted. If he had been educated at West Point he would have been a top notch soldier. As it was he had the misfortune to have been promoted to a rank beyond his capacity. He would have made an excellent brigadier general or a superb colonel. In politics he went far and with a little better luck he might have gone much further. He played more than a small part in generating the populist movement which gave rise in turn to William Jennings Bryan's "New Democracy," Theodore Roosevelt's "Square Deal," Woodrow Wilson's "New Freedom," and Franklin D. Roosevelt's "New Deal." If Butler had been born a generation or two later than he was he would have been a powerful, and perhaps a successful, rival to Bryan or one of the Roosevelt cousins.

Bibliography

Abbot, Willis J., *Watching the World Go By*. Boston: Little, Brown and Company, 1933.

Abbott, John S. C., "Heroic Deeds of Heroic Men." *Harper's Monthly*, April 1865, Vol. XXX.

The History of the Civil War in America (two vols.) New York: Henry Bill, 1863, 1867.

Adams, Brooks, "The Platform of the New Party." *North American Review*, July 1874, Vol. CXIX.

Adams, Charles Francis, *Richard Henry Dana* (two vols.) Boston: Houghton, Mifflin and Company, 1890.

Studies Military and Diplomatic. New York: The Macmillan Company, 1911.

Adams, Charles Francis, Jr., *Charles Francis Adams*. Boston: Houghton, Mifflin and Company, 1900.

An Autobiography. Boston: Houghton Mifflin Company, 1916.

Alexander, Augustus W., *Grant as a Soldier*. St. Louis: Published by the Author, 1887.

Ambler, Charles H., *Francis H. Pierpont . . . Father of West Virginia*. Chapel Hill; University of North Carolina Press, 1937.

Ames, Blanche Butler, *The Butler Ancestry of Gen. Benjamin Franklin Butler*. Lowell: Privately Printed, 1895.

Ammen, Daniel, *The Atlantic Coast*. New York: Charles Scribner's Sons, 1883.

The Old Navy and the New. Philadelphia: J. B. Lippincott Company, 1891.

Andrews, Matthew Page, *History of Maryland*. New York: Doubleday, Doran & Company, Inc., 1929.

Anonymous, "Our General." *Atlantic Monthly*, July 1863, Vol. XII.

Life and Public Services of Major-General Butler. Philadelphia: T. B. Peterson & Brothers, 1864.

Major Gen. Butler at Home (pamphlet, title page missing, acquired by the Boston Public Library, May 29, 1865).

"Wilmington During the Blockade," *Harper's Monthly,* September 1866, Vol. XXXIII.

Why I Cannot Vote for Ben. Butler by a Carpet Bag Voter of the 5th District, (pamphlet) no date, no publisher (Published during the 1868 congressional campaign).

"The Butler Canvass," *North American Review,* January 1872, Vol. CXIV.

Annals of the War. Philadelphia: The Times Publishing Company, 1879.

"Limited Sovereignty in the United States," *Atlantic Monthly,* February 1879, Vol. XLIII.

"Our Military Past and Future," *Atlantic Monthly,* November 1879, Vol. XLIV.

Arnold, Isaac N., *Abraham Lincoln and the Overthrow of Slavery.* Chicago: Clarke & Co., 1866.

Austin, George Lowell, *The History of Massachusetts.* Boston: B. B. Russell; Estes & Lauriat, 1876.

Baber, George, "Johnson, Grant, Seward, Sumner," *North American Review,* July 1887, Vol. CXLV.

Badeau, Adam, *Military History of Ulysses S. Grant.* (3 vols.) New York: D. Appleton and Company, 1881.

Basler, Roy (editor), *The Collected Works of Abraham Lincoln* (9 vols.) New Brunswick, N.J.: Rutgers University Press, 1955.

Beauregard, Pierre G. T., "Drury's Bluff and Petersburg," *North American Review,* March 1887, Vol. CXLIV.

"The Battle of Petersburg," *North American Review,* October 1887, Vol. CXLV.

Bennett, Lerone, Jr., "Was Abe Lincoln a White Supremacist?" *Ebony,* February 1968.

Bigelow, L. J., *Bench and Bar.* New York: Harper and Brothers, 1871.

Bill, Alfred Hoyt, *The Beleaguered City.* New York: Alfred A. Knopf, 1946.

Bishop, Joseph B., "The Secret Ballot in Thirty-three States," *The Forum,* January 1892, Vol. XII.

Blaine, James G., *Twenty Years of Congress* (two vols.) Norwich, Conn.: The Henry Bill Publishing Company, 1884, 1886.

Blakeman, A. Noel (editor), *Personal Recollections of the War of the Rebellion* (Vol. II) New York: G. P. Putnam's Sons, 1897.

Bland, T. A., *Life of Benjamin F. Butler*. Boston: Lee and Shepard, 1879.

Blodgett, Geoffrey, *The Gentle Reformers*. Cambridge: Harvard University Press, 1966.

Boutwell, George S., *Reminiscences of Sixty Years* (two vols.) New York: McClure, Phillips & Co., 1902.

Bowen, James L., *Massachusetts in the War*. Springfield, Mass.: Bowen & Son, 1892.

Bowers, Claude G., *The Tragic Era*. Boston: Houghton Mifflin Company, 1929.

Bradford, Gamaliel, *Wives*. New York: Harper & Brothers, 1925. *Damaged Souls*. Boston: Houghton Mifflin Company, 1931.

Bridgman, Raymond L., *The Independents of Massachusetts in 1884*. Boston: Cupples, Upham & Co., 1885.

Briggs, Emily Edson, *The Olivia Letters*. New York and Washington, D. C.: The Neale Publishing Company, 1906.

Brockett, M. D., *Men of Our Day*. Philadelphia: Ziegler & McCurdy, 1872.

Brodie, Fawn M., *Thaddeus Stevens*. New York: W. W. Norton & Company, 1959.

Brown, George William, *Baltimore and the Nineteenth of April, 1861*. Baltimore: Johns Hopkins University, 1887.

Brown, T. Allston, *History of the American Stage*. New York: Dick & Fitzgerald, 1870.

Buchanan, Joseph R., *Story of a Labor Agitator*. New York: The Outlook Company, 1903.

Buck, Paul H., *The Road to Reunion*. Boston: Little, Brown and Company, 1937.

Buck, Solon J., *The Agrarian Crusade*. New Haven: Yale University Press, 1920.

Burton, H. W., *The History of Norfolk, Virginia*. Norfolk: Norfolk, Virginia, Job Press, 1877.

Butler, Benjamin F., *The Character and Results of the War* (Pamphlet). New York: Loyal Publication Society, 1863.

A "Chaplain's Campaign" (not) with General Butler (Pamphlet). Lowell: Charles Hunt, 1865.

Campaign before Richmond (Pamphlet). Boston: Wright & Potter, Printers, 1865.

How We May Relieve Ourselves from Taxation (Pamphlet). Washington, D. C.: F. & J. Rives & George A. Bailey, 1868.

Reconstruction in Georgia (Pamphlet), Washington, D. C.: F. & J. Rives & George A. Bailey, 1869.

Reduction of the Army (Pamphlet). Washington, D. C.: F. & J. Rives & George A. Bailey, 1869.

The Present Relation of Parties (Pamphlet). Lowell, Mass.: Marden & Rowell, 1870.

The Treaty of Washington (Pamphlet). Lowell, Mass.: Marden & Rowell, 1871.

Frauds on the Revenues of the Government (Pamphlet). Washington, D. C.: Government Printing Office, 1874.

Letter of General Benj. F. Butler to Hon. E. R. Hoar (Pamphlet, dated October 1876). Lowell, Mass.: Published by request, 1876.

The Private Volunteer Soldier (Pamphlet). Boston: Rockwell and Churchill, 1876.

Speech on the necessity for a change in Party Aministration of Federal Politics (Pamphlet). Boston: Rockwell and Churchill, 1880.

"Presidential Inability," *North American Review*, November 1881, Vol. CXXXIII.

Argument before the Tewksbury Investigation Committee (Pamphlet). Boston: The Democratic Central Committee (of Massachusetts), 1883.

Address to his Constituents August 12, 1884 (Pamphlet). Boston: J. E. Farwell & Co., 1884.

Minority Report of Gen'l. Benj. F. Butler and his Argument before the National Democratic Convention, Chicago, 1884 (Pamphlet). Boston: J. E. Farwell & Co., 1884.

"Vice-Presidential Politics in '64," *North American Review*, October 1885, Vol. CXLI.

"The Behring Sea Controversy," *North American Review*, May 1892, Vol. CLIV.

Butler's Book. Boston: A. M. Thayer & Co., 1892.

Crawford, Theron Clark, *James G. Blaine*. Philadelphia: Edgewood Publishing Co., 1893.

Cunningham, Frank H., *Familiar Sketches of the Phillips Exeter Academy*. Boston: James R. Osgood and Company, 1883.

Curran, M. P., *Life of Patrick A. Collins*. Norwood, Mass.: The Norwood Press, 1906.

Curtis, George Ticknor, et al., *Discussions on the Constitution Proposed to the People of Massachusetts by the Convention of 1853*. Boston: Little, Brown and Company, 1854.

Curtis, William E., *The True Abraham Lincoln*. Philadelphia: J. B. Lippincott Company, 1903.

Dana, Charles A., *Recollections of the Civil War*. New York: D. Appleton and Company, 1898.

David, Henry, *The History of the Haymarket Affair*. New York: Farrar & Rinhehart, Inc., 1936.

Davis, Jefferson, *Rise and Fall of the Confederacy* (two vols.) New York: D. Appleton and Company, 1881.

Dawes, Anna Laurens, *Charles Sumner*. New York: Dodd, Mead and Company, 1892.

Day, D. L., *My Diary*. Milford, Mass.: King & Billings, 1884.

De Forest, John William, *A Volunteer's Adventures*. New Haven: Yale University Press, 1946.

Dennett, Tyler (Editor), *Lincoln and the Civil War in the Diaries and Letters of John Hay*. New York: Dodd, Mead & Company, 1939.

Dewitt, David Miller, *The Impeachment and Trial of Andrew Johnson*. New York: The Macmillan Company, 1903.
    The Assassination of Abraham Lincoln. New York: The Macmillan Company, 1909.

Dibble, F. L., *Vagaries of Sanitary Science*. Philadelphia: J. B. Lippincott Company, 1893.

Dodge, H. Augusta, *Gail Hamilton's Life in Letters* (two vols.) Boston, Lee and Shepard, 1901.

Dodge, Theodore Ayrault, *A Bird's-Eye View of Our Civil War*. Boston, Houghton Mifflin Company, 1911.

Donovan, J. W., *Modern Jury Trials and Advocates*. New York: Banks & Brothers, 1881.

Douglas, Henry Kyd, *I Rode with Stonewall*. Chapel Hill: University of North Carolina Press, 1940.

Bibliography — Page 305

Canfield, Eugene B., "Porter's Mortar Schooners," *Civil War Times,* October 1967, Vol. VI.

Carter, Hodding, *The Angry Scar.* Garden City, N. Y.: Doubleday & Company, 1959.

Chadsey, Charles E., *The Struggle between President Johnson and Congress over Reconstruction.* New York: Columbia University Press, 1896.

Chandler, Peleg W., *Memoir of the Hon. John Albion Andrew.* Cambridge, Mass.: John Wilson and Son, 1880.

Channing, Edward, *A History of the United States* (Vol. VI). New York: The Macmillan Company, 1925.

Chase, S. P., *Diary and Correspondence of Salmon P. Chase* (in the *Annual Report of the American Historical Association for the Year 1902,* Vol. II). Washington, D. C.: Government Printing Office, 1903.

Chestnut, Mary Boykin, *A Diary from Dixie.* New York: D. Appleton and Company, 1905.

Chittenden, L. E., *Recollections of President Lincoln and His Administration.* New York: Harper & Brothers, 1891.

Church, William Conant, *Ulysses S. Grant.* New York: G. P. Putnam's Sons, 1897.

Clapp, William W., Jr., *A Record of the Boston Stage.* Boston: James Munroe and Company, 1853.

Clark, Edward H. G., *General Butler.* New York: People's Party Document, 1884.

Colby, Elbridge, *Theodore Winthrop.* New York: Twayne Publishers, Inc., 1965.

Conway, Moncure Daniel, *Autobiography* (two vols.) Boston: Houghton, Mifflin and Company, 1904.

Conwell, Russell H., *Address before the Aurora Club, July 31st, 1874.* Boston: Published by the Aurora Club, 1874.

Coolidge, Louis A., *Ulysses S. Grant.* Boston: Houghton Mifflin Company, 1917.

Coulter, E. Merton, *The Confederate States of America.* Baton Rouge, La.: Louisiana State University Press, 1950.

Cox, Jacob D., "How Judge Hoar Ceased to be Attorney-General," *Atlantic Monthly* August 1895, Vol. LXXVI.

Crafts, W. A., *The Southern Rebellion.* (two vols.) New York: Samuel Walker & Co., 1866, 1867.

Draper, John William, *History of the American Civil War* (three vols.) New York: Harper & Brothers, 1867, 1868, 1870.

Du Bois, W. E. B., *Black Reconstruction.* New York: Harcourt, Brace and Company, 1935.

Dudley, Dean, *Officers of Our Union Army.* Boston: L. Prang & Co., 1862.

Dunbar-Nelson, Alice, "People of Color in New Orleans," *Journal of Negro History,* January 1917, Vol. II.

Dunning, William A., *Essays on the Civil War and Reconstruction and Related Topics.* New York: The Macmillan Company, 1898.

"The Undoing of Reconstruction," *Atlantic Monthly,* October 1901, Vol. XXCVIII.

Reconstruction Political and Economic. New York: Harper & Brothers, 1907.

Dwight, Theodore F. (Editor), *Critical Sketches of Some of the Federal and Confederate Commanders.* Boston: Houghton, Mifflin and Company, 1895.

Eaton, John, *Grant, Lincoln and the Freedmen,* New York: Longmans, Green and Co., 1907.

Edson, Theodore, *The Parish Register of St. Anne's Church.* Lowell, Mass.: Morning Mail Print, 1885.

Eggleston, George Cary, *The History of the Confederate War* (two vols.) New York: Sturgis & Walton Company, 1910.

Evans, Clement, *Confederate Military History* (Vol. X) Atlanta: Confederate Publishing Co., 1899.

Evans, Robley D., *A Sailor's Log.* New York: D. Appleton and Company, 1901.

Farragut, Loyall, *The Life of David Glasgow Farragut.* New York: D. Appleton and Company, 1879.

Felt, Charles W., *Butler among his Farmer, Mechanic and Laborer Constituents* (Pamphlet) Northboro, Mass.: Farmer Printing Office, 1878.

A Two Thousand Dollar Bill for Sale (Pamphlet) Northboro, Mass.: Farmer Printing Office, 1883.

Ficklen, John Rose, *History of Reconstruction in Louisiana.* Baltimore: The Johns Hopkins Press, 1910.

Fisk, John, *The Mississippi Valley in the Civil War*. Boston: Houghton, Mifflin and Company, 1900.

Fite, Emerson D., *The Presidential Campaign of 1860*. New York: The Macmillan Company, 1911.

Fleming, Walter L., *Documentary History of Reconstruction* (two vols.) Cleveland: The Arthur H. Clark Company, 1906, 1907.
The Sequel of Appomatox. New Haven: Yale University Press, 1920.

Ford, Worthington Chauncey (Editor), *A Cycle of Adams Letters: 1861–1865*. Boston, Houghton Mifflin Company, 1920.
(Editor) *Letters of Henry Adams*. Boston: Houghton Mifflin Company, 1930.

Forney, John W., *Anecdotes of Public Men* (two vols.) New York: Harper & Brothers, 1873, 1881.

Franklin, John Hope, *From Slavery to Freedom*. New York: Alfred A. Knopf, 1947.

Freeman, Douglas Southall, *R. E. Lee* (four vols.) New York: Charles Scribner's Sons, 1935.

Fuess, Claude M., *The Life of Caleb Cushing* (two vols.) New York: Harcourt, Brace and Company, 1923.
Carl Schurz. New York: Dodd, Mead & Company, 1932.

Garfield, James A., *Reply to the Hons. Frederic A. Pike and B. F. Butler* (Pamphlet) Washington, D. C.: F. & J. Rives & Geo. A. Bailey, 1868.

Garrett, William Robertson, and Robert O. Halley, *The Civil War from a Southern Standpoint*. Philadelphia: George Barrie & Sons, 1905.

Gillett, Frederick H., *George Frisbie Hoar*. Boston: Houghton Mifflin Company, 1934.

Gobrecht, J. C., *History of the National Home for Disabled Volunteer Soldiers*. Dayton, Ohio: United Brethren Printing Establishment, 1875.

Gordon, E. C., *The Battle of Big Bethel* (Pamphlet) Richmond, Va.: Carlton McCarthy & Co., 1883.

Gordon, George H., *A War Diary of Events in the Great Rebellion*. Boston: James R. Osgood and Company, 1882.

Gorham, George C., *Life and Public Services of Edwin M. Stanton* (two vols.) Boston: Houghton, Mifflin and Company, 1899.

Grant, U. S., *Personal Memoirs of U. S. Grant* (two vols.) New York: Charles L. Webster & Company, 1885, 1886.

Greeley, Horace, *The American Conflict* (two vols.) Hartford, Conn.: O. D. Case & Company, 1865, 1867.

Greeley, Horace and John F. Cleveland, *A Political Text–Book for 1860.* New York: The Tribune Association, 1860.

Griffin, John Q. A., *A Portrait of Benjamin F. Butler by a House Painter.* Pamphlet reprinted from the *Charlestown* (Mass.) *Advertiser,* September 7, 1859.

Gurowski, Adam, *Diary* (three vols.) Washington, D. C.: W. H. & O. H. Morrison, 1866.

Hale, Edward Everett, *Memories of a Hundred Years* (two vols.) New York: The Macmillan Company, 1902.

Halstead, Murat, *National Political Conventions of the Current Presidential Campaign.* Columbus, Ohio: Follett, Foster and Company, 1860.

Hamilton, Gail (Pseud. for Mary Abigail Dodge), *Biography of James G. Blaine.* Norwich, Conn.: The Henry Bill Publishing Company, 1895.

Hamlin, Charles Eugene, *The Life and Times of Hannibal Hamlin.* Cambridge, Mass.: Riverside Press, 1899.

Hanson, John W., *The Sixth Massachusetts Regiment.* Boston: Lee and Shepard, 1866.

Harris, Alexander, *A Review of the Political Conflict in America.* New York: T. H. Pollock, 1876.

Harris, Elbert L., *Benjamin F. Butler and the Negro.* Unpublished master's thesis, 1939, on deposit in the Howard University Library, Washington, D. C.

Hart, Albert Bushnell, *Salmon Portland Chase.* Boston: Houghton, Mifflin and Company, 1899.

(Editor) *Commonwealth History of Massachusetts* (four vols.) New York: The States History Company, 1930.

Hassler, William W., "Professor T. S. C. Lowe," *Civil War Times,* August 1967, Vol. VI.

Haynes, Fred E., *Third Party Movements Since the Civil War.* Iowa City, Iowa: The State Historical Society, 1916.

Headley, P. C., *Massachusetts in the Rebellion.* Boston: Walker, Fuller and Company, 1866.

Hedrick, Mary A., *Incidents of the Civil War.* Lowell, Mass.: S. W. Huse & Co., 1888.

Hendrick, Burton J., *Lincoln's War Cabinet*. Boston: Little, Brown and Company, 1946.

Hesseltine, William B., *Ulysses S. Grant*. New York: Dodd, Mead & Company, 1935.

Lincoln and the War Governors. New York: Alfred A. Knopf, 1955.

Higginson, T. W., "Regular and Volunteer Officers," *Atlantic Monthly,* September 1864, Vol. XIV.

Hill, Frederick Trevor, "The Impeachment of Andrew Johnson," *Harper's Monthly* November 1906, Vol. CXIII.

Hoar, George F., *Autobiography of Seventy Years* (two vols.) New York: Charles Scribner's Sons, 1903.

Hoffman, Wickham, *Camp, Court, and Siege*. New York: Harper & Brothers, 1877.

Holland, J. G., *The Life of Abraham Lincoln*. Springfield, Mass.: Gurdon Bill, 1866.

Holzman, Robert S., *Stormy Ben Butler*. New York: Collier Books, 1961.

Horn, Stanley F., *The Invisible Empire*. Boston: Houghton Mifflin Company, 1939.

Horowitz, Murray M., *Ben Butler: the Making of a Radical*. Ann Arbor, Mich.: University Microfilms, 1967.

Hosmer, James Kendall, *The Appeal to Arms*. New York: Harper & Brothers, 1907.

Outcome of the Civil War. New York: Harper & Brothers, 1907.

Howe, Julia Ward, *Reminiscences*. Boston: Houghton, Mifflin and Company, 1900.

Howe, M. A. DeWolfe, *Portrait of an Independent*. Boston: Houghton Mifflin Company, 1932.

Hudson, H. N., *General Butler's Campaign on the Hudson,* Boston: J. S. Cushing & Co., 1883.

Hudson, William C., *Random Recollections of an Old Political Reporter*. New York: Cupples & Leon Company, 1911.

Hughes, Sarah Forbes (Editor) *Letters and Recollections of John Murray Forbes* (two vols.) Boston: Houghton, Mifflin and Company, 1899.

Humphreys, Andrew Atkinson, *Virginia Campaigns of '64 and '65*. New York: Charles Scribner's Sons, 1883.

Irwin, Richard B., *History of the Nineteenth Army Corps.* New York: G. P. Putnam's Sons, 1892.

Jackson, L. P., "The Origin of Hampton Institute," *Journal of Negro History* April 1925, Vol. X.

Johnson, Edward Rossiter, *Camp–Fire and Battle–Field.* New York: Bryan, Taylor & Co., no date.

Johnson, Laura Winthrop, *Life and Poems of Theodore Winthrop.* New York: Henry Holt and Company, 1884.

Johnson, Robert Underwood, *Remembered Yesterdays.* Boston: Little, Brown and Company, 1923.

Johnson, Robert Underwood, and Clarence Clough Buel, *Battles and Leaders of the Civil War* (four vols.) New York: The Century Co., 1884–1888.

Johnson, Robert Wood, "The Maginot Line of America," *Harper's Magazine,* August 1948, Vol. CXCVII.

Judson, Harry Pratt, "American Politics: A Study of Four Careers," *Review of Reviews,* March 1893, Vol. VII.

Kane, Harnett T., *Queen New Orleans.* New York: William Morrow & Company, 1949.

Keyes, E. D., *Fifty Years' Observation of Men and Events.* New York: Charles Scribner's Sons, 1884.

Kimball, William, "The Little Battle of Big Bethel," *Civil War Times,* June 1967, Vol. VI.

King, W. C., and W. P. Derby, *Camp–Fire Sketches.* Springfield, Mass.: W. C. King & Co., 1887.

Kingsbury, Susan M. (Editor), *Labor Laws and Their Enforcement.* New York: Longmans, Green, 1911.

Klein, Frederic S., "Butler at Bermuda Hundred," *Civil War Times,* November 1967, Vol. VI.

Lee, Fitzhugh, *General Lee.* New York: D. Appleton and Company, 1894.

Leech, Margaret, *Reveille in Washington.* New York: Harper & Brothers, 1941.

Leonard, Clara T., *The Present Condition of Tewksbury* (Pamphlet) Boston: Rand, Avery & Co., 1883.

Lester, Edward, *The Life and Public Services of Charles Sumner.* New York: United States Publishing Company, 1874.

Lewis, Lloyd, *Sherman.* New York: Harcourt, Brace and Company, 1932.

Lockwood, H. C., "The Capture of Fort Fisher," *Atlantic Monthly,* May, June 1871, Vol. XXVII.

Lodge, Henry Cabot, *A Fighting Frigate and Other Essays and Addresses.* New York: Charles Scribner's Sons, 1902.

Lossing, Benson J., *The Civil War in America* (three vols.) Philadelphia: George W. Childs, 1866, 1868, 1870.

Lothrop, Thornton Kirkland, *William Henry Seward.* Boston: Houghton, Mifflin and Company, 1899.

McCall, Samuel W., *Thaddeus Stevens.* Boston: Houghton, Mifflin and Company, 1899.

Macartney, Clarence E., *Lincoln and His Generals.* Philadelphia: Dorrance and Company, 1925.

McClellan, Carswell, *Grant versus the Record.* Boston: Houghton, Mifflin and Company, 1887.

McCulloch, Hugh, *Men and Measures of a Half a Century.* New York: Charles Scribner's Sons, 1888.

Mackenzie, William L., *The Lives and Opinions of Benj'n Franklin Butler and Jesse Hoyt.* Boston, Cook & Co., 1845.

McLaughlin, James F., *The American Cyclops, the Hero of New Orleans and Spoiler of Silver Spoons.* Baltimore: Kelley & Piet, 1868.

McManus, Thomas, *The Battle Fields of Louisiana Revisited a Second Time.* Hartford, Conn.: The Fowler & Miller Co., 1898.

McMaster, John B., *A History of the People of the United States during Lincoln's Administration.* New York: D. Appleton and Company, 1927.

McPherson, Edward, *The Political History of the United States . . . during the Great Rebellion.* Washington, D. C.: Philp & Solomons, 1865.
    The Political History of the United States . . . during Reconstruction. Washington, D. C., 1871.

Macrae, David, *The Americans at Home.* New York: E. P. Dutton & Co., Inc., 1952.

Mahan, A. T., *The Gulf and Inland Waters.* New York: Charles Scribner's Sons, 1883.
    Admiral Farragut. New York: D. Appleton and Company, 1892.

Marshall, Jesse Ames (Compiler) *Private and Official Cor-*

respondence of Gen. Benjamin F. Butler During the Period of the Civil War. Privately issued, 1917.

Martin, Edward Sanford, *The Life of Joseph Hodges Choate* (two vols.) New York: Charles Scribner's Sons, 1921.

Martyn, Carlos, *Wendell Phillips.* New York: Funk & Wagnalls, 1890.

Mayer, George H., *The Republican Party* (second edition). New York: Oxford University Press, 1967.

Meneely, A. Howard, *The War Department, 1861.* New York: Columbia University, 1928.

Merriam, George S., *The Life and Times of Samuel Bowles* (two vols.) New York: The Century Co., 1885.

Merrill, Louis Taylor, *General Benjamin F. Butler and the Campaign of 1868* (Pamphlet) Chicago: University of Chicago Libraries, 1939.

Meserve, H. C., *Lowell.* New Bedford, Mass.: The National Association of Cotton Manufacturers, 1923.

Milton, George Fort, *The Age of Hate.* New York: Coward-McCann, Inc., 1930.

The Eve of Conflict. Boston: Houghton Mifflin Company, 1934.

Mitgang, Herbert (Editor), *Lincoln as they Saw Him,* New York: Rinehart & Co., 1956.

Moore, Frank (Editor), *The Rebellion Record* (11 vols.) New York: G. P. Putnam, D. Van Nostrand, 1861–1871.

Moore, Joseph West, *The American Congress.* New York: Harper & Brothers, 1895.

Morgan, James, *Our Presidents.* New York: The Macmillan Company, 1924.

Morrill, W. B., *Exercises at the Centennial . . . of . . . Phillips Exeter Academy.* Exeter, N.H.: News-Letter Press, 1884.

Morse, John T., Jr., *Abraham Lincoln* (2 vols.) Boston: Houghton, Mifflin and Company, 1899.

Memoir of Colonel Henry Lee. Boston: Little, Brown and Company, 1905.

Muzzey, David Saville, *James G. Blaine.* New York: Dodd, Mead & Company, 1934.

Nash, Howard P., Jr., *Third Parties in American Politics.* Washington, D. C.; Public Affairs Press, 1958.

"Yellow Jack," *Tradition,* August 1962, Vol. V.

Nevins, Allan, *Ordeal of the Union* (2 vols.) New York: Charles Scribner's Sons, 1947.

Nichols, Roy Franklin, *The Democratic Machine.* New York: Columbia University, 1923.

Nichols, Thomas Low, *Forty Years of American Life 1821–1861.* New York: Stackpole Sons, 1937.

Nicolay, John G., *The Outbreak of the Rebellion.* New York: Charles Scribner's Sons, 1881.

Nicolay, John G., and John Hay, *Abraham Lincoln* (10 vols.) New York: The Century Co., 1890.

Oberholzer, Ellis Paxson, *Abraham Lincoln.* Philadelphia: George W. Jacobs & Company, 1904.

History of the United States (Vol. IV) New York: The Macmillan Company, 1931.

Official Proceedings of the Democratic National Convention held in 1860 at Charleston and Baltimore. Cleveland: Plain Dealer, 1860.

Official Proceedings of the National Democratic Convention of 1884. New York: Douglas Taylor's Democratic Press, 1884.

Official Records of the Union and Confederate Armies (130 vols.) Washington, D. C.: Government Printing Office, 1890–1901.

Official Records of the Union and Confederate Navies in the War of the Rebellion (30 vols.) Washington, D. C.: Government Printing Office, 1894–1922.

Official . . . Proceedings of the . . . Convention Assembled May 4, 1853 to Revise . . . the Constitution of . . . Massachusetts. Boston: White & Potter, 1853.

Parton, James, *General Butler in New Orleans.* New York: Mason Brothers, 1864.

"The 'Strikers' of the Washington Lobby" Atlantic Monthly, August 1869, Vol. XXIV.

Pearson, Henry Greeleaf, *The Life of John A. Andrew* (2 vols.) Boston, Houghton, Mifflin and Company, 1904.

Perry, Benjamin, *Reminiscences of Public Men.* Greenville, S. C.: Shannon & Co., 1889.

Perry, Bliss, *Life and Letters of Henry Lee Higginson.* Boston: Atlantic Monthly Press, 1921.

Phelps, Albert, "New Orleans and Reconstruction." *Atlantic Monthly,* July 1901, Vol. LXXXVIII.

Phillips, Wendell, *Who Shall Rule Us?* (Pamphlet) Boston: Rand, Avery & Co., 1878.

Piatt, Donn, *Memories of the Men Who Saved the Union.* New York and Chicago: Belford, Clarke & Company, 1887.

Pierce, Edward L., "The Contrabands at Fortress Monroe," *Atlantic Monthly,* November 1861, Vol. VIII.

"The Freedmen at Port Royal," *Atlantic Monthly,* September 1863, Vol. XII.

Memoir and Letters of Charles Sumner (4 vols.) Boston: Roberts Brothers, 1877.

Pierrepont, Edwards, *Review . . . of Gen. Butler's Defense . . . in Relation to the New Orleans Gold.* New York: Wm. C. Bryant & Co., 1865.

Pollard, Edward A., *The Lost Cause.* New York: E. B. Treat & Co., 1866.

Poore, Ben: Perley, *Perley's Reminiscences* (2 vols.) Philadelphia: Hubbard Brothers, 1886.

Porter, David D., *Naval History of the Civil War.* New York: The Sherman Publishing Company, 1886.

Porter, Horace, "Campaigning with Grant," *The Century,* December 1896–October 1897, Vols. LIII, LIV, New Series XXXI, XXXII.

Pratt, Fletcher, *Ordeal by Fire* (Rev. ed.) New York: William Sloane Associates, 1948.

Radcliffe, George L. P., *Governor Thomas H. Hicks of Maryland and the Civil War.* Baltimore: Johns Hopkins Press, 1902.

Randall, J. G., *Constitutional Problems under Lincoln.* New York: D. Appleton and Company, 1926.

The Civil War and Reconstruction. Boston: D. C. Heath and Company, 1937.

Lincoln the President (2 vols.) New York: Dodd, Mead & Company, 1945.

Rhodes, James Ford, *History of the United States* (8 vols.) New York: The Macmillan Co., 1899–1919.

History of the Civil War. New York: The Macmillan Company, 1917.

Rice, William Gorham, and Francis Lynde Stetson, "Was New

York's Vote Stolen?" *North American Review,* January 1914, Vol. CXCIX.

Richardson, James D., *Messages and Papers of the Presidents.* Washington, D. C.: Bureau of National Literature and Art, 1900.

Riddle, Albert Gallatin, *Recollections of War Times.* New York: G. P. Putnam's Sons, 1895.

Ringwalt, J. L., *Anecdotes of General Ulysses S. Grant.* Philadelphia, J. B. Lippincott Company, 1886.

Roberts, A. Sellow, "The Federal Government and Confederate Cotton," *American Historical Review,* Vol. XXXII, 1927.

Robinson, Harriet J. H., *"Warrington" Pen Portraits.* Boston: Published by Mrs. William S. Robinson, 1877.

Robinson, William S. (Pseud. Warrington), "General Butler's Campaign in Massachusetts," *Atlantic Monthly,* December 1871, Vol. XXVIII.
The Salary Grab, . . . with special reference to the responsibility of Gen. B. F. Butler. Boston and New York: Lee and Shepard, 1873, Lee, Shepard, and Dillingham, 1873.
Robinson Scrapbooks (14 vols.) Selections of Robinson's articles compiled by himself, in the Rare Book Room of the Boston Public Library.

Rogers, Joseph M., "Men Who Might Have Been President," *North American Review,* May 1896, Vol. CLXII.

Ross, Edmund G., *History of the Impeachment of Andrew Johnson.* Santa Fé, New Mexico: New Mexican Printing Co., 1896.

Rowell, Eliphalet, *Six Months in the Military Department of Virginia and North Carolina.* Portland, Maine: Lefavor-Tower Company, 1902.

Russell, Charles Edward, *Blaine of Maine.* New York: Cosmopolitan Book Corporation, 1931.

Schouler, William, *A History of Massachusetts in the Civil War* (Vol. I) New York: E. P. Dutton & Co., 1868.

Seilhamer, George O., *History of the Republican Party.* New York: Judge Publishing Co., no date.

Sennott, George, *Sennott on Andrew and Butler* (Pamphlet) Boston: Redding and Company, 1862.

Smith, Goldwyn, *Reminiscences.* New York: The Macmillan Company, 1910.

Smith, R. M., *The Fall of New Orleans.* Richmond, Va.: Public Printer, 1864.

Smith, William Ernest, *The Francis Preston Blair Family in Politics.* (2 vols.) New York: The Macmillan Company, 1933.

Smith, William Farrar, *From Chattanooga to Petersburg Under Generals Grant and Butler.* Boston: Houghton, Mifflin and Company, 1893.

Soley, James Russell, *The Blockade and the Cruisers.* New York: Charles Scribner's Sons, 1883.

Admiral Porter. New York: D. Appleton and Company, 1903.

Southwood, Marion, *"Beauty and Booty," the Watchword of New Orleans.* New York, M. Doolady, 1867.

Spears, John Randolph, *David G. Farragut.* Philadelphia: George W. Jacobs & Company, 1905.

Stanton, Henry B., *Random Recollections.* New York: Harper & Brothers, 1887.

Stanwood, Edward, *James Gillespie Blaine.* Boston: Houghton Mifflin Company, 1905.

"Election Superstitions and Fallacies," *Atlantic Monthly,* October 1912, Vol. CX.

Stillé, Charles J., *History of the United States Sanitary Commission.* Philadelphia: J. B. Lippincott & Co., 1866.

Storey, Moorfield, *Charles Sumner.* Boston: Houghton, Mifflin and Company, 1900.

Storey, Moorfield, and Edward W. Emerson, *Ebenezer Rockwood Hoar.* Boston: Houghton Mifflin Company, 1911.

Supplement to the Congressional Globe, . . . the trial of Andrew Johnson. Fortieth Congress, Second Session. Washington, D. C.; F. & J. Rives & George A. Bailey, 1868.

Swinton, William, *History of the Seventh Regiment . . . of New York.* New York and Boston: Fields, Osgood & Co., 1870.

Taylor, Richard, *Destruction and Reconstruction.* New York: D. Appleton and Company, 1879.

Thayer, William Roscoe, "Lincoln and Some Union Generals," *Harper's Monthly,* December 1914, Vol. CXXX.

Life and Letters of John Hay (2 vols.) Boston: Houghton Mifflin Company, 1915.

Tinker, Edward Larocque, *Creole City.* New York: Longmans, Green & Co., 1953.

Todd, William C., *Biographical and Other Articles.* Boston: Lee and Shepard, 1901.

Towle, George M., "Some Secession Leaders," *Harper's Monthly,* April 1863, vol. XXVI.

Tuckerman, Charles K., *Recollections of Notable People.* New York: Dodd, Mead & Company, 1895.

Victor, Orville J., *Incidents and Anecdotes of the War.* New York: James D. Torrey, 1862.

Ware, Edith Ellen, *Political Opinion in Massachusetts during the Civil War and Reconstruction.* New York: Columbia University Press, 1916.

Watson, William, *Life in the Confederate Army.* London: Chapman and Hall, Limited, 1887.

Weeden, William B., *War Government Federal and State 1861– 1865.* Boston: Houghton Mifflin and Company, 1906.

Welles, Gideon, "Admiral Farragut and New Orleans," *Galaxy,* December 1871, Vol. XII.

"The Opposition to Lincoln in 1864," *Atlantic Monthly,* March 1878, Vol. XLI.

"Lincoln's Triumph in 1864," *Atlantic Monthly,* April 1878, Vol. XLI.

Diary of Gideon Welles. (3 vols.) Boston: Houghton Mifflin Company, 1911.

Wesley, Charles H., "Lincoln's Plan for Colonizing the Emancipated Negro," *Journal of Negro History,* January 1919, Vol. IV.

West, Richard S., Jr., *Gideon Welles.* Indianapolis: The Bobbs-Merrill Company, 1943.

Lincoln's Scapegoat General. Boston: Houghton Mifflin Company, 1965.

Willard, Joseph, *Half a Century with Judges and Lawyers.* Boston: Houghton Mifflin and Company, 1895.

Williams, George W., *A History of the Negro Troops in the War of the Rebellion.* New York: Harper & Brothers, 1888.

Williams, T. Harry, *Lincoln and the Radicals.* Madison, Wisc.: University of Wisconsin Press, 1941.

Williams, Thomas, "Letters of General Thomas Williams," *American Historical* Review, Vol. XIV, 1909.

Wilson, James Harrison, *Life and Services of W. F. Smith.* Wilmington, Del.: The John M. Rogers Press, 1904.

Wilson, Joseph T., *The Black Phalanx.* Hartford, Conn.: American Publishing Co., 1889.

Winston, Robert W., *Andrew Johnson.* New York: Henry Holt and Company, 1928.

Robert E. Lee. New York: William Morrow & Company, 1934.

Winthrop, Theodore, "New York Seventh Regiment," *Atlantic Monthly,* June 1861, Vol. VII.

"Washington as a Camp," *Atlantic Monthly,* July 1861, Vol. VIII.

Wolfson, George M., "Butler's Relations with Grant and the Army of the James in 1864," *The South Atlantic Quarterly,* October 1911, Vol. X.

Wood, William, *Captains of the Civil War.* New Haven, Conn.: Yale University Press, 1921.

Woodward, W. E., *Meet General Grant.* New York: Horace Liveright, Inc., 1928.

Index

Abbott, Josiah G., 50, 51
Abbott, Willis J., 293
Adams, Charles Francis, 164, 257
Adams, Henry, 248
Advertiser, Boston, Mass., 72, 80, 265, 277, 278, 280, 284, 291, 296
Aëdes aegypti mosquito, 160
Alaska, 260
Albany, New York, 226
Alexander, A. W., 197
Alexandria, Virginia, 103
Allen, Stephen M., 182
Allis, Edward P., 291
Alta Vela Island, 239
Alton, Illinois, 226
America (hymn), 26
American Anti-Slavery Society, 117
American House, 68
American Legion, 299
Ames, Adelbert, 35
Ames, Oakes, 253, 254
Ames, Seth, 25
Ammen, Daniel, 213
Andover, Mass., 34, 258
Andover-Newton Theological Seminary, 258
Andrew, John A., 66, 68, 69, 70, 71, 72, 73, 74, 75, 80, 81, 82, 84, 89, 90, 91, 92, 110, 120, 124, 125, 126, 127, 128, 203
Andrews, Colonel, C.S.A., 122
Annapolis, Md., 74, 81, 82, 83, 84, 85, 86, 88, 89, 90, 91, 92, 93, 95, 114
Annapolis and Elk Ridge Railroad, 87
Annapolis, Department of, 91, 101

Annapolis Junction, 87, 88
Anti-Masonic party, 50
Anti-Monopoly party, 18, 268, 291, 295
Appomatox River, 191, 193
Arkansas, 220
Army Appropriations Act, 235
Army Appropriations bill, 262
Army of Northern Virginia, 191, 214
Army of the Gulf, 134, 156, 165, 168
Army of the James, 183, 191, 192, 193, 194, 196, 197, 207, 209, 215, 217
Army of the Potomac, 130, 134, 182, 191, 192, 193, 198
Army Organization Act, 125
Army, United States, 262
Articles of Impeachment, 235, 239, 241, 244
Ashley, James M., 230, 231
"Assassination Committee," 231, 237
Assistant Secretary of the Navy, 208, 215
Associated Press, 251
Astor House, 75
Astoria, New York, 103
Atherton, Charles G., 45
Atlantic Blockading Squadron, 119
Atlantic Monthly, 108, 249, 268
Auburn, New York, 226
Australian ballot, 39
Avenue A, New York City, 205
Avery, William W., 59, 60

321